S0-BNB-322

The American Way of Death

by

JESSICA MITFORD

FAWCETT CREST · NEW YORK

THE AMERICAN WAY OF DEATH

Published by Fawcett Crest Books, a unit of CBS Publications, the Consumer Publishing Division of CBS Inc., by arrangement with Simon and Schuster, a division of Gulf & Western Corporation.

ISBN: 0-449-23985-3

Printed in the United States of America

First Fawcett Crest printing: July 1964

New Fawcett Crest edition: April 1979

23 22 21 20 19 18 17 16 15 14 13

Dedicated to my husband
ROBERT TREUHAFT
*with much gratitude for his
untiring collaboration in all phases
of the preparation of this book.*

Funerals are becoming more and more a part of the American way of life.

—HOWARD C. RAETHER, *Executive Secretary*,
National Funeral Directors Association

Contents

FOREWORD

This would normally be the place to say (as critics of the American funeral trade invariably do), "I am not, of course, speaking of the vast majority of ethical undertakers." But the vast majority of ethical undertakers is precisely the subject of this book. To be "ethical" merely means to adhere to a prevailing code of morality, in this case one devised over the years by the undertakers themselves for their own purposes. The outlook of the average undertaker, who does adhere to the code of his calling, is to me more significant than that of his shadier colleagues, who are merely small-time crooks such as may be found operating in any sphere of business. Scandals, although they frequently erupt (misuse by undertakers of the coroner's office to secure business, bribery of hospital personnel to "steer" cases, the illegal re-use of coffins, fraudulent double charges in welfare cases), are not typical of the trade as a whole, and therefore are not part of the subject matter of this book.

Another point often made by critics of the modern American funeral is that, if there are excesses in funerary matters, the public is to blame. I am unwilling on the basis of present evidence to find the public guilty; this defendant has only recently begun to present his case.

I have not included the atypical funerals, quaint death customs still practiced by certain Indian tribes, the rites accorded Gypsy kings and queens, the New Orleans jazz funerals, the great movie and gangland funerals which had their heyday in the thirties and still occur from time to time. I have regretfully avoided these byways, intriguing though they are, for the main highway—the "average," "typical" American funerary practices, surely fully as curious as any of the customs derived from ancient folklore or modern variants.

ACKNOWLEDGMENTS

Large portions of this book could well be labeled, "By Robert Treuhaft, as told to Jessica Mitford." My husband, the family expert on funerals because of his participation in the Bay Area Funeral Society, worked with me for many months gathering material. He spent long hours in the library of the San Francisco College of Mortuary Science, bringing home all sorts of treasures found therein—embalming textbooks, old issues of funeral trade magazines, manuals on casket salesmanship. He pioneered the subject of cemeteries, about which almost nothing has been written except in industry journals. He gave invaluable direction to the selection and organization of the subject matter. I should never have attempted this book without his help.

When I first started work on *The American Way of Death,* some of my friends and advisers were frankly appalled at the choice of subject; but my agent, Miss Candida Donadio, was enthusiastic about the idea from the beginning. So was Mr. Roul Tunley, himself something of an authority on the subject. Their encouragement was most welcome and meant a great deal to me, especially during the first stages of the writing.

The following people in the funeral industry were kind enough to furnish much information: Mr. Robert Mac-Neur, Mr. and Mrs. Nicholas Daphne, Mr. Francis Wilson, Mr. Del Reynolds, all owners of funeral establishments; Mr. Wilber Krieger and Dr. Charles H. Nichols of the National Foundation of Funeral Service; Mr. Bruce Hotchkiss and Mr. Howard C. Raether of the National Funeral Directors Association; Mr. Leon Utter, dean, and Mr. Arthur Colton, librarian, of the San Francisco College of Mortuary Science; Mr. L. C. Ashton, owner of a London funeral establishment.

Among those with special knowledge of various aspects of the American funeral who generously contributed their ideas are Dr. Jesse Carr, Bishop James Pike, Rabbi Sidney Akselrad, the Reverend Mr. Laurance Cross, Professor Edmund Volkart.

For much of the economics material, and for the chart on page 47, I am indebted to Mr. Philip Eden, economist and assistant research director of the International Longshoremen's and Warehousemen's Union. Mr. Martin Harwayne, C.P.A., helped me to unravel some of the mysteries of the operation of "nonprofit" cemeteries.

Mr. Melvin Belli introduced me to the Chelini case, and lent me his transcript of the trial. Mr. Bernard Asbell corresponded with me about Franklin D. Roosevelt's funeral and sent me the issue of the *Southern Funeral Director* with Mr. Patterson's account of the proceedings. Mr. Justin Kaplan suggested that I should read Emily Post on funerals. Mr. Rufus Rhoades gave me permission to describe his personal experience with undertakers. Mr. Paul Egly lent me his file on Forest Lawn, and Mr. Nicholas Petris let me borrow his material on the ash-scattering bill. Mr. Ralph Graves sang me the singing commercial which appears in the chapter on funerals in England, and Mr. W. W. Chambers (whose letterhead says he is "one of the largest undertakers in the world") gave me permission to use it.

Mrs. Dorothy Demorest, education director of the Bay Area Funeral Society, lent me her collection of newspaper clippings, articles and letters about funerals—a truly rare assortment; she also made some very useful suggestions about the subject matter. Dr. and Mrs. Josiah Bartlett, Dr. Carl Wennerstrom and Mr. C. Errol Fletcher contributed many ideas about the funeral reform movement. Mr. Irving Baldinger, Mr. Abe Magrisso and Mr. Donald Rubin gave me much information about funerals and the labor movement.

The how-to-do-it material in the appendix is the work of Mr. Ernest Morgan, who kindly gave me permission to extract the information from his excellent publication, *A Manual of Simple Burial.*

Among those who volunteered help with the research were Mr. Peter Rand, Mr. Mark Lapin, Mrs. Judy Viorst, Mrs. Lannes Davis, Mrs. Joyce Turner, Mr. Arnold Cutler. Mrs. Sheila Bush supplied valuable information for the chapter on funerals in England, and my sisters Nancy and Deborah contributed a certain amount of misinformation on this subject.

Mrs. Elizabeth Bacon read the manuscript at various stages of its preparation, and made some very helpful criticisms and suggestions. Mrs. Barbara Sharwood and Mrs. Barbara Kahn did a most efficient job of typing the manuscript. Mr. Frederick Anderson directed the work of compiling the index.

Lastly, I must thank the many friends with fertile brains who plied me with suggestions for chapter titles: The High Cost of Leaving, Mourning Becomes Expensive, Remains to Be Seen, A Funny Thing Happened on the Way to the Mausoleum, Dig That Crazy Grave. Even more fervently do I thank my editor, Mr. Robert Gottlieb of Simon and Schuster, who made so many important contributions to the book—not the least of which was to dissuade me from using any of these chapter titles.   — J.M.

1

THE AMERICAN WAY OF DEATH

*How long, I would ask, are we to be subjected to the ty-
ranny of custom and undertakers? Truly, it is all vanity and
vexation of spirit—a mere mockery of woe, costly to all,
far, far beyond its value; and ruinous to many; hateful, and
an abomination to all; yet submitted to by all, because
none have the moral courage to speak against it and act in
defiance of it.*   —LORD ESSEX

O DEATH, where is thy sting? O grave, where is thy
victory? Where, indeed. Many a badly stung survivor,
faced with the aftermath of some relative's funeral, has
ruefully concluded that the victory has been won hands
down by a funeral establishment—in disastrously unequal
battle.

Much has been written of late about the affluent society
in which we live, and much fun poked at some of the irrational "status symbols" set out like golden snares to
trap the unwary consumer at every turn. Until recently,
little has been said about the most irrational and weirdest
of the lot, lying in ambush for all of us at the end of the
road—the modern American funeral.

If the Dismal Traders (as an eighteenth-century English
writer calls them) have traditionally been cast in a comic
role in literature, a universally recognized symbol of
humor from Shakespeare to Dickens to Evelyn Waugh,

they have successfully turned the tables in recent years to
perpetrate a huge, macabre and expensive practical joke
on the American public. It is not consciously conceived of
as a joke, of course; on the contrary, it is hedged with
admirably contrived rationalizations.

Gradually, almost imperceptibly, over the years the
funeral men have constructed their own grotesque cloud-
cuckoo-land where the trappings of Gracious Living are
transformed, as in a nightmare, into the trappings of Gracious Dying. The same familiar Madison Avenue language,
with its peculiar adjectival range designed to anesthetize
sales resistance to all sorts of products, has seeped into
the funeral industry in a new and bizarre guise. The
emphasis is on the same desirable qualities that we have
all been schooled to look for in our daily search for excellence: comfort, durability, beauty, craftsmanship. The
attuned ear will recognize too the convincing quasi-
scientific language, so reassuring even if unintelligible.

So that this too, too solid flesh might not melt, we are
offered "solid copper—a quality casket which offers superb value to the client seeking long-lasting protection,"
or "the Colonial Classic Beauty—18 gauge lead coated
steel, seamless top, lap-jointed welded body construction."
Some are equipped with foam rubber, some with inner-
spring mattresses. Elgin offers "the revolutionary
'Perfect-Posture' bed." Not every casket need have a silver
lining, for one may choose between "more than 60 color
matched shades, magnificent and unique masterpieces"
by the Cheney Casket-lining people. Shrouds no longer
exist. Instead, you may patronize a grave-wear couturière
who promises "handmade original fashions—styles from
the best in life for the last memory—dresses, men's suits,
negligees, accessories." For the final, perfect grooming:
"Nature-Glo—the ultimate in cosmetic embalming." And,
where have we heard that phrase "peace of mind protection" before? No matter. In funeral advertising, it is
applied to the Wilbert Burial Vault, with its 3/8-inch pre-
cast asphalt inner liner plus extra-thick, reinforced
concrete—all this "guaranteed by Good Housekeeping."

Here again the Cadillac, status symbol par excellence, appears in all its gleaming glory, this time transformed into a pastel-colored funeral hearse.

You, the potential customer for all this luxury, are unlikely to read the lyrical descriptions quoted above, for they are culled from *Mortuary Management* and *Casket and Sunnyside,* two of the industry's eleven trade magazines. For you there are ads in your daily newspaper, generally found on the obituary page, stressing dignity, refinement, high-caliber professional service and that intangible quality, *sincerity.* The trade advertisements are, however, instructive, because they furnish an important clue to the frame of mind into which the funeral industry has hypnotized itself.

A new mythology, essential to the twentieth-century American funeral rite, has grown up—or rather has been built up step by step—to justify the peculiar customs surrounding the disposal of our dead. And, just as the witch doctor must be convinced of his own infallibility in order to maintain a hold over his clientele, so the funeral industry has had to "sell itself" on its articles of faith in the course of passing them along to the public.

The first of these is the tenet that today's funeral procedures are founded in "American tradition." The story comes to mind of a sign on the freshly sown lawn of a brand-new Midwest college: "There is a tradition on this campus that students never walk on this strip of grass. This tradition goes into effect next Tuesday." The most cursory look at American funerals of past times will establish the parallel. Simplicity to the point of starkness, the plain pine box, the laying out of the dead by friends and family who also bore the coffin to the grave—these were the hallmarks of the traditional funeral until the end of the nineteenth century.

Secondly, there is the myth that the American public is only being given what it wants—an opportunity to keep up with the Joneses to the end. "In keeping with our high standard of living, there should be an equally high standard of dying," says the past president of the Funeral

Directors of San Francisco. "The cost of a funeral varies
according to individual taste and the niceties of living the
family has been accustomed to." Actually, choice doesn't
enter the picture for the average individual, faced, generally for the first time, with the necessity of buying a
product of which he is totally ignorant, at a moment
when he is least in a position to quibble. In point of fact
the cost of a funeral almost always varies, not "according
to individual taste" but according to what the traffic will
bear.

Thirdly, there is an assortment of myths based on half-
digested psychiatric theories. The importance of the
"memory picture" is stressed—meaning the last glimpse
of the deceased in open casket, done up with the latest in
embalming techniques and finished off with a dusting of
makeup. A newer one, impressively authentic-sounding,
is the need for "grief therapy," which is beginning to go
over big in mortuary circles. A historian of American
funeral directing hints at the grief-therapist idea when
speaking of the new role of the undertaker—"the drama-
turgic role, in which the undertaker becomes a stage manager to create an appropriate atmosphere and to move the
funeral party through a drama in which social relation-
ships are stressed and an emotional catharsis or release
is provided through ceremony."

Lastly, a whole new terminology, as ornately shoddy as
the satin rayon casket liner, has been invented by the funeral industry to replace the direct and serviceable vocabulary of former times. Undertaker has been supplanted
by "funeral director" or "mortician." (Even the classified
section of the telephone directory gives recognition to this;
in its pages you will find "Undertakers—see Funeral
Directors.") Coffins are "caskets"; hearses are "coaches,"
or "professional cars"; flowers are "floral tributes";
corpses generally are "loved ones," but mortuary etiquette
dictates that a specific corpse be referred to by name only
—as, "Mr. Jones"; cremated ashes are "cremains."
Euphemisms such as "slumber room," "reposing room,"

and "calcination—the *kindlier* heat" abound in the funeral business.

If the undertaker is the stage manager of the fabulous production that is the modern American funeral, the stellar role is reserved for the occupant of the open casket. The decor, the stagehands, the supporting cast are all arranged for the most advantageous display of the deceased, without which the rest of the paraphernalia would lose its point—*Hamlet* without the Prince of Denmark. It is to this end that a fantastic array of costly merchandise and services is pyramided to dazzle the mourners and facilitate the plunder of the next of kin.

Grief therapy, anyone? But it's going to come high. According to the funeral industry's own figures, the *average* undertaker's bill in 1961 was $708 for casket and "services," to which must be added the cost of a burial vault, flowers, clothing, clergy and musician's honorarium, and cemetery charges. When these costs are added to the undertaker's bill, the total average cost for an adult's funeral is, as we shall see, closer to $1,450.

The question naturally arises, *is* this what most people want for themselves and their families? For several reasons, this has been a hard one to answer until recently. It is a subject seldom discussed. Those who have never had to arrange for a funeral frequently shy away from its implications, preferring to take comfort in the thought that sufficient unto the day is the evil thereof. Those who have acquired personal and painful knowledge of the subject would often rather forget about it. Pioneering "Funeral Societies" or "Memorial Associations," dedicated to the principle of dignified funerals at reasonable cost, have existed in a number of communities throughout the country, but their membership has been limited for the most to the more sophisticated element in the population—university people, liberal intellectuals—and those who, like doctors and lawyers, come up against problems in arranging funerals for their clients.

Some indication of the pent-up resentment felt by vast

numbers of people against the funeral interests was furnished by the astonishing response to an article by Roul Tunley, titled "Can You Afford to Die?" in *The Saturday Evening Post* of June 17, 1961. As though a dike had burst, letters poured in from every part of the country to the *Post*, to the funeral societies, to local newspapers. They came from clergymen, professional people, old-age pensioners, trade unionists. Three months after the article appeared, an estimated six thousand had taken pen in hand to comment on some phase of the high cost of dying. Many recounted their own bitter experiences at the hands of funeral directors; hundreds asked for advice on how to establish a consumer organization in communities where none exists; others sought information about pre-need plans. The membership of the funeral societies skyrocketed. The funeral industry, finding itself in the glare of public spotlight, has begun to engage in serious debate about its own future course—as well it might.

Is the funeral inflation bubble ripe for bursting? A few years ago, the United States public suddenly rebelled against the trend in the auto industry towards ever more showy cars, with their ostentatious and nonfunctional fins, and a demand was created for compact cars patterned after European models. The all-powerful auto industry, accustomed to *telling* the customer what sort of car he wanted, was suddenly forced to *listen* for a change. Overnight, the little cars became for millions a new kind of status symbol. Could it be that the same cycle is working itself out in the attitude towards the final return of dust to dust, that the American public is becoming sickened by ever more ornate and costly funerals, and that a status symbol of the future may indeed be the simplest kind of "funeral without fins"?

2

THE FUNERAL TRANSACTION

A funeral is not an occasion for a display of cheapness. It is, in fact, an opportunity for the display of a status symbol which, by bolstering family pride, does much to assuage grief. A funeral is also an occasion when feelings of guilt and remorse are satisfied to a large extent by the purchase of a fine funeral. It seems highly probable that the most satisfactory funeral service for the average family is one in which the cost has necessitated some degree of sacrifice. This permits the survivors to atone for any real or fancied neglect of the deceased prior to his death. . . .
— *National Funeral Service Journal,*
August 1961

THE SELLER of funeral service has, one gathers, a preconceived, stereotyped view of his customers. To him, the bereaved person who enters his establishment is a bundle of guilt feelings, a snob and a status seeker. The funeral director feels that by steering his customer to the higher-priced caskets, he is giving him his first dose of grief therapy. In the words of the *National Funeral Service Journal*: "The focus of the buyer's interest must be the casket, vault, clothing, funeral cars, etc.—the only tangible evidence of how much has been invested in the funeral—the only real status symbol associated with a funeral service."

Whether or not one agrees with this rather unflattering appraisal of the average person who has suffered a death in the family, it is nevertheless true that the funeral transaction is generally influenced by a combination of circumstances which bear upon the buyer as in no other type of business dealing: the disorientation caused by bereavement, the lack of standards by which to judge the value of the commodity offered by the seller, the need to make an on-the-spot decision, general ignorance of the law as it affects disposal of the dead, the ready availability of insurance money to finance the transaction. These factors predetermine to a large extent the outcome of the transaction.

The funeral seller, like any other merchant, is preoccupied with price, profit, selling techniques. As Mr. Leon S. Utter, dean of the San Francisco College of Mortuary Science, writes in *Mortuary Management's Idea Kit:* "Your selling plan should go into operation as soon as the telephone rings and you are requested to serve a bereaved family. . . . Never preconceive as to what any family will purchase. You cannot possibly measure the intensity of their emotions, undisclosed insurance or funds that may have been set aside for funeral expenses."

The selling plan should be subtle rather than high-pressure, for the obvious "hard sell" is considered inappropriate and self-defeating by modern industry leaders. Two examples of what *not* to say to a customer are given in the *Successful Mortuary Operation & Service* Manual: "I can tell by the fine suit you're wearing, that you appreciate the finer things, and will want a fine casket for your Mother," and "Think of the beautiful memory picture you will have of your dear Father in this beautiful casket."

At the same time nothing must be left to chance. The trade considers that the most important element of funeral salesmanship is the proper arrangement of caskets in the Selection Room (where the customer is taken to make his purchase). The sales talk, while preferably dignified and restrained, must be designed to take maximum advantage of this arrangement.

The uninitiated, entering a casket selection room for the first time, may think he is looking at a random grouping of variously priced merchandise. Actually, endless thought and care are lavished on the development of new and better selection room arrangements, for it has been found that the placing of the caskets materially affects the amount of the sale. There are available to the trade a number of texts devoted to the subject, supplemented by frequent symposiums, seminars, study courses, visual aids, scale model selection rooms complete with miniature caskets that can be moved around experimentally. All stress the desired goal: selling consistently in a "bracket that is above average."

The relationship between casket arrangement and sales psychology is discussed quite fully by Mr. W.M. Krieger, managing director of the influential National Selected Morticians Association, in his book *Successful Funeral Management.* He analyzes the blunder of placing the caskets in order of price, from cheapest to most expensive, which he calls the "stairstep method" of arrangement. As he points out, this plan "makes direct dollar comparisons very easy." Or, if the caskets are so arranged that the most expensive are the first ones the buyer sees, he may be shocked into buying a very cheap one. A mistake to be avoided is an unbalanced line with too many caskets in a low price range: "The unbalanced line with its heavy concentration of units under $300 made it very easy for the client to buy in this area with complete satisfaction."

In developing his method of display, Mr. Krieger divides the stock of caskets for convenience into four "quartiles," two above and two below the median price, which in his example is $400. The objective is to sell in the third, or just above median, quartile. To this end the purchaser is first led to a unit in this third quartile—about $125 to $150 *above* the median sale, in the range of $525 to $550. Should the buyer balk at this price, he should next be led to a unit providing "strong contrast, both in price and quality," this time something well below the median, say in the $375 to $395 range. The psychological reasons for this are explained. They are twofold. While the difference in quality is demonstrable, the price is not *so* low as to make the buyer feel

belittled. At the same time, if the buyer turns his nose up
and indicates that he didn't want to go *that* low, now is
the time to show him the "rebound unit"—one priced
from $5 to $25 *above* the median, in the $405 to $425
bracket.

Mr. Krieger calls all this the "Keystone Approach," and
supplies a diagram showing units 1, 2, and 3, scattered
with apparent artless abandon about the floor. The
customer, who has been bounced from third to second
quartile and back again on the rebound to the third,
might think the "Human Tennis Ball Approach" a more
appropriate term.

Should the prospect show no reaction either way on
seeing the first unit—or should he ask to see something
better—the rebound gambit is, of course, "out." "In" is
the Avenue of Approach. It seems that a Canadian Royal
Mountie once told Mr. Krieger that people who get lost
in the wilds always turn in a great circle to their right.
Probably, surmises Mr. Krieger, because 85 per cent of
us are right-handed? In any event, the Avenue of Approach is a main, wide aisle leading to the right in the
selection room. Here are the better-quality third-and
fourth-quartile caskets.

For that underprivileged, or stubborn, member of
society who insists on purchasing below the median
(but who should nevertheless be served "graciously and
with just as much courtesy and attention as you would
give to the buyer without a limit on what he can spend")
there is a narrow aisle leading to the *left,* which Mr.
Krieger calls "Resistance Lane." There is unfortunately
no discussion of two possible hazards: what if an extremely affluent prospect should prove to be among the
15 per cent of *left*-handed persons, and should therefore
turn automatically into Resistance Lane? How to
extricate him? Conversely, if one of the poor or stubborn,
possibly having at some time in his past been lost in
Canada, should instinctively turn to the broad, right-hand
Avenue of Approach?

The Comprehensive Sales Program offered by Successful Mortuary Operation to its participating members is designed along the same lines as Mr. Krieger's plan, only it is even more complicated. Everything is, however, most carefully spelled out, beginning with the injunction to greet the clients with a warm and friendly handshake, and a suggested opening statement, which should be "spoken slowly and with real sincerity: 'I want to assure you that I'm going to do everything I can to be helpful to you!' "

Having made this good beginning, the funeral director is to proceed with the Arrangement Conference, at each stage of which he should "weave in the service story"—in other words, impress upon the family that they will be entitled to all sorts of extras, such as ushers, cars, pall-bearers, a lady attendant for hairdressing and cosmetics, and the like—all of which will be included in the price of the casket which it is now their duty to select. These preliminaries are very important for "the Arrangement Conference can *make* or *break* the sale."

The diagram of the selection room in this manual resembles one of those mazes set up for experiments designed to muddle rats. It is here that we are introduced to the Triangle Plan, under which the buyer is led around in a triangle, or rather in a series of triangles. He is started off at position A, a casket costing $587, which he is told is "in the $500 range"—although, as the manual points out, it is actually only $13 short of $600. He is informed that the average family buys in the $500 range—a statement designed to reassure him, explain the authors, because "most of the people believe themselves to be *above* average." Supposing the client does not react either way to the $587 casket. He is now led to position B on the diagram—a better casket priced at $647. However, this price is not to be mentioned. Rather, the words "sixty dollars additional" are to be used. Should the prospect still remain silent, this is the cue to continue *upward* to the most expensive unit.

Conversely, should the client demur at the price of $587, he is to be taken to position C—and told that "he can *save* $100" by choosing this one. Again, the figure of $487 is not to be mentioned. If he now says nothing, he is led to position D. Here he is told that "at sixty dollars additional, we could use this finer type, and all of the services will be just exactly the same." This is the crux of the triangle plan; the recalcitrant buyer has now gone around a triangle to end up unwittingly within forty dollars of the starting point. It will be noted that the prices all end in the number seven, "purposely styled to allow you to quote as: 'sixty dollars additional' or 'save a hundred dollars.' "

The buyer is not likely to have caught the significance of this guided tour. As a customer he finds himself in an unusual situation, trapped in a set of circumstances peculiar to the funeral transaction. His frame of mind will vary, obviously, according to the circumstances which led him to the funeral establishment. He may be dazed and bewildered, his young wife having just been killed in an accident; he may be rather relieved because a crotchety old relative has finally died after a long and painful illness. The great majority of funeral buyers, as they are led through their paces at the mortuary—whether shaken and grief-stricken or merely looking forward with pleasurable anticipation to the reading of the will—are assailed by many a nagging question: What's the *right* thing to do? I am arranging this funeral, but surely this is no time to indulge my own preferences in taste and style; I feel I know what she would have preferred, but what will her family and friends expect? How can I avoid criticism for inadvertently doing the wrong thing? And, above all, it should be a nice, decent funeral—but what *is* a nice, decent funeral?

Which leads us to the second special aspect of the funeral transaction: the buyer's almost total ignorance of what to expect when he enters the undertaker's parlor. What to look for, what to avoid, how much to spend. The funeral industry estimates that the average individual has to arrange for a funeral only once in fifteen years. The cost of the funeral is the third largest expenditure, after a house and a car, in the life of an ordinary American family. Yet even in the case of the old relative, whose death may have been fully expected and even welcomed, it is most unlikely that the buyer will have discussed the funeral with anybody in advance. It just would not seem right to go round saying, "By the way, my uncle is very ill and he's not expected to live; do you happen to know a good, reliable undertaker?"

Because of the nature of funerals, the buyer is in a quite different position from one who is, for example, in the market for a car. Visualize the approach. The man of prudence and common sense who is about to buy a car consults a Consumers' Research bulletin or seeks the advice of his friends; he knows in advance the dangers of rushing into a deal blindly.

In the funeral home, the man of prudence is completely at sea without a recognizable landmark or bearing to guide him. It would be an unusual person who would examine the various offerings and then inquire around about the relative advantages of the Monaco casket by Merit and the Valley Forge by Boyertown. In the matter of cost, a like difference is manifest. The funeral buyer is generally not in the mood to compare prices here, examine and appraise quality there. He is anxious to get the whole thing over with—not only is he anxious for this, but the exigencies of the situation demand it.

The third unusual factor which confronts the buyer is the need to make an on-the-spot decision. Impulse buying, which should, he knows, be avoided in everyday life, is here a built-in necessity. The convenient equivocations of commerce—"I'll look around a little, and let you know," "Maybe, I'll call you in a couple of weeks if I decide to take it," "My partner is going to Detroit next month, he may pick one up for me there"—simply do not apply in this situation. Unlike most purchases, this one cannot be returned in fifteen days and your money refunded in full if not completely satisfied.

Not only is the funeral buyer barred by circumstances from shopping around in a number of establishments; he is also barred by convention and his own feelings from complaining afterwards if he thinks he was overcharged or otherwise shabbily treated. The reputation of the TV repairman, the lawyer, the plumber is public property and their shortcomings are often the subject of dinner party conversation. The reputation of the undertaker is relatively safe in this respect. A friend, knowing I was writing on the subject, reluctantly told me of her experience in arranging the funeral of a brother-in-law. She went to a long-established, "reputable" undertaker. Seeking to save the widow expense, she chose the cheapest redwood casket in the establishment and was quoted a low price. Later, the salesman called her back to say the brother-in-law was too tall to fit into this casket, she would have to take one that cost $100 more. When my friend objected, the salesman said, "Oh, all right, we'll use the redwood one, but we'll have to cut off his feet." My friend was so shocked and disturbed by the nightmare quality of this conversation that she never mentioned it to anybody for two years.

Popular ignorance about the law as it relates to the disposal of the dead is a factor that sometimes affects the funeral transaction. People are often astonished to learn that in no state is embalming required by law except in certain special circumstances, such as when the body is to be shipped by common carrier.

The funeral men foster these misconceptions, sometimes by coolly misstating the law to the funeral buyer and sometimes by inferentially investing with the authority of law certain trade practices which they find it convenient or profitable to follow. This free and easy attitude to the law is even to be found in those institutes of higher learning, the Colleges of Mortuary Science, where the fledgling undertaker receives his training. For example, it is the law in most states that when a decedent bequeaths his body for use in medical research, his survivors are bound to carry out his directions. Nonetheless an embalming textbook, *Modern Mortuary Science,* disposes of the whole distasteful subject in a few misleading words: "Q: Will the provisions in the will of a decedent that his body be given to a medical college for dissection be upheld over his widow? A: No . . . No-one owns or controls his own body to the extent that he may dispose of the same in a manner which would bring humiliation and grief to the immediate members of his family."

I had been told so often that funeral men tend to invent the law as they go along (for there is a fat financial reward at stake) that I decided to investigate this situation at first hand. Armed with a copy of the California code, I telephoned a leading undertaker in my community with a concocted story: my aged aunt, living in my home, was seriously ill—not expected to live more than a few days. Her daughter was coming here directly; but I felt I ought to have some suggestions, some arrangements to propose in the event that . . . Sympathetic monosyllables from my interlocutor. The family would want something very simple, I went on, just cremation. Of course, we can arrange all that, I was assured. And since we want only cremation, and there will be no service, we should prefer not to buy a coffin. The undertaker's voice at the other end of the phone was now alert, although smooth. He told me, calmly and authoritatively, that it would be "illegal" for him to enter into such an arrangement. "You mean, it would be against the law?" I asked. Yes, indeed. "In that case, perhaps we could take the body straight to the crematorium in our station wagon?" A shocked silence, followed by an explosive outburst: "Madam, the average lady has neither the facilities nor the inclination to be hauling dead bodies around!" (Which was actually a good point, I thought.)

I tried two more funeral establishments, and was told substantially the same thing: cremation of an uncoffined body is prohibited under California law. This was said, in all three cases, with such a ring of conviction that I began to doubt the evidence before my eyes in the state code. I re-read the sections on cremation, on health requirements; finally I read the whole thing from cover to cover. Finding nothing, I checked with an officer of the Board of Health, who told me there is no law in California requiring that a coffin be used when a body is cremated. He added that indigents are cremated by some county welfare agencies without benefit of coffin.

It is, however, true that most privately owned crematoria have their own privately established rule that they will not cremate without a coffin. After all, why not? Many are in the casket-selling business themselves, and those that are not depend for their livelihood on the good will of funeral directors who are.

Cemetery salesmen are also prone to confuse fact with fiction to their own advantage in discussing the law. Cemeteries derive a substantial income from the sale of "vaults." The vault, a cement enclosure for the casket, is not only a money-maker; it facilitates upkeep of the cemetery by preventing the eventual subsidence of the grave as the casket disintegrates. In response to my inquiry, a cemetery salesman (identified on his card as a "memorial counselor") called at my house to sell me what he was pleased to call a "pre-need memorial estate," in other words, a grave for future occupancy. After he had quoted the prices of the various graves, the salesman explained that a minimum of $120 must be added for a vault, which, he said, is "required by law."

"Why is it required by law?"

"To prevent the ground from caving in."

"But suppose I should be buried in one of those Eternal caskets made of solid bronze?"

"Those things are not as solid as they look. You'd be surprised how soon they fall apart."

"Are you *sure* it is required by law?"

"I've been in this business fifteen years; I should know."

"Then would you be willing to sign this?" (I had been writing on a sheet of paper, "California State Law requires a vault for ground burial.")

The memorial counselor gathered up his colored photographs of memorial estates and walked out of the house.

The fifth unusual factor present in the funeral transaction is the availability to the buyer of relatively large sums of cash. The family accustomed to buying every major item on time—car, television set, furniture—and to spending to the limit of the weekly paycheck, suddenly finds itself in possession of insurance funds and death benefit payments, often from a number of sources. It is usually unnecessary for the undertaker to resort to crude means to ascertain the extent of insurance coverage. A few simple and perfectly natural questions put to the family while he is completing the vital statistics forms will serve to elicit all he needs to know. For example, "Occupation of the deceased?" "Shall we bill the insurance company directly?"

The undertaker knows, better than a schoolboy knows the standings of the major league baseball teams, the death benefit payments of every trade union in the community, the social security and workmen's compensation scale of death benefits, the veterans' and servicemen's death benefits: social security payment, up to $255; if the deceased was a veteran, $250 more and free burial in a national cemetery; burial allowance of $400 and up for military personnel and U. S. Civil Service employees; $700 for retired railroad workers; additional funeral allowance of $300 to $800 under various state workmen's compensation laws if the death was occupationally connected, and so on and on.

The undertaker has all the information he needs to proceed with the sale. The widow, for the first time in possession of a large amount of ready cash, is likely to welcome his suggestions. He is, after all, the expert, the one who knows how these things should be arranged, who will steer her through the unfamiliar routines and ceremonies ahead, who will see that all goes as it should.

At the lowest end of the scale is the old-age pensioner, most of whose savings have long since been spent. He is among the poorest of the poor. Nevertheless, most state and county welfare agencies permit him to have up to $1,000 in cash; in some states he may own a modest home as well, without jeopardizing his pension. The funeral director knows that under the law of virtually every state the funeral bill is entitled to preference in payment as the first charge against the estate. (Efforts in some states to pass legislation limiting the amount of the priority for burial costs to, say, $500 have been frustrated by the funeral lobby.) There is every likelihood that the poor old chap will be sent out in high style unless his widow is a very, very cool customer indeed.

The situation that generally obtains in the funeral transaction was summed up by former Surrogate's Court Judge Fowler of New York in passing upon the reasonableness of a bill which had come before him: "One of the practical difficulties in such proceedings is that contracts for funerals are ordinarily made by persons differently situated. On the one side is generally a person greatly agitated or overwhelmed by vain regrets or deep sorrow, and on the other side persons whose business it is to minister to the dead for profit. One side is, therefore, often unbusinesslike, vague and forgetful, while the other is ordinarily alert, knowing and careful."

There are people, however, who know their own minds perfectly well and who approach the purchase of a funeral much as they would any other transaction. They are, by the nature of things, very much in the minority. Most frequently they are not in the immediate family of the deceased but are friends or representatives of the family. Their experiences are interesting because to some extent they throw into relief the irrational quality of the funeral transaction.

Mr. Rufus Rhoades, a retired manufacturer of San Rafael, California, was charged with arranging for the cremation of a ninety-two-year-old friend who died in a rest home in 1961. He telephoned the crematorium, and was quoted the price of $75 for cremation plus $15 for shipping the ashes to Santa Monica, where his friend's family had cemetery space. He suggested hiring an ambulance to pick up the body, but this idea was quickly vetoed by the crematorium. He was told that he would have to deal through an undertaker, that the body could not be touched by anyone but a licensed funeral director, that a "container" would have to be provided. This he was unaware of; and no wonder, for these are "regulations" of the crematorium, not requirements of California law.

Mr. Rhoades looked in the San Rafael telephone directory, and found five funeral establishments listed. He picked one at random, called, and was told that under no circumstances could price be discussed over the telephone as it was "too private a matter"; that he should come down to the funeral home. There he found that the cheapest price, including "a low priced casket and the complete services" was $480. Mr. Rhoades protested that he did not *wish* the complete services, that there was to be no embalming, that he did not want to see the coffin. He merely wanted the body removed from the rest home and taken to the crematorium, some five miles away. Balking at the $480, Mr. Rhoades returned home and telephoned the other four funeral establishments. The lowest quotation he could obtain was $250.

Not unnaturally, Mr. Rhoades feels that he paid a fee of $50 a mile to have his friend's body moved from the rest home to the crematorium. The undertaker no doubt felt, for his part, that he had furnished a service well below his "break even" point, or, in his own terminology, "below the cost at which we are fully compensated."

There was the case of a young widow whose husband died of cancer in 1950 after a long illness in Oakland, California. His death was fully expected by both of them, and they had discussed the matter of his funeral. The day he died, the widow left town to stay with her mother, leaving the funeral arrangements in the hands of their attorney, who was also a close friend. There was to be no religious service, just cremation and disposal of the ashes. Cremation, the attorney learned, would cost $60. The body had already been moved from the hospital to a nearby funeral establishment, so the attorney telephoned the undertaker to instruct him to deliver it to the crematorium. To his astonishment, he was told the minimum price for this would be $350—"including our complete services." There ensued a long conversation full of cross-purposes; for what "service" could now possibly be rendered to the dead man, to his widow who was thousands of miles away, or indeed to anybody? The funeral director insisted that this was the lowest price at which he would be fully compensated. Compensated for what? demanded the attorney. For the complete services . . . and so it went, until the attorney blew up and threatened to complain to the hospital that they had recommended an unscrupulous funeral establishment. At that point, the undertaker reduced his price to $150.

The point of view of the funeral director must here be explored. I talked with Mr. Robert MacNeur, owner of the largest funeral establishment in the Oakland area, with a volume of 1,000 funerals a year. Their cheapest offering is the standard service with redwood casket, at $485. "My firm has never knowingly subjected a person to financial hardship," Mr. MacNeur declared. "We will render a complete funeral service for nothing if the circumstances warrant it. The service is just the same at no charge as it is for a $1,000 funeral."

Mr. MacNeur produced a copy of the "Grant Miller Cooperative Plan," in which this philosophy is spelled out, and is here quoted in full: "Grant Miller Mortuaries have served the families of this community for over sixty years. It has always been their policy to provide funeral service regardless of financial circumstances. If a family finds the First Standard Arrangement including the finer type Redwood Casket at $485 to be beyond their present means or wishes, Grant Miller Mortuaries stand ready to reduce costs in accordance with the following cooperative plan chart, rather than use one or a series of cheap or inferior caskets."

The price chart which accompanies this shows the buyer that if he cannot afford to pay $485 for the cheapest casket in the house, he can have it, with the complete service, for $422.50. If he cannot afford that,

he can pay $360, or $297.50, or $235, or $117.50, and
so on down the line to "$0" for "persons in Distress
Circumstances." It is the undertaker, of course, who
decides who is eligible for these dispensations.

The retired manufacturer and the young widow happened to be extremely well off financially. They were not
entitled to, neither did they solicit, any sort of charitable
contribution from the funeral establishments or any
reduction of the charges because of "distress circumstances." But as business people they were astonished
that the undertakers should expect them to pay several
hundred dollars for merchandise and services they wanted
no part of, as a kind of assessment or contribution to
the operation of the funeral establishment. The undertakers, it should be added, were equally incredulous, and
possibly hurt, that these people should question their
method of doing business.

The guiding rule in funeral pricing appears to be
"from each according to his means," regardless of the
actual wishes of the family. A funeral director in San
Francisco says, "If a person drives a Cadillac, why should
he have a Pontiac funeral?" The Cadillac symbol figures
prominently in the funeral men's thinking. There is a
funeral director in Los Angeles who says his rock-bottom
minimum price is $200. But he reserves to himself the
right to determine who is eligible for this minimum-priced
service. "I won't sell it to some guy who drives up in a
Cadillac." This kind of reasoning is peculiar to the funeral
industry. A person can drive up to an expensive
restaurant in a Cadillac and can order, rather than the
$10 dinner, a 25-cent cup of tea and he will be served.
It is unlikely that the proprietor will point to his elegant
furnishings and staff, and will demand that the Cadillac
owner should order something more commensurate with
his ability to pay so as to help defray the overhead of the
restaurant.

There is, however, one major difference between the
restaurant transaction and the funeral transaction. It is
clear that while the Cadillac owner may return to the

restaurant tomorrow with a party of six and order $10 dinners all around, this will not be true of his dealings with the undertaker. In the funeral business it's strictly one to a customer. Very likely many a funeral director has echoed with heartfelt sincerity the patriotic sentiments of Nathan Hale: "My only regret is that I have but one life to give for my country." The television industry touts the advantages of a TV set in every room; auto salesmen urge the convenience of several cars for every family; cigarette manufacturers urge "a carton for the home and one for the office"; but if the undertaker fails to move in and strike while the iron is hot, the opportunity is literally lost and gone forever. (The only exception to this is noted by the Clark Metal Grave Vault people, who in their advertisements advance the startling thought: "DISINTERMENTS—RARE BUT REWARDING. It needn't be a problem. *It can lead to repeat business.* . . .")

The funeral industry faces a unique economic situation in that its market is fixed, or inelastic; and as the death rate steadily declines, the problems become sharper.

3

FUNERAL COSTS

In 1960, Americans spent, according to the only available government estimate, $1.6 billion on funerals, setting thereby a new national and world record. The $1.6 billion is, as we shall see, only a portion of what was actually spent on what the death industry calls "the care and memorialization of the dead." Even this partial figure, if averaged out among the number of deaths, would amount to the astonishing sum of $942 for the funeral of every man, woman, child and stillborn babe who died in the United States in 1960.

The $1.6 billion figure that is given for our national burial bill is furnished by the U.S. Department of Commerce census of business under the heading "personal expenditure for death expense." Since it includes personal expenditures only, it does not include burial expenditures by cities and counties and by private and public institutions for the burial of indigents, welfare recipients and persons confined in public institutions, nor does it include burial expenditures by the armed forces for military personnel. How much do these public expenditures amount to annually? Nobody knows, for there is no centrally maintained source of information. The burial of indigents, for example, is a matter of city or county concern. There are some 3,000 counties in the United States, and among them there is a wildly disparate variation in costs and procedures. Some counties contract with funeral directors for casket, service and burial for as little as $70, some pay as much as $300 for casket and service alone. Other local authorities manufacture their own coffins and bury their indigent dead without the intervention of a private funeral director.

Another substantial item of funeral expense which is not included in the Department of Commerce figure of $1.6 billion is the cost of shipping the dead by train or plane. These charges must be considerable; one in ten of all the dead are shipped elsewhere for burial. Train fare for a corpse is double the cost of a single first-class ticket for a live passenger. Air transport is, as one might expect, becoming the preferred means of carriage for the modishly attired corpse, and on any day of the year not less than one hundred and fifty of these may be counted jetting their way to their various destinations. The standard rate for air shipment of human remains is two and one-half times the rate for other air freight; the average transcontinental fare for a dead body is $255.78. How much is spent annually for the transportation of the dead? The airlines won't tell you, the railroads don't seem to know, nor does any agency of the government.

Another item not included in the Department of Commerce figures is funeral flowers. These account for a good bit more than half of the dollar volume of all sales by retail florists in the United States.

Lastly, the Department of Commerce statistics leave out of account entirely the very considerable amounts spent each year by Americans who in increasing numbers buy graves and mausoleum crypts for future occupancy.

This mushrooming business is known in cemetery parlance as "pre-need" selling. "Pre-need" sales, although they now run into hundreds of millions of dollars annually, are nowhere reflected in the available national data on funeral expenditures.

It would be a conservative guess that these extras, if added to the Commerce Department's base figure of $1.6 billion, would bring the nation's burial bill to well over $2 billion. A little over three-fourths of all funerals are what the industry calls "regular adult funerals." The remainder are limited service funerals for infants and limited fee funerals for indigents and servicemen, handled by contract with government agencies. The Department of Commerce figure of $1.6 billion averages out to $1,160 for each regular adult funeral. The more realistic figure of $2 billion yields a nationwide average of $1,450 for the disposition of the mortal remains of an adult American.

Figures in the millions tend to startle, in the billions to numb the brain. Is $2 billion a lot or a little for a nation as rich and populous as the United States to pay for the disposal of its dead? The funeral men think on the whole it is rather a small sum. They like to compare it with the national liquor bill, or the national tobacco bill.

Less biased observers might think that $2 billion is rather a lot, even if it is less than we spend on whiskey or cigarettes. It might be more instructive to compare what we spend to bury the dead with what we spend for the health and welfare of the living.

Personal expenditures for all higher education—tuition, books, and living expenses for 3.6 million students enrolled in colleges and graduate schools in 1960—came to $1.9 billion, which is a little less than Americans spent to bury 1.7 million dead in the same year. We pay doctors more ($4.6 billion) but dentists less ($1.9 billion) than we spend on funerals. The cost of providing medical care for the aged, the 17 million Americans who are 65 or older, under a medical-hospital insurance program, would be less than the annual cost of dying in the United States. The Federal government spends less each year for conservation and development of natural resources than we spend on funerals. Americans spend more on funerals than they spend on police protection ($1.8 billion) or on fire protection ($1 billion).

Funeral people, confronted with the charge that they are responsible for the staggering cost of dying, loudly protest their innocense; how can it be *their* fault, if fault it be? they say. It is up to the individual family to decide how much to spend on a funeral, and if Americans spend more on death than they spend on higher education or conservation, that's only because funeral buyers are exercising their inalienable right to spend their money as they choose.

"How much should a funeral cost?" says Mr. Wilbur Krieger, managing director of the National Selected Morticians. "That's like asking how much should I pay for a house or how much for a car. You can buy at all prices." Most funeral advertising stresses the same thought: "The decision of how much to spend for a funeral always rests with the family." "A funeral should cost exactly what you desire, for the cost and selection is entirely in your hands."

Very occasionally, somebody within the industry will spill the beans. Such a one was W. W. Chambers, self-styled "slab-happy" mortician of Washington, D.C., a self-made man who built a million-dollar mortuary empire. "It's the most highly specialized racket in the world," he declared, testifying before a Congressional committee in 1947. "It has no standard prices; whatever can be charged and gotten away with is the guiding rule. My competitors don't like my habit of advertising prices in black and white, because they'd rather keep the right to charge six different prices for the same funeral to six different people, according to what they can pay. Why, some of these bums charge a family $90 to bury a poor little baby in a casket that costs only $4.50." Scoffing at the suggestion that an undertaker is a "professional man,"

Chambers said any good plumber could learn how to embalm in sixty days. He added that he could embalm a human body for 40 cents and an elephant for $1.50.

Mr. Chambers's views are frequently echoed by the man on the other side of the Arrangements Conference table, the funeral customer. A railroad worker writes, "They really do not use a gun to hold you up, but they sure do everything else. This thing happened to a friend of ours; now I am only talking about people in very ordinary circumstances. To make a long story short, the whole thing cost $1,200." A lawyer in Akron, Ohio: "It has long been my belief that American funeral directors exploit the grief of a bereaved family, as well as empty their pockets." A retired carpenter, in the quavering hand of the very old: "I have just buried a sister and it cost $900 just for the undertaker. I cannot see why it would cost so much. I cannot for the life of me see why we feel that we must spend anywhere from $400 up for a casket with silver handles, box springs, etc., which we put in the ground and cover with dirt. What we pay for a so-called decent burial, a man could buy a good lathe with its intricate parts. Where a metal casket is just stamped and welded metal. To dig a grave here in Philadelphia cost my niece $90 and it was done with a steam shovel. Also here in Penna you must have a concrete box in which to place the casket. They told us, 'It's a law.' It looks as though the morticians are out to get you at all turns. You say to yourself, I won't buy a lot and I will save the cost of a lot and the concrete box and the digging of the grave. But some of them say you must be embalmed and placed in a casket before they will cremate you."

I have read hundreds of letters like these. More than five thousand have poured into the San Francisco Bay Area Funeral Society from all parts of the country since the appearance of an article in a national magazine describing the Society's program for simple and dignified funerals at low cost. A wide gulf seems to separate these indignant customers from the funeral men who assure us that "the decision of how much to spend always rests with the family."

Thirty-five years ago a detailed study of funeral costs was undertaken under the sponsorship of the Metropolitan Life Insurance Company, which appropriated $25,000 for the work.

The director of the survey, Mr. John C. Gebhart, made this observation: "The business practices of the funeral director have always been shrouded in mystery. There is probably no form of commercial enterprise about which the public is in such complete ignorance."

The Gebhart study was an attempt, the first and only one of broad scope, to unravel the mystery and to present a comprehensive view of the burial business in all its aspects.

The question was posed: "Do present funeral charges fall with undue severity upon those least able to incur them?" The answer, contained in some 300 pages of statistical tables and interpretation, is a resounding "Yes."

The study was commissioned after a quarter of a century of frustrated attempts by the company to protect its policyholders from victimization by undertakers.* As early as 1903, social workers were complaining that the undertakers invariably managed to find out the amount of industrial insurance carried by the deceased, and then made sure that their bills were sufficiently large to absorb all of the insurance money available.

Two years later, in 1905, Mr. Haley Fiske, vice-president of Metropolian, sent a letter to all the company's superintendents and assistant superintendents, ordering them to refuse information to undertakers, to discourage their attendance at the office, and to make it easy for claimants to get their own papers and money

---

*When I mentioned the Gebhart report in a conversation with Mr. Wilber Krieger, the managing director of National Selected Morticians, he commented rather drily that Metropolitan's sponsorship of the study was not entirely a matter of altruism; that Metropolitan, as the largest seller of burial insurance in the United States, stood to boost its sales by reminding the public that dying costs a lot.

without the "help" of a solicitous undertaker: "You can often drop a word of advice against extravagance in funerals. Above all make it plain that a claimant needs no help or influence in order to collect insurance; that he or she is welcome to come alone and will receive all the more attention for doing so; and that there is no reason ever why they should give their policies to undertakers as security or tell undertakers what the amount of the insurance is; and you can make sure that none of our men furnish such information. You can give them a written certificate that a policy is in force on the life at the date of death wthout stating the amount. In short we ought to do everything possible to protect our policyholders and to help them make the money go as far as it will. . . ." He adds testily, "This letter is intended to be mandatory as well as advisory."

In spite of this directive to its employees, Metropolitan found that undertakers continued to skim off all that could be skimmed from the insurance money accruing to survivors.

Another approach was attempted. Metropolitan now sought to work directly with the Undertakers Association for the purpose of establishing standard rates and services. "It was pointed out that if any considerable number of undertakers were willing to offer standard rates, the company would be prepared to duly notify its policyholders of the names and addresses of such undertakers and of the conditions under which they would furnish funerals." The Undertakers replied characteristically with one of their matchless flights into semantic obscurantism, mutilating beyond recognition words like "ethics" and "professional": "The Association deems it inexpedient to meet with your plans, owing to the fact that to do so would be in direct opposition to the most important factor in our Code of Ethics, which relates to advertising goods and prices. The Association has always aimed to improve and place our calling on a professional basis, and to start in and advocate the advertising of goods and prices, we consider would be derogatory to our profession."

Finding itself blocked at every turn in its attempts to protect policyholders from extortionate funeral charges, Metropolitan in 1926 initiated its study. An independent Advisory Committee on Burial Survey was established, drawn from religious groups, the professions, and the burial industry itself. The committee must have been sorely tried from time to time in the course of its work; a detailed questionnaire seeking information about prices, directed to some 23,000 undertaking establishments, drew only a 2 per cent response. "It was found impossible to make any statistical use of the material submitted."

Luckily, the Advisory Committee had access to an alternate source of information—Metropolitan's 20 million industrial policyholders. A painstaking examination of thousands of their funeral bills revealed the key to funeral pricing, summed up in a phrase that occurs again and again in the Gebhart study: "They charge what the traffic will bear." It was found, moreover, that the burden of burial costs fell most heavily on the poorest families.

Mr. Gebhart had high hopes for the effect his disclosures would have. Never was crystal ball more clouded than the one in which he saw the funeral industry taking steps to cut prices as a result of his work: "The cost finding study is already culminating in a movement (by the undertakers) which will lead to a marked reduction in funeral costs." The cost of dying has instead risen in a straight line, at a 45-degree angle, outstripping by a considerable margin the cost of living (see chart). Burial costs have more than tripled since his optimistic words were committed to print.

About once every decade in the last fifty years the complacency of the undertaking business has been shattered by magazine and newspaper exposés of the high cost of dying and the exploitation of bereavement. There is no evidence that these have had the slightest effect on funeral costs, which have continued serenely to rise in the wake of each outcry. One reason for this has been the lack of a vehicle for organized protest and action by the consumer (one wishes there were some other word to describe the

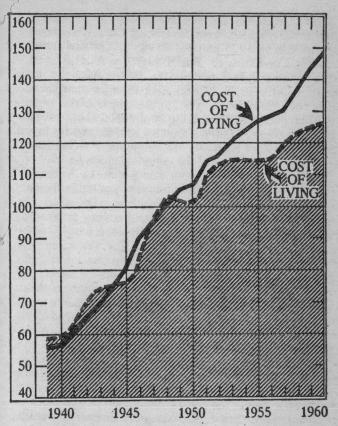

The figure 100 halfway up the left side of the chart is an index number representing the cost of living and dying in the base period, 1947-49. The broken line shows the rise in the cost of living during the years 1939 to 1960. The solid black line shows the rise of the cost of dying in the same period.

Source: Computed from data of U.S. Departments of Labor, Commerce, and Health, Education and Welfare.

buyer of funerals). Another is the lack of solid statistical and economic data to work with.

There has been no serious attempt at a general study of funeral costs in the United States since Gebhart. The Federal government agencies—Social Security Administration, Railroad Retirement Board, Civil Service Commission and Veterans Administration—which pay out hundreds of millions of dollars annually in burial allowances, have not the slightest idea of what the consumer actually pays for burial services, and, except for the Veterans Administration through its contract burial program,* make no effort to protect the beneficiaries from exploitation by funeral directors. The Bureau of Labor Statistics has not in the past included burial costs in its cost of living index (there are, however, indications that it may be preparing to do so in the future). Universities and foundations have likewise neglected the funeral cost problem. The field, then, has been left by default to the funeral directors, who from time to time publish cost studies which leave something to be desired from the standpoint of accuracy and objectivity.

The few investigations that have been conducted— sporadic, inadequately financed, usually confined to a single community or a single group—indicate that funerals continue to bankrupt the families of workers and that undertakers continue to appropriate insurance money intended for the survivors, the only difference being that there is today a great deal more insurance money around for them to grab.

The 1947 Centralia, Illinois, mine disaster, in which 111 men were killed, proved a bonanza for the undertakers of that community. The *United Mineworkers Journal* angrily reported, "The Centralia undertakers moved in like ghouls," and spoke of the "unconscionable greed that literally followed the victims to their graves and mulcted the surviving dependents of sizable sums from the Welfare Fund death gratuity and state compensation they received." An investigation by the U. S. Coal Mines Ad-

*See Chapter Notes.

ministration revealed that funeral charges levied against the widows of the miners averaged $732.78. All but six of the funerals (94.6 per cent) cost more than $500; 24 ranged in price from $900 to $1,178.50. The undertakers' total take was around $80,000. Examination of the individual bills showed a wild disparity between amounts charged for substantially identical services. A "bronze metallic casket" cost one family $645, while a "gray metal casket" of cheaper construction was billed at $835. The "standard service" charge, exclusive of casket, ranged from $690 for a $976.30 funeral to $395 for a $545.15 funeral.

The community rallied to the aid of the miners' families. AFL hod carriers dug and filled the graves without charge—and the undertakers showed this fraternal contribution on their bills as a "credit" of $10, deducted from their own charge for the standard service. To add insult to injury, when the undertakers were approached by other businessmen in the town for a contribution to the Centralia Miners Relief Fund, they made their donations in the form of discounts on the funeral bills—from $11.85 on a $567 funeral to $22.50 on a $937.50 funeral.

The attitude of funeral industry leaders to the behavior of their colleagues in Centralia sheds some light on the "ethical standards of the profession." I asked Mr. Wilber Krieger whether any steps had been taken within the industry to discipline the Centralia undertakers. He answered most indignantly that in his opinion they had committed no transgression, they had in no way violated any code of ethics. On the contrary, they had risen nobly to the emergency, had worked long and hard to provide funeral service for the dead miners. "They served those families as they wished to be served." The prices charged did not seem out of line to Mr. Krieger; in any event, he said, this was a private matter between the widows and the funeral directors, and would never have become the subject of Government investigation had it not been for a few troublemakers in the mine workers' union.

Not only the victims of sweeping community disasters

feel the financial blows inflicted by the cost of modern funerals. Surveys by labor unions of funeral expenses incurred by their members reveal an uncanny correlation between available insurance or death benefit and funeral bill. For example, the Retail, Wholesale and Department Store Union, Local 65, of New York reports that where the member had been earning an average of $70 a week, and left a death benefit of $1,000, the funeral bill frequently amounted to $900 to $1,000. For those earning $85 a week, and receiving a death benefit of $1,500, the funeral bill was more commonly at the level of $1,200 to $1,500.

Labor union officials with responsibility for administering pension funds are becoming increasingly aware of the problem, and some are beginning to wonder who—the undertaker or the union member's family—is the principal beneficiary of their efforts to bargain for increased death payments. The *AFL-CIO Industrial Union Digest* says:

Certainly organized labor can ill afford to sit on its hands—and for reasons quite apart from the purely ethical. The New York State Insurance Department, for example, reports that in 1958 the 1,020 welfare and pension funds in the state jointly administered by labor and management and whose benefits were covered by insurance carriers paid out $11,914,-349 to the beneficiaries of deceased workers. *Seventy-five percent, or some eight million dollars, of that amount was siphoned off by undertakers.* The picture is probably about the same for the rest of the country. Without perhaps realizing it, organized labor, through its many welfare and pension plans, is thus helping to subsidize the burial industry.

It must not be inferred, from what has been said, that undertakers are by nature a special, evil breed, more greedy or more grasping than practitioners of other trades. As individuals I found them to be a rather jolly lot, no better and no worse than the run of people you would find at a Kiwanis or Rotary meeting. All of them, however, are in thrall to the peculiar economic situation that has developed within the industry.

There is in the undertaking business, as presently organized, a fantastic amount of waste, disorganization and inefficiency, for which the customer is expected to pay. Gebhart noted this peculiarity in his 1927 report:

Most of the waste in the burial industry is attributable to the multiplicity of funeral directors and manufacturers of burial goods. During the past 25 years the "demand" for funeral service, as limited by the death rate, has remained stationary, while the industry has expanded rapidly. Expansion in total volume of business has only been possible by selling more goods and more expensive goods to the same number of customers. . . . Even the extravagant charges on the part of certain undertakers are largely due to an effort to make a living out of a very small volume of business.

The situation within the industry has not changed appreciably in the intervening years. In contrast to the general trend of business in the direction of ever-greater concentration and size, the trend in the funeral industry has been in the opposite direction. A proliferation of funeral establishments in the last eighty years, in the face of a steadily declining death rate, has brought about a most unfavorable situation for the trade.

Thus in 1880 there were 993,000 deaths and 5,100 funeral establishments, giving each a potential clientele of 194 cases per year. By 1960 the number of funeral establishments had grown almost fivefold, to 25,000, each new one bigger and more lavishly appointed than the last, and they had to share a mere 1,700,000 deaths, for an average of fewer than 70 cases each per year. It is easy to see how, with the business so thinly distributed, there is an ever-present compulsion to make each sale a big one, to regard each opportunity as a golden one. The field is, without question, absurdly overcrowded.

What seems to have happened is that the undertaking population, while increasing roughly in proportion to the increase in the general population, neglected to take into account that the death rate, which was 19 per thousand in 1880, would by 1960 be exactly halved. By now, of course, the funeral directors have learned that while other businessmen eagerly scan the booming population figures and project them in planning for the future, they must gloomily confine themselves to the column headed "deaths per annum." They can comfort themselves, however, with the thought that in this department 1960's total of 1.7 million was the best since 1918, when the influenza epidemic helped make a record number of 1.8 million cadavers available to the trade. Mr. Wilber Krieger reports a hopeful trend: "We are coming to the end of a line, we cannot continue to expand the span of life for people indefinitely. It has to turn down. . . . Funeral directors that I'm meeting are telling me that there is a slight increase in mortality rate. So perhaps this trend that was forecast by a market analyst is becoming evident even a little ahead of his schedule."

So many undertakers competing for so few funerals should create, one would expect, a buyer's market, leading to lower prices. The opposite, we know, has occurred, and funeral prices have increased sinfully in the last fifty years. This paradoxical state of affairs can be explained in part, but not entirely, by the special features of the funeral transaction, discussed in the previous chapter, which strip the customer of the bargaining advantages he would normally enjoy in a competitive market.

The truth of the matter is that price competition in the funeral business has in many parts of the country been stifled virtually to extinction by price-fixing agreements. Since price-fixing agreements are illegal under the antitrust laws, there can be no question of the undertakers in a given area getting together and publishing a minimum price schedule.

How, then, is it done? It is no secret that members of local associations of funeral directors, usually at the city or county level, arrive at an understanding that "the lowest price at which the funeral director will be fairly compensated" in the given area is "X" dollars. This figure is arrived at by estimating the "average overhead per case" in the area.

"Average overhead per case," as used in undertaking circles, is a fictitious figure compounded of guesswork and hope. Each undertaker estimates his own average per case by totaling expenses for the previous year (labor costs, rent, equipment, depreciation, etc.), adding to it his estimate of the value of his own time, plus in some cases his hoped-for-profit, and dividing the total by the number of adult funerals he handled in the previous year. These estimates are pooled and from them is produced the average.

In one area (where the matter is, as of this writing, under investigation by antitrust lawyers), the average overhead is estimated to be $475. The wholesale cost of the cheapest coffin sold in this area is $40. Add this to the overhead, and $515 becomes the "lowest price at which the funeral director will be fully compensated" for his cheapest funeral. This becomes the established minimum price at which a funeral is offered by the conforming funeral directors. Once the line is set for the minimum casket and service, there is no attempt to fix prices for the higher-priced caskets. In fact above the area minimum there is no uniformity, and a casket selling for $895 in one establishment may be found in another priced at $1,195.

The participating undertakers attempt to hold the line by publicizing the overhead cost figures, by reminding their brethren that he who sells for less than $515 (except of course in cases deserving of charity) is hurting not only himself but all other funeral directors in the area as well.

Generally speaking, these arrangements are of greatest benefit to the smaller operators, the 60 per cent who average about one funeral a week, the 95 per cent who conduct fewer than 300 in the course of a year, whose very existence depends upon an effective shield from competition. The larger establishments, having lower operating expenses per case, benefit also; but they, and the chain operators who are beginning to emerge in this once highly individualized business, are the ones who first become restive under the restraints upon competition and who have in some areas already upset the applecart by advertising low-cost funerals.

When this happens, the little men who control the state associations of funeral directors can be counted on to move into action with the biggest guns they can find, which is like trying to plug a leak by blasting it with heavy artillery. In 1961 Mr. Nicholas Daphne, one of San Francisco's largest operators, was expelled from the California Funeral Directors Association, charged with a breach of ethics. The transgression which drew the penalty was advertising $150 funerals, at a time when other San Francisco undertakers were trying to hold the line at $500 for a minimum funeral service. Related to this charge was another: Daphne had contracts with two funeral societies to furnish low-cost funerals for their members.

Daphne's expulsion from the Association became front-page news in San Francisco. He was featured in national magazines as a friend of the consumer, doing battle against the price fixers and the monopolists. His already prosperous business prospered even more mightily. Then Forest Lawn of Los Angeles, whose mortuary handles over 6,000 funerals a year (one hundred times the volume of the average undertaker), took Daphne's ouster as its cue to blast the Association for its ban on price advertising. It resigned from the state association in a burst of publicity and followed up by blanketing Los Angeles with hundreds of billboards bearing the simple legend "Undertaking: $145." Utter-McKinley, a competitor with a chain of 16 mortuaries in the Los Angeles area, was not slow to respond, and soon hundreds of new billboards were uttering: "Undertaking: $100." Surveying the wreckage left in the wake of Daphne's expulsion, *Mortuary Managament* was moved to comment gloomily, "Like the Cuban invasion—ill-timed, improperly planned, mishandled. The intentions were honorable but the results disastrous."

No matter what the eventual development of the funeral

industry—whether it remains overcrowded and inefficient or moves, as seems inevitable, in the direction of the large supermarket type of operation—there is cold comfort for the consumer. Once having driven out their small competitors, there is no reason to believe the big-volume concerns will demonstrate a more tender regard for the pocketbooks of their customers than has traditionally been the case in the Dismal Trade.

4

THE ARTIFACTS

*Men have been most phantasticall in the singular contriv-
ances of their corporall dissolution. . . .*
—Sir Thomas Browne, *Urne-Buriall*

"The No. 280 reflects character and station in life. It is
superb in styling and provides a formal reflection of
successful living." This is quoted from the catalogue of
Practical Burial Footwear of Columbus, Ohio, and refers
to the Fit-A-Fut Oxford, which comes in patent, calf,
tan or oxblood with lace or goring back. The same firm
carries the Ko-Zee, with its "soft, cushioned soles and
warm, luxurious slipper comfort, but true shoe smartness."
Just what practical use is made of this footwear is
spelled out. Burial footwear demonstrates "consideration
and thoughtfulness for the departed." The closed portion
of the casket is opened for the family, who on looking see
that "the ensemble is complete although not showing.
You will gain their complete confidence and good will."
The women's lingerie department of Practical Burial
Footwear supplies a deluxe package, in black patent
box with gold-embossed inscription, of "pantee, vestee"

and nylon hose, "strikingly smart—ultimate in distinction." Also for the ladies is the "new Bra-form, Post Mortem Form Restoration," offered by Courtesy Products at the demonstrably low price of $11 for a package of 50—they "accomplish so much for so little."

Florence Gowns Inc. of Cleveland, Ohio, exhibited their line of "streetwear type garments and negligees" together with something new, a line of "hostess gowns and brunch coats," at a recent convention of the National Funeral Directors Association. (However, the devotional set exhibit at the same meeting, put on by Ray Funeral Supplies of Grand Rapids, Michigan, while it included "The Last Supper" in new paints and finishes, failed to come through with a "Last Brunch.")

The latest in casket styles range from classic (that is, the "urn theme,") to colonial to French provincial to futuristic—the "Transition" casket, styled for the future—surely, something here to please everybody. The patriotic theme comes through very strong just now, finding its most eloquent expression in Boyertown Burial Casket Company's "Valley Forge." This one is "designed to reflect the rugged, strong, soldierlike qualities associated with historic Valley Forge. . . . Its charm lies in the warm beauty of the natural grain and finish of finest Maple hardwoods. A casket designed indeed for a soldier—one that symbolizes the solid, dependable, courageous American ideals so bravely tested at Valley Forge." The Valley Forge casket is pictured in a full-page color spread in the October, 1961, issue of *Casket and Sunnyside,* resting on a scarlet velvet drapery, flanked by some early American cupboards. For all its soldierlike qualities it looks most comfortable, with its nice beige linen pillow and sheets. On the wall behind it hangs a portrait of George Washington who is looking, as usual, rather displeased.

For the less rugged, the bon vivant who dreams of rubbing shoulders with the international smart set, the gay dog who would risk all on the turn of a card, there is the "Monaco," a Duraseal metal unit by the Merit Company of Chicago, "with Sea Mist Polished Finish, interior richly lined in 600 Aqua Supreme Cheney velvet, magnificently quilted and shirred, with matching jumbo bolster and coverlet." Set against a romantic background depicting a brilliant Riviera sky, its allure heightened by suggestions of tropical ferns and a golden harp, this model can be had for not much more than the cost of a round-trip flight to Monte Carlo.

And for the homebody who is neither rugged nor daring, but is interested in solid comfort, Mr. Leslie Gruber, president of Major Casket Company, announces that their medium-priced metal caskets are now equipped with the "Beautyrama Adjustable Soft-Foam Bed. Quality mattress fabric is used and height adjustment is accomplished by patented means which eliminate cranking. Modified during a year of product development," he continues, "the bed is soft and buoyant, but will hold firm without slipping. . . . Beautyrama beds will be standard at no additional cost on the entire Major half couch, hinge cap and 20-gauge Sealtite line." Major will continue to use Sealy innerspring mattresses (we are assured) in its quality line of 18-gauge and copper Sealtite Caskets.

Children's caskets, "specially made for boys and girls," come in blue and white or pink and gold. These can be displayed on "attractive formica-covered biers."

Well, there is a great deal more to it. The observer, confronted for the first time by the treasures and artifacts of this unfamiliar world, may well feel something akin to the astonishment of Bernal Díaz at his first glimpse of the hitherto undiscovered court of Montezuma: "We were amazed," he declared, "and some of the soldiers even asked whether the things we saw were not a dream."

To venture a little further into the baroque wonderland of the mortuary: "The Final Touch that Means so Much" describes Geneva Sculptured Hardware (decorative handles and hinges), with its "natural beauty and mood-setting styles, a completely new concept of sculptured hardware to compliment [*sic*]* caskets; for emphasis, to heighten their attractiveness, and above all to make your completed product desirable—the final touch toward increased sales."

Then there is Brocatelle, one of Batesville Casket Company's decorator fabrics, "hand-loomed in the traditional European manner, custom designed, typical of the rich, heavy-figured fabrics used by royalty during the seventeenth, eighteenth and nineteenth centuries. These fabrics are color oriented with sculptured panels of complementary hues, an interpretation of the finest art and sculpture, usually found only in the world's leading decorator houses."

The burial vault is a relative newcomer in funeral wares. As late as 1915 it was used in only 5 to 10 per cent of all funerals—a far cry from today's proud slogan of a leading vault manufacturer, "A Wilbert Burial Vault Every Minute" (based, a footnote tells us, on an eight-hour workday). Since the word "vault" may connote to the uninitiated a burial chamber, a word of explanation is in order. The vault we are describing here is designed as an outer receptacle to protect the casket and its contents from the elements during their eternal sojourn in the grave. Vaults are made of a variety of materials; they may be of concrete, pre-asphalt-lined; of aluminum; of a copper, asphalt and concrete mixture; of fiber glass. In any case, a good vault is a "symbolic expression of affection." They are getting more beautiful by the year, may be had in a variety of colors including polished stripes, and are frequently decorated with all sorts of lovely things—foreverness symbols like Trees of Life or setting suns leading one to speculate as to whether the time may not be ripe for the introduction of a sur- or super- or supra-vault to protect the vault. And so on and on, like

---

*I do not like repeated use of *sic*. It seems to impart a pedantic, censorious quality to the writing. I have throughout made every effort to quote the funeral trade publications accurately; the reader who is fastidious about usage will hereafter have to supply his own *sics*.

those little wooden eggs-within-eggs we used to find in our Christmas stockings.

Cemeteries now compete with the funeral directors for the lucrative vault business. Many today *require* the use of vaults in all burials, for the ostensible reason that the vault prevents the caving in of the grave due to the eventual disintegration of the casket. The selling point made to the customer is, of course, the eternal preservation of the dead. It seems that the Midwest is a particularly fruitful territory for the sale of metal vaults. "Must be a psychological reason brought about by thoughts of extreme heat and cold, stormy weather, snow, and frozen ground," muses *Mortuary Management*.

An appropriate showcase setting for all these treasures assumes a special importance. Gone forever are the simple storefront undertaking establishments of earlier days. They have been replaced by elaborate structures in the style of English country houses, French provincial châteaux, Spanish missions, split-level suburban executive mansions, or Byzantine mosques—frequently, in a free-wheeling mixture of all these. A Gothic chapel may be carpeted with the latest in wall-to-wall two-inch-thick extra-pile Acrilan, and Persian rugs laid on top of this; its bronze-girt door may open onto an authentically furnished Victorian drawing room in one corner of which is a chrome-and-tile coffee bar. The slumber rooms in the same building may stress the light and airy Swedish modern motif.

The funeral home "chapel" has begun to assume more and more importance as the focal point of the establishment. In fact, many now call themselves "chapel." The nomenclature has gradually changed. From "undertaker" to "funeral parlor" to "funeral home" to "chapel" has been the linguistic progresson; *chapel* has the additional advantage of circumventing the word *funeral*. Chapel of the Chimes, Chapel of Memories, Little Chapel of the Flowers—these are replacing Snodgrass Funeral Home. The chapel proper is a simulated place of worship.

Because it has to be all things to all men, it is subject to a quick change by wheeling into place a "devotional chapel set" appropriate to the religion being catered to at the moment—a Star of David, a crucifix, a statue of the Virgin and so on. Advertisements and promotional brochures generally emphasize the chapel and its features: "Enter the chapel. Note how the sun pours its diffused glory through Gothic windows, and how the blue and amber, ruby and amethyst tones of glass play smilingly on walls and ceiling . . ." (Chapel of the Chimes brochure).

The slumber rooms are elusively reminiscent of some other feature of American life. What familiar, recurring establishments also boast such eclecticism of design, from medieval to futuristic, invariably combined with the most minute attention to comfort? In what category of building are you sure to find voluptuous carpeting underfoot, floor-length draw drapes, skillfully arranged concealed lighting to please the eye, temperature expertly adjusted by push button for maximum well-being—the soothing atmosphere of restful luxury pervading all? The answer was suggested by a funeral director with whom I was discussing costs. His prices are, as is customary in the trade, predicated on the cost of the casket, and he was explaining the items which go to make up the total. "So then you've got a slumber room tied up for three days or more," he said. "Right there's a consideration: How much would it cost you to stay in a good motel for three days? Fifty dollars or more, right?"

Motels for the dead! That's it, of course—a swimming pool and TV the only missing features.

The selection room is the portion of the mortuary where the caskets are displayed and offered for sale. It is here that all of the previous efforts of the funeral director—his advertising, his living the good life in the community, the impression he has made on the bereaved family during the arrangement conference—will be crowned with success or doomed to failure. It is here that the actual price of the funeral will be settled.

The decor and lighting of the selection room and

particularly the arrangement of merchandise are matters of greatest importance, for these, as we have seen, materially condition and affect the conduct of the transaction itself. As an interior decorator wrote, "Being the financial foundation of mortuary income, caution should be exercised in every detail and appointment, employing the finest selling qualities of color, lighting effects, proper placement of caskets, and special background features; the psychological effect producing a feeling of security and confidence that results in the sale of higher grade caskets, and the return of families for additional service when needed."

Further on decor, one writer advises that warm colors are said to be *advancing* colors; cold colors are *receding* colors. She recommends cool backgrounds to set off the warm walnut, mahogany, copper shades of the caskets. Another prefers touches of red about the place, possibly decorative wallpaper panels, and a bone-white ceiling to give a good distribution of light. The matter of good lighting is most important, because in a dim light it is hard to distinguish between low-grade rayon and transparent velvet casket linings. Throughout, "color, life and light" will provide the right atmosphere for people "conditioned to modern environment." A *minimum* of forty square feet of floor space is needed to display a burial casket, although if possible sixty square feet should be allowed for each unit.

We have glimpsed the chapel, the slumber rooms, the casket selection room, all designed for public inspection and edification. We have examined some of the choice and curious artifacts and their uses.

There is one door we have not yet opened, through which the public may not enter and behind which certain procedures take place—procedures indispensable to the proper utilization of the funeral director's merchandise and premises. What goes on in that forbidden territory, and why, can only be understood in context if we "weave in the service story."

5

THE STORY OF SERVICE

THERE WAS A TIME when the undertaker's tasks were clear-cut and rather obvious, and when he billed his patrons accordingly. Typical late-nineteenth-century charges, in addition to the price of merchandise, are shown on bills of the period as: "Services at the house (placing corpse in the coffin) $1.25," "Preserving remains on ice, $10," "Getting Permit, $1.50." It was customary for the undertaker to add a few dollars to his bill for being "in attendance," which seems only fair and right. The cost of embalming was around $10 in 1880. An undertaker, writing in 1900, recommends these minimums for service charges: Washing and dressing, $5; embalming, $10; hearse, $8 to $10. As Habenstein and Lamers, the historians of the trade, have pointed out, "The undertaker had yet to conceive of the value of personal services offered professionally for a fee, legitimately claimed." Well, he has now so conceived with a vengeance.

When weaving in the story of service as it is rendered today, spokesmen for the funeral industry tend to become so carried away by their own enthusiasm, so positively lyrical and copious in their declarations, that the outsider may have a little trouble understanding it all. There are indeed contradictions. Preferred Funeral Directors International has prepared a mimeographed talk designed to inform people about service: "The American public receive the services of employees and proprietor alike, nine and one half days of labor for every funeral handled, they receive the use of automobiles and hearses, a building including a chapel and other rooms which require building maintenance, insurance, taxes and licenses, and depreciation, as well as heat in the winter, cooling in the summer and light and water." The writer goes on to say that while the process of embalming takes only about three hours, yet, "it would be necessary for one man to work two forty-hour weeks to complete a funeral service. This is coupled with an additional forty hours service required by members of other local allied professions, including the work of the cemeteries, newspapers, and of course, the most important of all, the service of your clergyman. These some 120 hours of labor are the basic value on which the cost of funerals rests."

Our informant has lumped a lot of things together here. To start with "the most important of all, the service of your clergyman," the average religious funeral service lasts no more than 25 minutes. Furthermore, it is not, of course, paid for by the funeral director. The "work of the cemeteries" presumably means the opening and closing of a grave. This now mechanized operation, which takes 15 to 20 minutes, is likewise not billed as part of the funeral director's costs. The work of "newspapers"? This is a puzzler. Presumably reference is made here to the publication of an obituary notice on the vital statistics page. It is, incidentally, surprising to learn that newspaper work is considered an "allied profession."

Just how insurance, taxes, licenses and depreciation are figured in as part of the 120 man-hours of service is hard to tell. The writer does mention that his operation features "65 items of service." In general, the funeral salesman is inclined to chuck in everything he does under the heading of "service." For example, in a typical list of "services" he will include items like "securing statistical data" (in other words, completing the death certificate and finding out how much insurance was left by the deceased), "the arrangements conference" (in which the sale of the funeral to the survivors is made), and the "keeping of records," by which he means his own bookkeeping work. Evidently there is some confusion here between items that properly belong in a cost-accounting system and items of *actual* service rendered in any given funeral. In all likelihood, idle time of employees is figured in and prorated as part of the "man-hours." The up-to-date funeral home operates on a 24-hour basis, and the mimeographed speech contains this heartening news:

The funeral service profession of the United States is proud of the fact that there is not a person within the continental limits of the United States who is more than two hours away from a licensed funeral director and embalmer in case of need. That's one that even the fire fighting apparatus of our country cannot match.

While the hit-or-miss rhetoric of the foregoing is fairly typical of the prose style of the funeral trade as a whole, and while the statement that 120 man-hours are devoted to a single man- (or woman-) funeral may be open to question, there really is a fantastic amount of service accorded the dead body and its survivors.

Having decreed what sort of funeral is right, proper and nice, and having gradually appropriated to himself all the functions connected with it, the funeral director has become responsible for a multitude of tasks beyond the obvious one of "placing corpse in the coffin" recorded in our nineteenth-century funeral bill. His self-imposed duties fall into two main categories: attention to the corpse itself, and the stage-managing of the funeral.

The drama begins to unfold with the arrival of the corpse at the mortuary.

Alas, poor Yorick! How surprised he would be to see how his counterpart of today is whisked off to a funeral parlor and is in short order sprayed, sliced, pierced, pickled, trussed, trimmed, creamed, waxed, painted, rouged and neatly dressed—transformed from a common corpse into a Beautiful Memory Picture. This process is known in the trade as embalming and restorative art, and is so universally employed in the United States and Canada that the funeral director does it routinely, without consulting corpse or kin. He regards as eccentric those few who are hardy enough to suggest that it might be dispensed with. Yet no law requires embalming, no religious doctrine commends it, nor is it dictated by considerations of health, sanitation, or even of personal daintiness. In no part of the world but in Northern America is it widely used. The purpose of embalming is to make the corpse presentable for viewing in a suitably costly container; and here too the funeral director routinely, without first consulting the family, prepares the body for public display.

Is all this legal? The processes to which a dead body may be subjected are after all to some extent circumscribed by law. In most states, for instance, the signature of next of kin must be obtained before an autopsy may be performed, before the deceased may be cremated, before the body may be turned over to a medical school for research purposes; or such provision must be made in the decedent's will. In the case of embalming, no such permission is required nor is it ever sought. A textbook, *The Principles and Practices of Embalming,* comments on this: "There is some question regarding the legality of much that is done within the preparation room." The author points out that it would be most unusual for a responsible member of a bereaved family to instruct the mortician, in so many words, to *"embalm"* the body of a deceased relative. The very term "embalming" is so seldom used that the mortician must rely upon custom in the matter. The author concludes that unless the family specifies otherwise, the act of entrusting the body to the care of a funeral establishment carries with it an implied permission to go ahead and embalm.

Embalming is indeed a most extraordinary procedure, and one must wonder at the docility of Americans who each year pay hundreds of millions of dollars for its perpetuation, blissfully ignorant of what it is all about, what is done, how it is done. Not one in ten thousand has any idea of what actually takes place. Books on the subject are extremely hard to come by. They are not to be found in most libraries or bookshops.

In an era when huge television audiences watch surgical operations in the comfort ot their living rooms, when, thanks to the animated cartoon, the geography of the digestive system has become familiar territory even to the nursery school set, in a land where the satisfaction of curiosity about almost all matters is a national pastime, the secrecy surrounding embalming can, surely, hardly be attributed to the inherent gruesomeness of the subject. Custom in this regard has within this century suffered a complete reversal. In the early days of American embalming, when it was performed in the home of the deceased, it was almost mandatory for some relative to stay by the embalmer's side and witness the procedure. Today, family members who might wish to be in attendance would certainly be dissuaded by the funeral director. All others, except apprentices, are excluded by law from the preparation room.

A close look at what does actually take place may explain in large measure the undertaker's intractable reticence concerning a procedure that has become his major *raison d'être*. Is it possible he fears that public information about embalming might lead patrons to wonder if they really want this service? If the funeral men are loath to discuss the subject outside the trade, the reader may, understandably, be equally loath to go on reading at this point. For those who have the stomach for it, let us part the formaldehyde curtain. Others should skip to page 74.

The body is first laid out in the undertaker's morgue—

or rather, Mr. Jones is reposing in the preparation room—
to be readied to bid the world farewell.

The preparation room in any of the better funeral establishments has the tiled and sterile look of a surgery, and
indeed the embalmer-restorative artist who does his
chores there is beginning to adopt the term "dermasur-
geon" (appropriately corrupted by some mortician-writers
as "demisurgeon") to describe his calling. His equipment,
consisting of scalpels, scissors, augers, forceps, clamps,
needles, pumps, tubes, bowls and basins, is crudely imitative of the surgeon's, as is his technique, acquired in a
nine- or twelve-month post-high-school course in an embalming school. He is supplied by an advanced chemical
industry with a bewildering array of fluids, sprays, pastes,
oils, powders, creams, to fix or soften tissue, shrink or
distend it as needed, dry it here, restore the moisture
there. There are cosmetics, waxes and paints to fill and
cover features, even plaster of Paris to replace entire
limbs. There are ingenious aids to prop and stabilize the
cadaver: a Vari-Pose Head Rest, the Edwards Arm and
Hand Positioner, the Repose Block (to support the shoulders during the embalming), and the Throop Foot Positioner, which resembles an old-fashioned stocks.

Mr. John H. Eckels, president of the Eckels College of
Mortuary Science, thus describes the first part of the embalming procedure: "In the hands of a skilled practitioner,
this work may be done in a comparatively short time and
without mutilating the body other than by slight incision
—so slight that it scarcely would cause serious inconve-
nience if made upon a living person. It is necessary to
remove the blood, and doing this not only helps in the
disinfecting, but removes the principal cause of disfigure-
ments due to discoloration."

Another textbook discusses the all-important time element: "The earlier this is done, the better, for every
hour that elapses between death and embalming will add
to the problems and complications encountered. . . ."
Just how soon should one get going on the embalming?
The author tells us, "On the basis of such scanty informa-

tion made available to this profession through its rudimentary and haphazard system of techinical research, we must conclude that the best results are to be obtained if the subject is embalmed before life is completely extinct—that is, before cellular death has occurred. (In the average case, this would mean within an hour after somatic death." For those who feel that there is something a little rudimentary, not to say haphazard, about this advice, a comforting thought is offered by another writer. Speaking of fears entertained in early days of premature burial, he points out, ("One of the effects of embalming by chemical injection, however, has been to dispel fears of live burial.") How true; once the blood is removed, chances of live burial are indeed remote.

To return to Mr. Jones, the blood is drained out through the veins and replaced by embalming fluid pumped in through the arteries. As noted in *The Principles and Practices of Embalming,* "every operator has a favorite injection and drainage point—a fact which becomes a handicap only if he fails or refuses to forsake his favorites when conditions demand it."—Typical favorites are the carotid artery, femoral artery, jugular vein, subclavian vein. There are various choices of embalming fluid. If Flextone is used, it will produce a "mild flexible rigidity. The skin retains a velvety softness, the tissues are rubbery and pliable. Ideal for women and children." It may be blended with B. and G. Products Company's Lyf-Lyk tint, which is guaranteed to reproduce "nature's own skin texture . . . the velvety appearance of living tissue." Suntone comes in three separate tints: Suntan; Special Cosmetic Tint, a pink shade "especially indicated for young female subjects"; and Regular Cosmetic Tint, moderately pink.

About three to six gallons of a dyed and perfumed solution of formaldehyde, glycerin, borax, phenol, alcohol and water is soon circulating through Mr. Jones, whose mouth has been sewn together with a "needle directed upward between the upper lip and gum and brought out slightly "for a more pleasant expression." If he should be bucktoothed, his teeth are cleaned with Bon Ami and coated with colorless nail polish. His eyes, meanwhile, are closed with flesh-tinted eye caps and eye cement.

The next step is to have at Mr. Jones with a thing called a trocar. This is a long, hollow needle attached to a tube. It is jabbed into the abdomen, poked around the entrails and chest cavity, the contents of which are pumped out and replaced with "cavity fluid." This done, and the hole in the abdomen sewn up, Mr. Jones's face is heavily creamed (to protect the skin from burns which may be caused by leakage of the chemicals), and he is covered with a sheet and left unmolested for a while. But not for long—there is more, much more, in store for him. He has been embalmed, but not yet restored, and the best time to start the restorative work is eight to ten hours after embalming, when the tissues have become firm and dry.

The object of all this attention to the corpse, it must be remembered, is to make it presentable for viewing in an attitude of healthy repose. "Our customs require the presentation of our dead in the semblance of normality . . . unmarred by the ravages of illness, disease or mutilation," says Mr. J. Sheridan Mayer in his *Restorative Art*. This is rather a larger order since few people die in the full bloom of health, unravaged by illness and unmarked by some disfigurement. The funeral industry is equal to the challenge: "In some cases the gruesome appearance of a mutilated or disease-ridden subject may be quite discouraging. The task of restoration may seem impossible and shake the confidence of the embalmer. This is the time for intestinal fortitude and determination. Once the formative work is begun and affected tissues are cleaned or removed, all doubts of success vanish. It is surprising and gratifying to discover the results which may be obtained."

The embalmer, having allowed an appropriate interval to elapse, returns to the attack, but now he brings into play the skill and equipment of sculptor and cosmetician. Is a hand missing? Casting one in plaster of Paris is a simple matter. "For replacement purposes, only a cast of the back of the hand is necessary; this is within the ability of the average operator and is quite adequate." If a lip or two, a nose or an ear should be missing, the embalmer has at hand a variety of restorative waxes with which to model replacements. Pores and skin texture are simulated by stippling with a little brush, and over this cosmetics are laid on. Head off? Decapitation cases are rather routinely handled. Ragged edges are trimmed, and head joined to torso with a series of splints, wires and sutures. It is a good idea to have a little something at the neck—a scarf or high collar—when time for viewing comes. Swollen mouth? Cut out tissue as needed from inside the lips. If too much is removed, the surface contour can easily be restored by padding with cotton. Swollen necks and cheeks are reduced by removing tissue through vertical incisions made down each side of the neck. "When the deceased is casketed, the pillow will hide the suture incisions . . . as an extra precaution against leakage, the suture may be painted with liquid sealer."

The opposite condition is more likely to present itself—that of emaciation. His hypodermic syringe now loaded with massage cream, the embalmer seeks out and fills the hollowed and sunken areas by injection. In this procedure the back of the hands and fingers and the under-chin area should not be neglected.

Positioning the lips is a problem that recurrently challenges the ingenuity of the embalmer. Closed too tightly, they tend to give a stern, even disapproving expression. Ideally, embalmers feel, the lips should give the impression of being ever so slightly parted, the upper lip protruding slightly for a more youthful appearance. This takes some engineering, however, as the lips tend to drift apart. Lip drift can sometimes be remedied by pushing one or two straight pins through the inner margin of the lower lip and then inserting them between the two front upper teeth. If Mr. Jones happens to have no teeth, the pins can just as easily be anchored in his Armstrong Face Former and Denture Replacer. Another method to maintain lip closure is to dislocate the lower jaw, which is then held in its new position by a wire run through holes which have been drilled through the upper and lower jaws at the midline. As the French are fond of saying, *il faut souffrir pour être belle.**

If Mr. Jones has died of jaundice, the embalming fluid will very likely turn him green. Does this deter the embalmer? Not if he has intestinal fortitude. Masking pastes and cosmetics are heavily laid on, burial garments and casket interiors are color-correlated with particular care, and Jones is displayed beneath rose-colored lights. Friends will say, "How *well* he looks." Death by carbon monoxide, on the other hand, can be rather a good thing from the embalmer's viewpoint: "One advantage is the fact that this type of discoloration is an exaggerated form of a natural pink coloration." This is nice because the healthy glow is already present and needs but little attention.

The patching and filling completed, Mr. Jones is now shaved, washed and dressed. Cream-based cosmetic, available in pink, flesh, suntan, brunette and blond, is applied to his hands and face, his hair is shampooed and combed (and, in the case of Mrs. Jones, set), his hands manicured. For the horny-handed son of toil special care must be taken; cream should be applied to remove ingrained grime, and the nails cleaned. "If he were not in the habit of having them manicured in life, trimming and shaping is advised for better appearance—never questioned by kin."

Jones is now ready for casketing (this is the present participle of the verb "to casket"). In this operation his right shoulder should be depressed slightly "to turn the body a bit to the right and soften the appearance of lying flat on the back." Positioning the hands is a matter of importance, and special rubber positioning blocks may be

---

*In 1963 *Mortuary Management* reports a new development: "Natural Expression Formers," an invention of Funeral Directors Research Company. "They may be used to replace one or both artificial dentures, or over natural teeth; have 'bite-indicator' lines as a closure guide. . . . Natural Expression Formers also offer more control of facial expression."

used. The hands should be cupped slightly for a more life-like, relaxed appearance. Proper placement of the body requires a delicate sense of balance. It should lie as high as possible in the casket, yet not so high that the lid, when lowered, will hit the nose. On the other hand, we are cautioned, placing the body too low "creates the impression that the body is in a box."

Jones is next wheeled into the appointed slumber room where a few last touches may be added—his favorite pipe placed in his hand or, if he was a great reader, a book propped into position. (In the case of little Master Jones a Teddy bear may be clutched.) Here he will hold open house for a few days, visitng hours 10 A.M. to 9 P.M.

All now being in readiness, the funeral director calls a staff conference to make sure that each assistant knows his precise duties. Mr. Wilber Krieger writes: "This makes your staff feel that they are a part of the team, with a definite assignment that must be properly carried out if the whole plan is to succeed. You never heard of a football coach who failed to talk to his entire team before they go on the field. They have drilled on the plays they are to execute for hours and days, and yet the successful coach knows the importance of making even the bench-warming third-string substitute feel that he is important if the game is to be won." The winning of *this* game is predicated upon glass-smooth handling of the logistics. The funeral director has notified the pallbearers whose names were furnished by the family, has arranged for the presence of clergyman, organist, and soloist, has provided transportation for everybody, has organized and listed the flowers sent by friends. In *Psychology of Funeral Service* Mr. Edward A. Martin points out: "He may not always do as much as the family thinks he is doing, but it is his helpful guidance that they appreciate in knowing they are proceeding as they should. . . . The important thing is how well his services can be used to make the family believe they are giving unlimited expression to their own sentiment."

The religious service may be held in a church or in the chapel of the funeral home; the funeral director vastly prefers the latter arrangement, for not only is it more convenient for him but it affords him the opportunity to show off his beautiful facilities to the gathered mourners. After the clergyman has had his say, the mourners queue up to file past the casket for a last look at the deceased. The family is *never* asked whether they want an open-casket ceremony; in the absence of their instruction to the contrary, this is taken for granted. Consequently well over 90 per cent of all American funerals feature the open casket—a custom unknown in other parts of the world. Foreigners are astonished by it. An English woman living in San Francisco described her reaction in a letter to the writer:

I myself have attended only one funeral here—that of an elderly fellow worker of mine. After the service I could not understand why everyone was walking towards the coffin (sorry, I mean casket), but thought I had better follow the crowd. It shook me rigid to get there and find the casket open and poor old Oscar lying there in his brown tweed suit, wearing a suntan makeup and just the wrong shade of lipstick. If I had not been extremely fond of the old boy, I have a horrible feeling that I might have giggled. Then and there I decided that I could never face another American funeral—even dead.

The casket (which has been resting throughout the service on a Classic Beauty Ultra Metal Casket Bier) is now transferred by a hydraulically operated device called Porto-Lift to a balloon-tired, Glide Easy casket carriage which will wheel it to yet another conveyance, the Cadillac Funeral Coach. This may be lavender, cream, light green —anything but black. Interiors, of course, are color-correlated, "for the man who cannot stop short of perfection."

At graveside, the casket is lowered into the earth. This office, once the prerogative of friends of the deceased, is now performed by a patented mechanical lowering device.

A "Lifetime Green" artificial grass mat is at the ready to conceal the sere earth, and overhead, to conceal the sky, is a portable Steril Chapel Tent ("resists the intense heat and humidity of summer and the terrific storms of winter . . . available in Silver Grey, Rose or Evergreen"). Now is the time for the ritual scattering of earth over the coffin, as the solemn words "earth to earth, ashes to ashes, dust to dust" are pronounced by the officiating cleric. This can today be accomplished "with a mere flick of the wrist with the Gordon Leak-Proof Earth Dispenser. No grasping of a handful of dirt, no soiled fingers. Simple, dignified, beautiful, reverent! The modern way!" The Gordon Earth Dispenser (at $5) is of nickel-plated brass construction. It is not only "attractive to the eye and long wearing"; it is also "one of the 'tools' for building better public relations" if presented as "an appropriate non-commercial gift" to the clergyman. It is shaped something like a saltshaker.

Untouched by human hand, the coffin and the earth are now united.

It is in the function of directing the participants through this maze of gadgetry that the funeral director has assigned to himself his relatively new role of "grief therapist." He has relieved the family of every detail, he has revamped the corpse to look like a living doll, he has arranged for it to nap for a few days in a slumber room, he has put on a well-oiled performance in which the concept of *death* has played no part whatsoever—unless it was inconsiderately mentioned by the clergyman who conducted the religious service. He has done everything in his power to make the funeral a real pleasure for everybody concerned. He and his team have given their all to score an upset victory over death.

Dale Carnegie has written that in the lexicon of the successful man there is no such word as "failure." So have the funeral men managed to delete the word death and all its associations from their vocabulary. They have from time to time published lists of In and Out words and phrases to be memorized and used in connection with the final return of dust to dust; then still dissatisfied with the result, have elaborated and revised the lists. Thus a 1916 glossary substitutes "prepare body" for "handle corpse." Today, though, "body" is Out and "remains" or "Mr. Jones" is In.

"The use of improper terminology by anyone affiliated with a mortuary should be strictly forbidden," declares Edward A. Martin. He suggests a rather thorough over-hauling of the language; his deathless words include: "ser-vice, not funeral; Mr., Mrs., Miss Blank, not corpse or body; preparation room, not morgue; casket, not coffin; funeral director or mortician, not undertaker; reposing room or slumber room, not laying-out room; display room, not showroom; baby or infant, not stillborn; deceased, not dead; autopsy or post-mortem, not post; casket coach, not hearse; shipping case, not shipping box; flower car, not flower truck; cremains or cremated remains, not ashes; clothing, dress, suit, etc., not shroud; drawing room, not parlor."

This rather basic list was refined in 1956 by Victor Landig in his *Basic Principles of Funeral Service.* He en-joins the reader to avoid using the word "death" as much as possible, even sometimes when such avoidance may seem impossible; for example, a death certificate should be referred to as a "vital statistics form." One should speak not of the "job" but rather of the "call." We do not "haul" a dead person, we "transfer" or "remove" him— and we do this in a "service car," not a "body car." We "open and close" his grave rather than dig and fill it, and in it we "inter" rather than bury him. This is done not in a graveyard or cemetery but rather in a "memorial park." The deceased is beautified, not with makeup, but with "cosmetics." Anyway, he didn't die, he "expired." An im-portant error to guard against, cautions Mr. Landig, is re-ferring to "cost of the casket." The phrase, "amount of in-vestment in the service" is a wiser usage here.

Miss Anne Hamilton Franz, writing in *Funeral Direc-tion and Management,* adds an interesting footnote on the use of the word "ashes" to describe (in a word) ashes.

She fears this usage will encourage scattering (for what is more natural than to scatter ashes?) and prefers to speak of "cremated remains" or "human remains." She does not like the word "retort" to describe the container in which cremation takes place, but prefers "cremation chamber" or "cremation vault," because this "sounds better and softens any harshness to sensitive feelings."

As for the Loved One, poor fellow, he wanders like a sad ghost through the funeral men's pronouncements. No provision seems to have been made for the burial of a Heartily Disliked One, although the necessity for such must arise in the course of human events.

6

THE RATIONALE

*A funeral service is a social function at which the deceased
is the guest of honor and the center of attraction. . . . A
poorly prepared body in a beautiful casket is just as incongruous as a young lady appearing at a party in a costly
gown and with her hair in curlers.*

—FREDERICK AND STRUB, *The Principles and
Practices of Embalming*

THE WORDS "costly gown" are operative ones in the above
paragraph, culled from a standard embalming school textbook. The same thought is often expressed by funeral
men: "Certainly, the incentive to select quality merchandise would be materially lessened if the body of the deceased were not decontaminated and made presentable,"
says *De-Ce-Co,* publication of a funeral supply company.
And Mr. T. E. Schier, president of the Settegast-Knopf
Funeral Home in Houston, Texas, says, "The majority
of the American people purchase caskets, not for the
limited solace from their beauty prior to funeral service,
or for the impression that they may create before their
friends and associates. Instead, they full-heartedly believe
that the casket and the vault give protection to that which
has been accomplished by the embalmer."

One might suppose—and many people do—that the
whole point of embalming is the long-term preservation

of the deceased. Actually, although phrases like "peace of mind protection" and "eternal preservation" crop up frequently in casket and vault advertising, the embalmers themselves know better. For just how long is an embalmed body preserved? The simple truth is that a body *can* be preserved for a very long time indeed—probably for many years, depending upon the strength of the fluids used, and the temperature and humidity of the surrounding atmosphere. Cadavers prepared for use in anatomical research may outlast the hardiest medical student. The trouble is, they don't look very pretty; in fact they tend to resemble old shoe leather.

The more dilute the embalming fluid, the softer and more natural-appearing the guest of honor. Therefore, the usual procedure is to embalm with about enough preservative to ensure that the body will last through the funeral—generally, a matter of a few days. "To the ancient embalmer permanent preservation was of prime importance and the maintenance of a natural color and texture a matter of minor concern; to us the creation and maintenance of a lifelike naturalness is the major objective, and post-burial preservation is incidental. . . . The Egyptian embalmer's subjects have remained preserved for thousands of years—while the modern embalmer sometimes has to pray for favorable climatic conditions to help him maintain satisfactory preservation for a couple of days." The same textbook, *The Principles and Practices of Embalming,* cautioning the neophyte embalmer on the danger of trying to get by with inadequate embalming, says, "But if we were to approach the average embalmer and tell him that the body he had just embalmed would have to be kept on display for a month or two during the summer, what would his reaction be? To fall in a dead faint from fright, no doubt."

No matter what the more gullible customers may be led to believe about eternal preservation in the privacy of the arrangements room conference, undertakers do not try to mislead the serious investigator about this. They will generally admit quite readily that their handiwork is not even intended to be permanent.

If long-term preservation is not the embalmer's objective, what then is?

Clearly, some rather solid-sounding justifications for the procedure had to be advanced, above and beyond the fact that embalming is good business for the undertaker because it helps him to sell more expensive caskets.

The two grounds chosen by the undertaking trade for defense of embalming embrace two objectives near and dear to the hearts of Americans: hygiene, and mental health. The theory that embalming is an essential hygienic measure has long been advanced by the funeral industy. A much newer concept, that embalming and restoring the deceased are necessary for the mental well-being of the survivors, is just now being developed by industry leaders; the observer who looks closely will discover a myth in the making here. "Grief therapy," the official name bestowed by the undertakers on this new aspect of their work, is at this point beginning to be a second line of defense for the embalmers.

The primary purpose of embalming, all funeral men will tell you, is a sanitary one, the disinfecting of the body so that it is no longer a health menace. More than one writer, soaring to wonderful heights of fantasy, has gone so far as to attribute the falling death rate in this century to the practice of embalming (which, if true, would seem a little shortsighted on the part of the practitioners): "It is a significant fact that when embalming was in its infancy, the death rate was 21 to every 1,000 persons per year, and today it has been reduced to 10 to every 1,000 per year." The writer magnanimously bestows "a great deal of credit" for this on the medical profession, adding that funeral directors are responsible for "about 50 percent of this wonderful work of sanitation which has so materially lowered the death rate." When embalmers get together to talk among themselves, they are more realistic about the wonderful work of sanitation. In a panel discussion reported by the *National Funeral Service Journal*,

Dr. I. M. Feinberg, an instructor at the Worsham College of Mortuary Science, said, "Sanitation is probably the farthest thing from the mind of the modern embalmer. We must realize that the motives for embalming at the present time are economic and sentimental, with a slight religious overtone."

Whether or not the undertakers themselves actually believe that embalming fulfills an important health function (and there is evidence that most of them really do believe it), they have been extraordinarily successful in convincing the public that it does. Outside of medical circles, people who are otherwise reasonably knowledgeable and sophisticated take for granted not only that embalming is done for reasons of sanitation but that it is required by law.

In an effort to sift fact from fiction and to get an objective opinion on the matter, I sought out Dr. Jesse Carr, Chief of Pathology at the San Francisco General Hospital and Professor of Pathology at the University of California Medical School. I wanted to know specifically how, and to what extent, and in what circumstances, an unembalmed cadaver poses a health threat to the living.

Dr. Carr's office is on the third floor of the San Francisco General Hospital, its atmosphere of rationality and scientific method in refreshing contrast to that of the funeral homes. To my question "Are undertakers, in their capacity of embalmers, guardians of the public health?" Dr. Carr's answer was short and to the point: "They are not guardians of anything except their pocketbooks. Public-health virtues of embalming? You can write it off as inapplicable to our present-day conditions." Discussing possible injury to health caused by the presence of a dead body, Dr. Carr explained that in cases of communicable disease a dead body presents considerably less hazard than a live one. "There are several advantages to being dead," he said cheerfully. "You don't excrete, inhale, exhale, or perspire." The body of a person who has died of a noncommunicable illness, such as heart disease or cancer, presents no hazard whatsoever, he explained.

In the case of death from typhoid, cholera, plague and other enteric infections, epidemics have been caused in the past by spread of infection by rodents and seepage from graves into the city water supply. The old-time cemeteries and churchyards were particularly dangerous breeding grounds for these scourges. The solution, however, lies in city planning, engineering and sanitation, rather than in embalming, for the organisms which cause disease live in the organs, the blood and the bowel, and cannot all be killed by the embalming process. Thus was toppled—for me, at least—the last stronghold of the embalmers; for until then I had confidently believed that their work had value, at least in the rare cases where death is caused by such diseases.

Dr. Carr has carried on his own campaign for a decent, commonsense approach to cadavers. The morgue in his hospital was formerly a dark retreat in the basement, "supposedly for aesthetic and health reasons; people think bodies smell and are unhealthy to have around." Objecting strongly to this, Dr. Carr had the autopsy rooms moved up to the third floor along with the offices. "The bodies aren't smelly, they're not dirty—bloody, of course, but that's a normal part of medical life," he said crisply. "We have so little apprehension of disease being spread by dead bodies that we have them up here right among us. It is medically more efficient, and a great convenience in student teaching. Ten to twenty students attend each autopsy. No danger here!"

A body will keep, under normal conditions, for twenty-four hours unless it has been opened. Floaters, explained Dr. Carr in his commonsense way, are another matter; a person who has been in the Bay for a week or more ("shrimps at the orifices, and so forth") will decompose more rapidly. They used to burn gunpowder in the morgue when floaters were brought in, to mask the smell, but now they put them in the deepfreeze, and after about four hours the odor stops (because the outside of the body is frozen) and the autopsy can be performed. "A good undertaker would do his cosmetology and then freeze," said Dr. Carr thoughtfully. "Freezing is modern and sensible."

Anxious that we should not drift back to the subject of the floaters, I asked about the efficacy of embalming as a means of preservation. Even if it is very well done, he said, few cadavers embalmed for the funeral (as distinct from those embalmed for research purposes) are actually preserved.

"An exhumed embalmed body is a repugnant, moldy, foul-looking object," said Dr. Carr emphatically. "It's not the image of one who has been loved. You might use the quotation 'John Brown's body lies a-moldering in the grave'; that really sums it up. The body itself may be intact, as far as contours and so on; but the silk lining of the casket is all stained with body fluids, the wood is rotting, and the body is covered with mold." The caskets, he said, even the solid mahogany ones that cost thousands of dollars, just disintegrate. He spoke of a case where a man was exhumed two and a half months after burial: "The casket fell apart and the body was covered with mold, long whiskers of penicillin—he looked ghastly. I'd rather be nice and rotten than covered with those whiskers of mold, although the penicillin is a pretty good preservative. Better in fact than embalming fluid."

Will an enbalmed corpse fare better in a sealed metal casket? Far from it. "If you seal up a casket so it is more or less airtight, you seal in the anaerobic bacteria—the kind that thrive in an airless atmosphere, you see. These are the putrefactive bacteria, and the results of their growth are pretty horrible." He proceeded to describe them rather vividly, and added, "You're a lot better off to be buried in an aerobic atmosphere, otherwise the putrefactive bacteria take over. In fact, you're really better off with a shroud, and no casket at all."

Like many another pathologist, Dr. Carr has had his run-ins with funeral directors who urge their clients to refuse to consent to post-mortem medical examinations. The funeral men hate autopsies; for one thing, it does make embalming more difficult, and also they find it harder to sell the family an expensive casket if the decedent has been autopsied. There are, said Dr. Carr, three or four good concerns in San Francisco who understand and approve the reasons for post-mortem examination, and these will help get the needed autopsy permission from the family, and are skilled technicians. "It's generally the badly trained or avaricious undertaker who is resistant to the autopsy procedure. They all tip the hospital morgue men who help them, but the resistant ones are obstructive, unskilled and can be nasty to the point of viciousness. They lie to the family, citing all sorts of horrible things that can happen to the deceased, and while they're usually very soft-spoken with the family, they are inordinately profane with hospital superintendents and pathologists. In one case where an ear had been accidentally severed in the course of an autopsy, the mortician threatened to *show* it to the family."

In a 1959 symposium in *Mortuary Management* on funeral director attitudes towards autopsies, some of this hostility to doctors erupts into print. One undertaker writes, "The trouble with doctors is that they think they are little tin Gods, and anything they want, we should bow to, without question. My feeling is that the business of the funeral director is to serve the family in the best way he knows how, and if the funeral director knows that an autopsy is going to work a hardship, and result in a body that would be difficult to show, or that couldn't be shown at all, then I think the funeral director has not only the right, but the duty, to advise the family against permitting an autopsy." Another, defending the pathologists ("After all, the medical profession as a whole is reasonably intelligent"), describes himself as a "renegade embalmer where the matter of autopsies is concerned." He points to medical discoveries which have resulted from post-mortem examination; but he evidently feels he is in a minority, for he says, "Most funeral directors are still 'horse and buggy undertakers' in their thinking and it shows up glaringly in their moronic attitude towards autopsies."

To get the reaction of the funeral men to the views expressed by Dr. Carr now became my objective. I was not so much interested, at this point, in talking to the run-of-the-mill undertaker, but rather to the leaders of the industry, those whose speeches and articles I had read in the trade press—in short, those who might be termed the theoreticians of American funeral service. They, I felt, would have at their fingertips any facts that might bolster the case for embalming, and would be in a position to speak authoritatively for the industry as a whole.

In this, I was somewhat disappointed. The discussions seemed inconclusive, and the funeral spokesmen themselves often appeared to be unclear about the points they were making.

My first interview was with Dr. Charles H. Nichols, a Ph.D. in education from Northwestern University, and since 1949 educational director of the National Foundation of Funeral Service. Among his published works are "The Psychology of Selling Vaults" and "Selling Vaults," which appeared in *The Vault Merchandiser* in 1954 and 1956 respectively. His duties at the Foundation include lecturing to undertakers at the School of Management on such subjects as "Counseling in Bereavement."

Dr. Nichols readily volunteered the information that embalming has made an enormous contribution to public health and sanitation, that if done properly it can disinfect the dead body so thoroughly that it is no longer a source of contamination. "But *is* a dead body a source of infection?" I asked. Dr. Nichols replied that he didn't know. "What about foreign countries where they do not as a rule embalm; is much illness caused by failure to do so?" Dr. Nichols said he didn't know.

Mr. Wilber Krieger is an important figure in funeral circles, for he is not only managing director of an influential trade association, National Selected Morticians, he is also director of the National Foundation of Funeral Service. To my question "Why is embalming universally practiced in the United States?" he answered that there is a public health factor; germs do not die with the host, and embalming disinfects. I told him of my conversation with Dr. Jesse Carr, and of my own surprise at learning that even in typhoid cases embalming is ineffective as a safety measure against contagion; upon which he burst out with "That's a typical pathologist's answer! That's the sort of thing you hear from so many of them." Pressed for specific cases of illness caused by failure to embalm, Mr. Krieger recalled the death from smallpox of a prominent citizen in a small Southern community where embalming was not practiced. Hundreds went to the funeral to pay their respects, and as a result a large number of them came down with smallpox. Unfortunately Mr. Krieger had forgotten the name of the prominent citizen, the town, and the date of this occurrence. I asked him if he would check up on these details and furnish me with the facts; however, he has not yet done so.

I had no better luck in a subsequent conversation with Mr. Howard C. Raether, executive secretary of the National Funeral Directors Association (to which the great majority of funeral directors belong) and Mr. Bruce Hotchkiss, vice-president of that organization and himself a practicing undertaker. In this case our conversation was recorded on tape. I asked what health hazard is presented by a dead body which has not been opened up, for purposes of either autopsy or embalming.

MR. RAETHER: Well, as an embalmer, Bruce, aren't there certain discharges that come from the body without it having been opened up?

MR. HOTCHKISS: Yes, most assuredly from—orally—depending upon the mode or condition preceding death.

Then I asked, "Can you give any place, then, where the public health has been endangered—give us the place and the time?"

They could not. We talked around the point for several minutes, but these two leaders of an industry built on the embalming process were unable to produce a single fact to support their major justification for the procedure. I told them what Dr. Carr had said about embalming and public health. "Do you have any comment on that?" I asked. Mr. Raether answered, "No; but we can take a look-see and try to give you some instances."

When the results of the look-see arrived, eight weeks later, in the form of an impressive-looking document titled "Public Health and Embalming," I was surprised to find that it was the work not of a medical expert but of Mr. Raether (who is a lawyer) himself. The approach was curiously oblique:

> I confronted some teachers in colleges of mortuary science with the opinion of your San Francisco pathologist that embalming in no way lessens the spread of communicable disease. Their first reaction was "who is he, what is his proof?" And, rightly so. Then they add that it is not contended embalming destroys all microbes.

What *is* contended? We are not told. Authority is cited that seems vaguely irrelevant. It is recommended that I read *Public Health in Boston, 1630-1822;* I am assured that the Dean of the American Academy of Funeral Service "has documented proof," but no further evidence is offered. This reminds me of the old trial lawyers' maxim: "When the law is against you, argue the facts; when the facts are against you, argue the law; when the law and the facts are against you, give the opposing counsel Hell."

A health officer, in the single reference to a source outside the funeral industry, is quoted as advancing a startlingly novel argument for embalming. It is efficacious, he declares, not only from a public health standpoint but "from the standpoint of man's ages-long concern with life after death." No further explanation is forthcoming, for this statement is in fact offered as the triumphant conclusion or punch line to the memorandum.

The only specific information furnished me by Mr. Raether to support his contention that embalming has value as a sanitary measure concerned the procedures

followed in a famous clinic. He said, "At the ———
Clinic they have a standing rule that no autopsy shall be
conducted on a body unless that body is embalmed—unless they need tissue immediately. This is a standing rule
for the protection of doctors and pathologists who might
be working with the body." Unversed though I am in the
procedures of doctors and pathologists, this sounded very
strange to me. I wrote to the clinic in question to ask if it
was true. Their answer: "Unfortunately, it appears that
Mr. Raether has been misinformed concerning the attitude of the ——— Clinic toward the embalming of
bodies. We have no rule which requires that bodies be
embalmed before an autopsy is performed. It is true that
frequently bodies are embalmed prior to the performance
of an autopsy, but this is done more for the convenience
of the funeral directors than because of any insistence on
our part."*

If the public health benefits of embalming are elusive,
ten times more so is the role of "grief therapy," fast becoming a favorite with the funeral men. Trying to pin
down the meaning of this phrase is like trying to pick up
quicksilver with a fork, for it apparently has no meaning
outside funeral trade circles. Although it sounds like a
term picked up from the vocabulary of psychiatry, psychiatrists of whom I inquired were unable to enlighten me
because they had never heard of it.

"Grief therapy" is most commonly used by funeral men
to describe the mental and emotional solace which, they
claim, is achieved for the bereaved family as a result of
being able to "view" the embalmed and restored deceased.
Dr. Charles Nichols told me it is a known fact that the
"final memory picture" is of "emotional and psychological
value to families served." I asked him how he knew this
to be so. He replied that his opinion was based on reading
and research in those areas. It was a commonplace concept, he said; he had read it in any number of places.

---

* The writer of the letter requested that the clinic not be identified.

Pressed for a psychiatric reference, he was unable to supply one.

The total absence of authoritative sources on the subject does not stop the undertakers and their spokesmen from donning the mantle of the psychiatrist when it suits their purposes. As an embalming textbook says, "In his care of each subject the embalmer has a heavy responsibility, for his skill and interest will largely determine the degree of permanent mental trauma to be suffered by all those closely associated with the deceased."

Lately the meaning of "grief therapy" has been expanded to cover not only the Beautiful Memory Picture, but any number of aspects of the funeral. Within the trade, it has become a catchall phrase, its meaning conveniently elastic enough to provide justification for all of their dealings and procedures. Phrases like "therapy of mourning," "grief syndrome" trip readily from their tongues. The most "therapeutic" funeral, it seems, is the one that conforms to their pattern, that is to say, the one arranged under circumstances guaranteeing a maximum profit.

For example, prearranged funerals, in which a person while still alive specifies the mode and cost of his final disposition, tend for obvious reasons to be much less expensive than those arranged by sorrowing survivors. Howard C. Raether took note of this fact at a recent National Funeral Directors Association convention. He was discussing an analysis of funeral sales: "If it were possible to tabulate all the prearranged funeral services on record, how do you suppose the average of all of them would compare with the average adult figure shown here?" (Average adult figure means average price of an adult's funeral). "Are you ready, willing and able to become part of a program that is going to lower the quality of the average funeral service selected to the point where you will find it difficult if not impossible to stay in business rendering the service you now give?" He added, "It is good for those who survive to have the right and duty to make the funeral arrangements. Making such arrangements, having such responsibilities, is essential. It is part of the grief syndrome, part of the therapy of mourning. It is a positive hook upon which the hat of funeral service is hung. Why should we tear it down by saying the funeral is for the deceased, therefore he or she should make the arrangements? . . . If funeral directors insist on soliciting pre-need funerals, they are in fact prearranging the funeral of their profession."

I had a long discussion with Mr. Raether about "grief therapy," in which I sought to know what medical, psychiatric backing he could produce to substantiate the funeral industry theory that viewing the restored and embalmed body has psychotherapeutic value. He spoke of grief and ceremony; he mentioned some clergymen of his acquaintance; but no qualified psychiatric reference was forthcoming.

Eventually I did receive from Mr. Raether, a five-page memorandum titled "Value of Funeral Service and Rites Including Viewing the Remains." Mr. Robert Habenstein, who together with Mr. William M. Lamers was commissioned by the National Funeral Directors Association to write *Funeral Customs the World Over* and *The History of American Funeral Directing*, is quoted at some length. He refers with approval to an article on bereavement and mental health by Professor Edmund H. Volkart of Stanford University, which appeared in *Explorations in Social Psychiatry*. Says Habenstein:

The lesson of this stimulating effort [Professor Volkart's article] is that bereavement needs best be understood not only in terms of genetic development of self vs. cross sectional pressures, but with reference to socio-cultural conditions. Other relevant variables are role configurations of bereaved persons (sociological), the import of religious beliefs (psychological), the functions and dysfunctions of funeral practices (social psychological-anthropological), the part played by empathic responses (psychiatric), and matters relating to community support of bereaved families (sociological).

I reread this several times, but it did not seem to contain an answer to my question about the therapeutic benefits of viewing the remains. In fact it is not until page 3 of the memorandum that we get down to this question. Mr. Raether writes as follows:

In an attempt to get a published work specifically on viewing of the "embalmed and restored body," I wrote to Reverend Paul E. Irion. He replied that while he could not think of one immediately, ". . . this is not to say by inference psychiatry would not recognize the value of such experience in many instances. Certainly ample foundation can be found for tracing the implications of such a point of view from psychiatric data."

Fortunately, Mr. Raether is as much at home tracing implications from psychiatric data as he is in the field of medical pathology. Not in the least abashed by his failure to produce a reference to a published authority, he now exchanges his pathologist's hat for that of an analyst of psychiatric case histories. His case histories all have happy endings for the undertaking trade:

Recently a funeral director told me of a woman who needed psychiatric treatment because her husband's funeral was with a closed casket, no visitation and burial in another state with her not present. The psychiatrist called him (the funeral director) to learn about the funeral, or lack of one. The patient was treated and has recovered and has vowed never to be part of another memorial type service.

Another case involves the widow of a university professor whose body was given to a medical school for anatomical purposes ten years ago. Today, she is waiting to get back that which remains of it and already has made plans for burial over 1000 miles from the medical school.

Mr. Raether rests his case with a quotation, "specifically on viewing the prepared, casketed body," from Dr. William M. Lamers, Jr., a recent medical school graduate completing his training in psychiatry as a resident at Cincinnati General Hospital, and by coincidence the son of the Mr. William Lamers who collaborated with Mr. Habenstein in the writing of two books commissioned by the National Funeral Directors Association.

Dr. Lamers says, "We know that viewing—in most instances—is valuable." *He* knows it, he says, from an experience in his own family and from "patients I have treated in the past few years," also from reading he has done in anthropological studies of funeral customs. He quotes La Rochefoucauld:"One can no more look steadily at death than at the sun," and goes on to say, "Yet, in viewing, we try in a way to look at death. In the funeral setting it is like looking at the sun through a dark filter. And as scientists have learned much from studying the sun we are starting to learn a great deal from studying death."

At this point, it seemed advisable to check with Professor Volkart, whose article in *Explorations in Social Psychiatry* was the only authoritative published work cited in Mr. Raether's memorandum that had any bearing on the matter at hand. Professor Volkart, who is professor of sociology at Stanford University and director of the Program in Medicine and the Behavioral Sciences, wrote to me as follows:

I know of no evidence to support the view that "public" viewing of an embalmed body is somehow "therapeutic" to the bereaved. Certainly there are no statistics known to me comparing the outcomes of such a process in the United States with the outcomes of England where public viewing is seldom done. Indeed, since the public viewing of the corpse is part and parcel of a whole complex of events surrounding funerals, it would be difficult, if not impossible, to ascertain either its therapeutic or contratherapeutic effect.

The phrase "grief therapy" is not in common usage in psychiatry, so far as I know. That the loss of any loved object frequently leads to depressions and mal-functioning of the organism is, of course, well known; what is not well-known or understood are the conditions under which some kind of intervention should be made, or even the nature of the intervention. My general feeling is that the phenomena of grief and mourning have appeared in human life long before there were "experts" of any kind (psychiatric, clerical etc.) and somehow most, if not all, of the bereaved managed to survive. The interesting problem to me is why it should be that so many modern Americans seem more incapable of managing loss and/or grief than other peoples, and why we have such reliance upon specialists. My own hunch is that morbid problems of grief arise only when the relevant lay persons (family members, friends, children, etc.) somehow fail to perform their normal therapeutic roles for the bereaved—or may it be that the bereaved often break down because they simply do not know how to behave under the circumstances? Very few of us, I think, would be capable of managing sustained, ambiguous situations.

Demonstrably flimsy and ridiculous as the justifications for universal embalming and "viewing" may be, they have nonetheless proved very effective and so far have been safe from authoritative contradiction. No government agency has ever challenged these patently fraudulent claims of undertakers for their product. In other areas of commerce there is some regulation of methods used to extract profit by playing on human emotions, hopes and fears. The cosmetics manufacturer may be barred by the Food and Drug Administration from making false statements about the efficacy of the hormones in his face cream, and the purveyor of quack cancer cures must move nimbly to stay one step ahead of the prosecutor; but no law presently exists to curb the specious claims of those who peddle grief therapy to the grieving.

7

THE ALLIED INDUSTRIES

THE UNDERTAKER, who pockets slightly more than half of the funeral dollar, has generally drawn the spotlight upon himself when the high cost of dying has come under scrutiny. But he is not the whole show. Behind the scenes, waiting for their cue, are the cemeteries, florists, monument makers, vault manufacturers. The casket manufacturing companies, to whom the undertakers are perennially and heavily in debt, are often lurking in the wings like ambitious understudies waiting to move in and assume control of the funeral establishments should financial disaster strike.

The cast in this drama is not always one big happy family. There are the usual backstage displays of irritation, pique, jealousy, a certain vying and jockeying for position. There are lawsuits and scathing denunciations which arise because of the stiff competition. These can be submerged in the interests of a common endeavor, for the show must go on, and the common goal must be served: that of extracting the maximum admission fee from the paying audience.

The casket companies report that the alarming condition of the industry's accounts receivable is "far more aggravated in the casket field than in any other manufacturing endeavor." In 1961 the funeral establishments owed the casketmakers more than $39 million, 20 per cent of the year's production, an amount equal to about 317,000 caskets of which, groaned the creditors, some 40 per cent had "already been interred!" Presumably making repossession a most inconvenient remedy for the creditor.

The answer to this problem is, of course, to sell in ever-higher brackets. As Herbert L. Stein, vice-president of the National Casket Company and president of the Casket Manufacturers Association, said, "Since the public's purse limits funeral expenditures and nature limits the number of funerals . . . skillful merchandising of quality goods is about the only avenue for upping profits anywhere along the line."

Selling the public on the "quality" of his merchandise can tax the ingenuity of the undertaker. The costliest caskets are those built of the thickest metal. The cheaper lines of metal caskets, constructed of thin sheet metal over a wooden frame, achieve the same look of massive elegance, and can hardly be distinguished (except by grateful pallbearers) from the heavyweights that weigh hundreds of pounds more and sell for thousands of dollars more. A writer in *Mortuary Management* described the average run of lightweight metal caskets as "nothing more or less than stovepipes. Stovepipe gauges are always misleading the public. . . . 'Metal is metal,' says John Public."

The method hit upon by the casketmakers to solve this knotty problem is essentially the method used by furniture manufacturers (whose direct descendants they are): that is, to make the cheaper lines so hideous that only customers who can afford the barest minimum will buy them. Mr. John Beck, president of the Balanced Line Casket and of Elgin Associates, carefully explains the position:

In most cases where funeral directors are not showing enough profit, they are showing too many low price metal caskets that look too good, are embellished up entirely too much for their price position. . . . We call the items "profit robbers." For right in the area where people do have the money to buy better funerals and will do so when given the proper selection and opportunity, the better sale is lost. The second area where opportunity is lost is in the sealer* area. If the lowest price sealer looks as good as the best one, of course most people will buy the lowest price one. . . . This is the region where greater profits can be made as this is the one where people who have the money to buy will do so if they are given the proper incentive.

And Mr. Leroy R. Derr, president of Boyertown Casket Company:

We can make cheaper caskets, certainly. You can make them and so can I. However, each one helps underwrite the failure of our funeral directors. Too many "cheapies" will ruin the funeral directors completely.

So well did the anti-cheapie program succeed that sales of metal caskets, which in 1950 accounted for only 28 per cent of the industry's sales, climbed by 1960 to 52 per cent of the unit sales and 67 per cent of the dollar volume of the casket industry.

The significance of this industry-engineered change in funeral fashions lies in the circumstance that the average wholesale cost of metal caskets is $158 each as compared with $60 for the cloth-covered wooden variety. Grained hardwood caskets, which wholesale on an average for about as much as metals, held their own, accounting for 14 per cent of sales in 1950 and 15 per cent in 1961. The metals, which can be mass-produced more cheaply than

*A sealer is a casket with a gasket.

the hardwoods, are, however, the ones that are pushed most vigorously by the manufacturers.

Here again, what is good for one segment of the burial business has its odd and painful repercussions in another. So enthusiastically are metal caskets pushed that fairly often they are sold even in cases where the deceased is to be cremated. This is most irksome to the crematories, whose equipment, designed for the expeditious combustion of wood, is not geared to the combustion of metal receptacles. One crematory operator told me how they solve the problem: the lightweight metal caskets are put into the retort, where they eventually buckle and partially melt. "The remains are actually baked," he explained. The heavier and costlier grades cannot be disposed of in this way because they are likely to ruin the equipment. The body is removed from this type of casket and cremated as is—which leaves the problem of disposing of the casket. "State law prohibits the re-use of them," the crematory operator said. "You can't very well take it out to the city dump, because what if the family should happen to pass by and see it there? So we have to break them up and scrap them."

The anti-cheapie program ran into a little trouble with the government in 1954. The Federal Trade Commission took note of it by filing a complaint against the Casket Manufacturers Association and its 160 members, charging them with "collusion to fix prices and concentrate business on higher price lines." The manufacturers, the FTC said, had reached a mutual agreement to expand production and sales of higher-priced caskets and to cut down on less costly models. The complaint further charged that association members had agreed on "uniform, artificial and noncompetitive retail prices" for their wares. The government contended that it was hampered in its investigation "by the destruction of documents by the Secretary of the Casket Manufacturers Association." The FTC eventually dismissed the case for lack of evidence.

The significance to the consumer of wholesale casket costs lies in the widespread use by many funeral establishments of the practice of "formula-pricing," which means in its simplest application that the price of the funeral is arrived at by marking up the wholesale casket cost anywhere from 400 to as much as 900 per cent or higher. The markup is usually steepest in the lower price ranges.

Funeral directors have always been jealous guardians of the secrets of wholesale costs. The first official act of the California Undertakers and Funeral Directors Association, at its founding convention in 1882, was the adoption of a resolution "that this Association earnestly request all manufacturers and wholesale dealers in undertakers' goods . . . to refrain from sending out catalogues and price lists to any parties who are not undertakers or funeral directors in good standing." Seventy years later this concern was still uppermost; *Mortuary Management* in 1952 reported, "The National Funeral Directors Association has for a number of years had a policy which states that all catalogues, catalogue sheets, and other advertisements which give wholesale prices for funeral merchandise, when mailed, should be sent in sealed envelopes as first class mail. The same policy applies to funeral directors who mail price lists offering shipping services, embalming services, etc. These lists or advertisements quoting wholesale or service prices to funeral directors should also be mailed in sealed envelopes by first-class mail. The reason for this policy is obvious."

Likewise jealously guarded from the public is reliable information about the take-overs of failing mortuaries by their creditors, the casket companies. This works something like the take-overs of English pubs by the breweries, in which the pub, owned by the brewer, becomes an outlet for the brewer's particular product exclusively. An Oakland funeral director hinted to me that some large scale behind-the-scenes operations were in progress in California and Nevada, involving the control and management by casket companies of what appear on the surface to be small, independent undertaking establishments. This enables the casket company to avoid having to pay the customary 10 per cent salesman's commission and to guarantee an exclusive market for his own product. "They often fire everyone, and move right in with their own staff," said my informant. "Then they sell the existing stock of caskets at wholesale and bring in their own."

I was anxious to get more information about this new development, and particularly to get firsthand the views of the California Funeral Directors Association. A discussion with Mr. Bruce Hotchkiss, former secretary of the Association, proved something less than enlightening.

Q. We understand there are situations where some casket companies operating in California have moved in to take control of some of the funeral directing establishments. Do you know whether that's true?

A. Well, this is the question, and you say it's happening particularly in Nevada and California and you would like the facts. The only answer that I can give you that—is that there are no facts.

Q. You mean it's not true?

A. Well—I—no, I didn't say that. I just said there are no facts. I can't give you the facts. I've heard the same thing, but we have no facts.

Q. If it is true that this is happening, do you feel that it's a bad or a good development, from the point of view of the funeral business?

A. For funeral service generally—I don't know; I—it would depend upon the individual, I suppose. I don't know. Anything that tends to monopoly I think would be not good.

Q. Well, this would have a tendency to force the establishment that's under control to buy from this particular casket manufacturer

A. No one likes to do that.

Q. Well, isn't that a matter of concern for the California Association? Wouldn't you want to look into that?

A. They've never discussed it. Leastwise as far as I know, they've never discussed it.

Q. So you don't know personally of any instances where that has taken place?

A. I do not. No.

Q. Well, it's something that I should think would be in the public interest to investigate, and the funeral service industry does act in the public interest—that's its position?

A. Quite frankly, I've never heard it discussed. As a matter of fact I *know* it has not been discussed by the Association. . . .

The conflict between cemetery and funeral director is of a different nature, for they are in direct competition for the dead man's dollar. The funeral director is here in the choice position, since he ordinarily gets to the prospect first. By the time he gets through with him, there won't be much money left over for a grave. The cemetery people come in a poor second, often finding that by the time their particular commodity is offered to the prospect the funeral director has skimmed the cream from the top. He has not only induced the bereaved family to spend its all on the casket, but he may steer them away from direct contact with the cemetery and take it upon himself to order a cheap grave by telephone. This can all be very annoying and not at all good for grave sales.

The American Cemetery reports a discussion on "immediate-need" selling in which suggestions were made about how the cemeteries can get around this problem. The first thing is to insist that the family should make a personal visit to the cemetery, and not to permit the purchase of the grave to be handled through the funeral director. Mr. David E. Linge, Executive Vice-President of Cedar Memorial Park, Cedar Rapids, Iowa, is quoted as saying: "We don't feel a funeral director's position is such that he can call a cemetery and say, 'Open a thirty-five-dollar single,' any more than we would call him and say, 'Provide the family with your hundred-dollar casket.' For that reason we will not take, under any circumstances, a sale over the telephone in an at-need situation."

The funeral director should, however, be asked to supply as much information as possible about the family —"their names, relationship to the deceased, financial background, social and economic status in the community." Once he has done so, the article continues, he can safely be dismissed while the arrangements proceed. At this time the funeral director is tactfully drawn away from the family group, since Mr. Linge feels that "as a matter of professional courtesy, he should not be present at the conference."

The family visit also gives the cemetery personnel an opportunity "to describe its other services, such as bronze memorials, flowers, mausoleum crypts and cremation facilities." If the family does not buy a memorial then and there, chances are they will do so in the very near future; for Cedar Memorial Park has a "carefully planned program to provide counsel and assistance for lot owners after the at-need sale has been made." The program works like this: first a letter is sent to the family announcing that the Cedar Park Memorial Counselor and Director of Family Counseling Service will call upon them shortly "to secure the information necessary for the Historical Record and present you with a photographic record of the services at Cedar Memorial." Three days later the counselor arrives at the home and "suggests the purchase of a bronze memorial." But that is not all; in the middle of the month following the service the counselor is after the family again, this time to invite them to a "counseling program" at the cemetery chapel. This in turn is followed up by yet another personal visit; "Dr. Dill always visits them if a memorial has not been selected."

Another cemetery writer describes the conflict of interest between undertaker and cemetery: "You are all familiar with the situation wherein the mortician gives a telephone order for your bare minimum, telling you to put it on his bill and not contact the family? He is trying to be a good fellow in the eyes of the family he is serving, but more than that, he is scared to death that if we see them, we'll oversell them, and he will suffer in his sale or will have to wait for his money.*

*Since this was written *Mortuary Management* stated editorially that it is the funeral director's traditional prerogative to "get first whack at

The cemeteries are not taking it lying down. They have developed their own potent counterweapon—"pre-need" sales, for which salesmen roam the neighborhoods of metropolis and suburb like thieving schoolboys in an orchard, snatching the fruit before it has fallen from the tree. They have outflanked their adversary here by getting to the prospect not hours ahead, but probably years ahead, of the undertaker. Worse yet, they are beginning to establish their own mortuaries for the new "one-stop" funeral.

Cemetery lobby and funeral lobby clashed head on recently in the Texas Legislature over the issue of "pre-need." The funeral directors had sponsored a measure to regulate pre-need selling; the degree of bitterness engendered can be gauged in this description of the Senate debate by a cemetery writer: "One of the funniest things that happened was when Senator George Parkhouse of Dallas asked Mr. Birdwill (representing the State Association of Funeral Directors) this: 'Isn't the main reason for this bill that when a person dies his family is more susceptible to buying than he is when he makes arrangements in advance? You want to get hold of people when they are in deep sorrow and they'll buy anything.' This really provoked an applause from several hundred cemetery operators attending this hearing and the presiding officer in the Senate had to bring the house down sharply and remind them where they were." No wonder that cemeteries rank high in the lists of "threats," "menaces," "problems plaguing the profession," that pepper the convention orations of the funeral directors.

Then there's the touchy problem of who gets to sell the vault. Vaultmanship is very big these days; 60 per cent of all Americans wind up in one of these stout rectangular metal or concrete containers, which may cost anywhere from $70 to a few thousand dollars. Vault selling is

---

the family." *Concept: The Journal of Creative Ideas for Cemeteries* was quick to take issue with this statement, calling it a "shocking blunder" and adding, "Regardless of the truth in the statement, isn't it improper to talk that way?"

ordinarily the prerogative of the funeral director, to whom the vault manufacturers address their message: "Think of your last ten clients. Think how many of that ten had the means and would actually have *welcomed* an opportunity to choose a *finer* vault. Makes sense, doesn't it, to *give* them that opportunity? You'll be surprised how many will *choose* this finer Clark Vault and be *grateful* to you for recommending it."

Vault men, when they get together among themselves, can be a convivial and jolly lot, prone to their own kind of family jokes; the Wilbert Burial Vault Company, for instance, gives an annual picnic featuring barbecued chicken, ribs, and "vaultburgers." This bonhomie does not extend to their relations with the cemetery people, whom they are constantly hauling into court. Lawsuits are raging in various parts of the country, brought by vault manufacturers against the cemeteries, to enjoin the latter from going into the business of selling vaults. The theory is that the cemeteries, operating as nonprofit organizations, have no business selling things. The monument makers, too, enter the fray with the same complaint, for the cemeteries have lately taken to banning the old-fashioned tombstones and selling their own bronze markers. They are slowly driving the monument makers out of business. In some cases the monument makers have secured injunctions prohibiting the cemeteries from selling monuments, markers or memorials of any kind. This is a cruel blow to the cemeteries, for they count heavily on the sale of bronze markers.

The cemeteries fight back by making things as rough as possible for both vault and monument companies. They may charge an arbitrary toll of $20 for use of their roads in connection with vault installations. They may require that all vaults be installed by cemetery personnel. They won't permit monument makers to install the foundations for their Smiling Christs, Rocks of Ages and other Items of Dignity, Strength and Lasting Beauty; instead, they insist that these be installed by the cemetery, which sets a stiff fee for the service.

The backstage squabbling among the various branches of the funeral business has long been a matter of concern to some of the more farsighted industry leaders, who are understandably fearful that the customer will eventually catch on.

These leaders believe that, rather than engage in such unseemly quarrels over the customer's dollar, they should instead concertedly strive to upgrade the standard of dying. A cemetery spokesman, decrying the friction between cemetery and undertaker, writes:

How simple it is to sell a product or an idea if we but believe in it! If we have the opportunity to foster the sentiment behind the funeral service, we must not fail to do so. Strengthen the idea behind the funeral customs, committals and the like. The family will receive additional mental satisfaction and comfort when the service is complete and in keeping with the deceased's station in life; and from a strictly mercenary angle, it will pay big dividends in establishing the thought of perpetuity and memorialization in the mind of the family.

He acknowledges the funeral director's pioneering role in conditioning the market:

Without question, the tremendous advancement in funeral customs in America must be credited to the funeral director and not to the demands of the public, not even ourselves. He has carried on assiduously an educational campaign which has resulted indirectly in a public desire for funeral sentiment and memorialization.

The lesson to be learned, then, is to promote harmony backstage for a smooth and profitable public performance. Another cemetery writer, reproving his fellow cemetery operators for their jealousy of "the success and dollar income of the funeral directors," suggests one good way in which the cemetery men can effect a *rapprochement* with these rivals: "Have a yearly meeting with them. Feed them a good dinner, distribute a small token. Last year, we

gave them all a set of cuff links made of granite from our
mausoleum. Last but not least set up a memorial council.
It won't cure all ills, but I can assure you it will help. I
believe it can control legislation. . . ."

The memorial council idea actually originated in another quarter, with the flower industry, which had long
been urging that industries which profit from funerals
unite in common cause. As the President of the Society
of American Florists said, "Funeral directors, as well
as florists, are in danger of being swept away along with
sentiment and tradition by those who do not realize the
true value of the traditional American funeral practice.
. . . Cooperation between florists and funeral director
is essential as it is only one step from 'no flowers' to 'no
funeral.' "

The florists, whose language is often pretty flowery,
convened the first meeting of the allied funeral industries
under the alliterative designation "Symposium on Sentiment." The announced purpose of the symposium was
"to combat the forces which are attacking sentiment,
memorialization and the rights of the individual in freedom of expression"—in blunter words, to combat the
religious leaders and the memorial societies who advocate
simpler, less expensive funerals. As the editor of the
American Funeral Director, weightiest of the industry's
trade journals, put it, "The present movement is broad
and sweeping. It threatens not only funeral directors, but
the entire American concept of memorialization. This
means that the supply men, cemeteries, florists, memorial
dealers and everyone else dedicated to the care and
memorialization of the dead have genuine cause for
alarm."

The sentimental gentlemen who rallied to the Symposium on Sentiment (they were in fact the only ones summoned) were an elite group, the top executives of the
funeral industry's major trade associations. The names
of the associations describe their respective areas of concern: National Funeral Directors Association, National
Selected Morticians, American Cemetery Association,

National Association of Cemeteries, Florists Telegraph Delivery Association, Monument Builders of America, and Casket Manufacturers Association.

The symposium heard a "Statement on Memorialization," prepared by the florists, who had quite a lot to say about the Dignity of Man, the United States as champion of freedom and leader of the democratic nations of the world, the importance of the individual, the profound traditions of the centuries, and so on: "The final rites, memorial tributes, the hallowed pageant of the funeral service all speak for the dignity of man. . . . Memorialization is love. It records a love so strong, so happy, so enduring that it can never die. It is the recognition of the immortality of the human spirit, the rightful reverence earned by the good life. It is the final testimony to the dignity of man." Just what else went on at the Symposium on Sentiment it is a little hard to say, for those participants in the hallowed pageant of the funeral service who attended the meeting have not told us what was said. I asked Mr. Howard Raether, who represented the funeral directors, what sort of agreements were reached. "No agreements." And are copies of the proceedings available? "No." Which is a pity, because from what one can learn of the florists and their ways, the symposium must have been a most colorful meeting.

8

THE MENACE OF P.O.

WISCONSIN FLORISTS, MORTICIANS COOPERATE TO FIGHT P.O.
—Headline in *Florists' Review*, June 1, 1961

WHAT IS P.O.? Your best friend won't tell you, because he won't know. It has nothing to do with perspiration and it does not stand for Petal Odor. It stands for the words "Please Omit," as in Please Omit Flowers, which is in turn a phrase people sometimes wish to have inserted in the newspaper notice of funeral.

P.O. is denounced as a Menace, a Peril, a Threat, a Problem and sometimes even a Specter in florists' trade journals, perhaps because 65 to 70 per cent* of the flower industry's revenue, or $414 million a year, derives from the sale of funeral flowers. This comes to a nation-wide *average* of over $246 for flowers per funeral. It sounds like an incredibly high figure; yet the florists themselves give it, and funeral directors have told me

*65% figure: "Sympathy flowers were estimated at 65% of all flower orders." *Florists' Review*, May 12, 1960. 70% figure: *Casket and Sunnyside*, June, 1961.

that it does not sound out of line to them. After all, if an ordinary citizen dies, his foreman, his union, some of his co-workers will likely send flowers, and so will his relatives and perhaps a few neighbors; and these offerings may cost from $10 up. If he was a sociable fellow, a churchgoer or a clubman, he will get proportionately more flowers from his cronies; and if he was a person of any prominence in the community, he will be deluged. This will all be in addition to the casket spray, "scarf" or blanket, etc., that his widow has purchased for anywhere from $25 to $250.

The funeral director sometimes gets rather fed up with all these flowers. To him falls the task of their care and supervision: receiving them, arranging them in the slumber room, setting them on racks in the funeral chapel, compiling a list of those who sent them, and eventually carting them off and disposing of them. There is little or no profit in this for him, for he is not supposed to receive a kickback from the florist, and in some states he is barred by law from owning his own flower shop.

A writer in *Canadian Funeral Service* comments: "I believe the funeral profession provides the largest single outlet for retail sales they [the florists] have, bar none. Yet it is the funeral director who hears all the remarks about 'paganism,' 'lavishness' and the like. I don't know any other situation where one business displays the products of another the way we are expected to do . . . receiving rooms for flowers . . . photos . . . attendant to set them up . . . $1,000 in stands, etc.—just to accommodate someone else's product. And you should hear them scream if they come in and find the flowers not too well set up. . . ."

Besides the chores involved, there are other disadvantages: the florist, betting on the fact that the bereaved family will hardly glance at the flowers, may send some very moribund specimens to the funeral. This practice has often been commented on by funeralgoers, and is evidently widespread enough to call for some criticism within the flower industry: "The greatest fault of some

florists is that of selling wilted, old blooms in funeral
pieces, because they feel that they will not be noticed or
returned. Yet these unethical florists are often loudest in
asking florists organizations to assist them in preventing
Please Omit Flowers notices." These unethical florists are
a problem for the funeral director since their festering
flowers can hardly fail to detract from the Beautiful
Memory Picture which he has worked so hard to create.

Equally distressing is the possibility that the widow
might decide on a full floral blanket. This, from the undertaker's point of view, is as bad as the traditional funeral
pall required by some churches, for it hides the lovely
casket completely, and at the very moment when there
is a maximum audience on hand to drink in its beauty and
note its enduring qualities.

These minor irritations between funeral directors and
florists have begun to fade in the face of a common
danger, the Menace of P.O. The custodians of the fragile
spring bloom, the tenders of the lily of the valley, the
summer rose, the winter snowdrop, can be most bellicose
on the subject of P.O. The anti-P.O. campaign is most
often discussed in military terms: "combatting current
attacks," "deploying our forces in the field," "massive
breakthrough," "crusade," etc. It gets more than a little
bloodthirsty; *Business Week*, commenting on a 1954
business slump in flowers, reported, "The wholesaler who
found business 'lousy' gave as his unhesitating explanation, 'Nobody's dying.' The slowed-up death rate makes
a big difference to an industry that gets nearly 85 per
cent of its $1.25 billion retail business from funerals and
weddings. Worse still, funeral notices in the newspapers
increasingly carry the message, 'Please Omit Flowers.' "

The funeral directors are key allies in the blitzkrieg
against P.O. because they control the wording of obituary
notices; according to a florists' survey, 92 per cent of the
death notices published in newspapers are given to the
papers by funeral directors. Florists spend a good deal
of time and money cementing the alliance by speaking
at conclaves of funeral directors, advertising in their

journals, and contributing articles to the funeral trade press. There is a certain amount of buttering up, as in an article addressed to funeral directors by the President of the Florists' Telegraph Delivery Association: "Your highest duty is creation. It is surely a function that is guided by the Great Creator, for in your hands has been placed the responsibility of creating a living Memory Picture." He warns of a common danger: "the attitude in some places that the present high standards of funeral service are unnecessary. Being close to the funeral directors in their daily work, F.T.D. florists feel that this attitude is dangerous and strikes at the very roots of our civilization." He lists "11 Ways To Meet 'Please Omit' Trend," the first way being "Say they may unthinkably offend sincere friends."

An appeal for the formation of a common front against the foe is contained in a full-page advertisement sponsored by F.T.D. which appears regularly (possibly, to some constant readers like myself, monotonously) in the pages of a number of funeral and cemetery trade magazines. It marshals the arguments to be used against P.O. and contains the hint of a threat of what can happen to the funeral director himself should he prove to be a deserter from the cause. An illustration designed to strike fear in the heart of a funeral director shows a completely bare chapel—pews, but no mourners; casket bier but no casket; flower vases but no flowers. The text:

PLEASE OMIT . . . WHAT?

What will they want to omit next? Ministers? Music? All but the plainest caskets? When does a funeral service stop comforting the bereaved—and become merely the mechanical fulfillment of an obligation? Once you start subtracting warmth and human feeling, where do you end—and what do you have left?

Think it over.

And the next time a client asks you about "Please Omit," remember that you and your florist friends serve the bereaved best by understanding their needs better, perhaps, than they may do themselves.

Your experience, your common sense and any good psychologist will tell you that most grieving people should have the extra warmth and comfort of living flowers. At an emotional moment, 'please omit' may seem like a simple solution to a torturing problem. It does not and cannot, however, serve the memory through the years.

That's why you're so right to recommend sympathy flowers and a full funeral service. They pay tribute to the life accomplishment of the deceased, and bring comfort to the bereaved when they need it most.

This solicitous concern for the psychological well-being of the bereaved family is considered a winning card by florists. "Softness comes back to her face as sorrow begins to slip away" is the caption for a picture of a young widow receiving some chrysanthemums; and the text continues, "Psychologists agree that funeral flowers comfort as almost nothing else can. . . . So you're on firm psychological ground when you recommend flowers." What psychologists? Psychologists like the proprietor of the Drive-In Floral Mart, who in a lecture to students at the Indiana College of Mortuary Science "stressed the importance of floral tributes in the therapy of grief for the mourners and in providing an outlet for the expressions of sympathy for friends of the deceased."

Spokesmen for the florists also express great solicitude for family friends who may be caused to suffer embarrassment by the publication of a Please Omit request. Such notices, they warn, may even rupture lifelong friendships; but an alert funeral director can help to prevent these dread consequences. Mr. Cecil Brown, Society of American Florists public relations representative, suggested an approach to the problem in a talk on "Sense in Sentiment": "The best place to combat this trend is in the counseling room. There the family places its faith in the funeral director, counting on his experience to arrange the funeral with dignity and good taste and in a way that creates a beautiful memory picture. Flowers, of course, are an integral part of this. When a client suggests omitting them, it is the duty of the funeral director to alert him to some of the unpleasantness which can follow in the wake of a 'Please Omit' notice. . . . The end result may well be a deterioration of relations between friends, who object to capitalizing on death in order to raise funds for charity. . . . A further unpleasant aspect is the embarrassment of friends who heed the admonition to omit flowers, only to find that others have not."

Not only are the mental health of the bereaved family, the peace of mind of their friends, and relations between family and friends all imperiled by the Please Omit notice —the very foundation of our country is at stake. As Mr. Brown went on to say, "It is to the benefit of all funeral directors to cooperate with florists in eliminating P.O., in order to preserve the sentiment now attached to funeral customs. Sentiment is one of the foundations upon which we have built our country, and history shows what happens when countries abandon it. It is our responsibility to preserve sentiment in order to protect our traditional American burial customs. Once they are gone, they can never be replaced."

The flower industry, shouldering this weighty responsibility to homeland and tradition for some three decades, has recorded some spectacular victories. True, in the early years of the fight against P.O., methods were a little crude, and sometimes brought down unseemly ridicule on the campaigners. *The New Yorker* reprinted an anti-P.O. letter from a florist to the St. Louis *Post-Dispatch* as an end-of-column filler under the heading O DEATH, WHERE IS THY ADVERTISING APPROPRIATION?:

We wish to express an objection to the reporting of an article concerning the death of ———— as it appeared in a recent issue of your paper.

At the close of this article you reported, "The family has asked that flowers be omitted and any tribute be given to the Red Cross or to the Mary Endowment Fund." We feel it is not clean business or necessary in reporting a situation, for one business to express the opinion that another business can afford to be penalized in the light of charity. We do not believe in doing a good job of reporting it was necessary to include this paragraph, and the omission of this request would not have changed your ability of reporting his passing.

As a member of the Allied Florists of St. Louis publicity committee, I know the *Post-Dispatch* has a generous share of our advertising funds, and the encouragement by your paper to "kindly omit flowers" can hasten the day when the funds available for advertising can be so restricted that the newspapers of this community can lose that source of revenue they have been receiving.

It is not of my mind to question the wishes of any person or family. I naturally am puzzled as to why we florists have been selected as a business which can afford to do without a portion of their business at the expense of charity. I have yet to see a newspaper article or a paid obituary notice suggesting the omission of candy, liquor, cosmetics or tobacco, with funds to be forwarded to charity. It is only in the light of what I consider good business that I draw this to your attention. D. S. Geddes, Jr.

The point made about advertising funds and good business was perhaps too starkly stated, and was perhaps a little too revealing. Clearly, a subtler approach, and one less likely to make the pages of humor magazines, was needed. A campaign was launched in the late fifties, backed by a $2-million-a-year advertising budget, to erase P.O. forever from the public prints. It is described by Marc Williams in *Flowers-by-Wire, The Story of The Florists' Telegraph Delivery Association:* "Before the end of 1957, Sales and Advertising conducted a national survey on the 'Please Omit' problem, which covered all the newspapers, radio and television stations in the United States. . . . Between 75 per cent and 85 per cent of the country's newspapers accepted such obituary notices." Armed with this information, the Florists' Information Council "was able to send its field men into the affected areas, to hold meetings with the advertising departments of the papers and also with the funeral directors to arrive at a solution."

The field men in their sorties into the affected areas wielded both clubs and carrots, the latter consisting of "a series of 85-line ads on the obituary pages of 70 news-papers . . . for obvious reasons, *The American Funeral Director* was listed for six insertions." Success was almost instantaneous: by 1959, the executive secretary of the Society of American Florists was able to report that "be-cause of Florists' Telegraph Delivery's financial aid, 241 cities had been visited by field men and 199 news-papers had agreed to refrain from using 'Please Omit' phrases."

This was followed up by another survey, results of which were reported to industry leaders in November, 1960, in a two-day session held "to give the committee members and guests ample time to scrutinize the many 'Please Omit' problem areas in which the Florists' In-formation Council is working." F.I.C.'s public relations representatives had called on 151 newspaper executives between July 1, 1959 and June 30, 1960 to discuss pol-icies regarding obituary notices. "The survey also revealed which newspapers are keeping their word as to policy on flowers," the report says darkly, information essential to the continuing success of the campaign because editors of delinquent papers can often be brought back into line with a "return call" from the field men.

The San Francisco papers, I had observed, never use "Please omit flowers" or "In lieu of flowers" in funeral no-tices, although they do publish requests for donations to worthy causes, usually in the words "Memorial contribu-tions to the ———— fund preferred." I was curious to know how the advertising department of a newspaper that has given its word to the florists would handle a request from an individual to print the forbidden phrase in a death notice.

I telephoned one of the large San Francisco dailies, and was connected with Miss Black. ("Miss Black" is, I learned, a fictitious name assigned to the employee who handles this department; I was struck with the passing thought that, to be up with the times in the changing funereal color scheme, the newspaper might consider changing her name to Miss Honey Beige, or Miss Peach

Pink.) I explained to Miss Black that I was telephoning on behalf of a friend whose mother had just died and who had asked me to arrange for newspaper notices of the funeral. She briskly told me that the proper person to take care of the notice is the funeral director. "There is no funeral director," I answered. "My friend's mother was cremated, and there will be a memorial service." Miss Black said she could not accept the notice from anybody other than a funeral director; I said I bet she could, and in this case she would have to. Miss Black excused herself to go and consult her supervisor. She returned to the phone several minutes later to report that the supervisor said the notice could be accepted in this case, subject only to later confirmation of the death by the crematorium, a routine precaution against practical jokers.

Now we got to the point. "The notice is to read 'Please omit flowers,' " I said.

"Well, we never put it that way. How about 'Memorial Contributions Preferred,' or 'Memorial gifts . . .' "? suggested Miss Black.

"No, I don't think that will do. The family wouldn't like to ask for charitable contributions on an occasion like this. Besides, my friend's mother left exact instructions in her will about the wording of the notice, and she specified that it should say, 'Please omit flowers.' "

Sounds of Miss Black being in deep water. "I'm sorry, ma'am, that would be against our policy. We are not allowed to accept ads that are derogatory about anyone, or about any*thing.*"

"But this isn't derogatory about anyone."

"It's derogatory about flowers."

"There is nothing unkind about flowers in that notice. As a matter of fact, my friend's mother adored flowers. She just doesn't want them cluttering up her funeral, that's all."

Miss Black was firm; she spoke about newspaper policy, she said she had her instructions. I was firm; I spoke about freedom of the press and the rights of the individual, but to no avail. Later, I telephoned the head of the department; he was firm, too. "We couldn't publish a notice like that," he said. "Why, the florists would be right on our necks!"

I called the other newspapers in the area, and got the same reaction.

While major accomplishments are being chalked up, there are nevertheless occasional setbacks. When President Eisenhower's mother-in-law died in September, 1960, the only funeral flowers were a white carnation cross sent by the President and one spray from members of the immediate family. The Washington *Post* carried this announcement: "The President and Mrs. Eisenhower requested that no flowers be sent and that contributions to charities be made instead." (For some reason *The New York Times* did not, in its story, see fit to print this portion of the President's statement.)* The florists were stung to the quick. Association executives rushed into action to get newspapers, television and radio stations to suppress the President's request. The *Florists' Review* says, "This was most important because many newspapers and TV and radio stations have already set their policy to not include 'In lieu of flowers' requests in their obituary notices. It was felt that such policies should be called to their attention. . . . The Society of American Florists is still doing everything within its power to remedy the dangerous effects which the President's unintentional bombshell exploded within the industry." Gratitude was expressed "to all industry members who immediately took action to support the florists' industry at this critical time." But efforts to obtain a retraction from the White House were in vain, and in fact brought down criticism from that arbiter of good taste, *Mortuary Management*: "Sending a wire to the White House over a matter that could have rank commercial overtones was, in our opinion, very bad taste. A breach of good manners will be remembered long

*However, the *Times* is among the major newspapers that are holding out and that will accept "Please Omit" notices. Among others are the New York *Herald Tribune* and the Washington *Post*.

after the public has forgotten this one 'Please Omit' notice."

On the whole, though, continued vigilance pays off. The least hint that a criticism of overspending on funeral flowers may be publicly voiced brings squadrons of florists' field men on the double to the affected area. Fortunately for the occasional library browser, they sometimes allow themselves to boast in print about the results of their successful forays into potentially hostile territory. Thus the *Florists' Review*:

It is a rare occurrence when florists can be grateful that funeral flowers are omitted. But such was the case when an article titled 'Can You Afford to Die?' appeared in the June 17 (1961) issue of the *Saturday Evening Post,* a popular consumer magazine with a circulation running into the millions. . . .

The important point here is that this omission of funeral flowers did not just happen. Derogatory references to flowers did not appear in the article because of intensive behind-the-scenes efforts of the Florists' Information Committee of the Society of American Florists. By working closely with the magazine's advertising department, the F.I.C. successfully headed off statements which would have been extremely damaging to the industry.

The article goes on, rather unkindly, to report that in spite of the fact that the florists' committee had tried its best to include Howard C. Raether, executive secretary of the National Funeral Directors Association, in the behind-the-scenes meetings, the latter was unsuccessful:

Despite all his efforts, the magazine went ahead with its original plans and refused to eliminate the article or to make changes suggested by him.

There is a moral to it all:

The article definitely illustrates a point that florists have been bringing to the attention of funeral directors—that the

P.O. problem can easily spread from flowers to the services offered by funeral directors.

This war of the roses, like its earlier counterpart, was more than a little embellished in the telling. Having been the lucky recipient of a manuscript copy of the beleaguered *Saturday Evening Post* article, I checked this against the published version, and found but three deletions:

1) "Not long ago the flowers in the bill of one far from wealthy man in Washington, D.C. came to $1,000 alone. . . ."

2) "Furthermore they [ministers] urged that flowers on such occasions be kept to a minimum and that friends express their sympathy by gifts to favorite causes that benefit the whole community. . . ."

3) " 'We wanted a few flowers but not the elaborate set pieces which were impossible to give away to hospitals after the ceremony.'. . ."

Just how the florists engineered these clever little changes remains a mystery. The editor of the *Post* told me he was completely flabbergasted by the article in *Florists' Review,* and had turned the magazine upside down to find out what happened. He added that during his seven years at the *Post* he had never heard of anything happening to an article which remotely resembled the tampering indicated by the florists.

9

GOD'S LITTLE MILLION-DOLLAR ACRE

*In the interment industry there have been a great many
revolutionary changes taking place in the last twenty years.
More progress has been made during this period than had
been made in the previous two thousand years. . . . Today we face an era of unprecedented development in our
industry through the use of progressive methods, materials
and educational techniques.*
           —*Concept: The Journal of Creative Ideas for
           Cemeteries*

THERE'S GOLD in them thar verdant lawns and splashing
fountains, in them mausoleums of rugged strength and
beauty, in them distinctive personalized bronze memorials,
in them museums and gift shops. *Concept: The Journal of
Creative Ideas for Cemeteries*—the very title vibrates with
the thunder of progress—circulates to some 5,000 of
America's 9,000 actively operating cemeteries, to whom it
imparts many an idea on how the gold can best be mined
and minted.

The cemetery as a moneymaking proposition is new in
this century. The earliest type of burial ground in America
was the churchyard. This gave way in the nineteenth century to graveyards at the town limits, largely municipally
owned and operated. Whether owned by church or munici-
pality, the burial ground was considered a community
facility; charges for graves were nominal, and the burial
ground was generally not expected to show a profit.

Prevailing sentiment that there was something special and sacred about cemetery land, that it deserved special consideration and should not be subjectd to such temporal regulation as taxation, was reflected in court decisions and state laws. A cemetery company is an association formed for "a pious and public use," the United States Supreme Court said in 1882, and more recently the New Jersey Supreme Court ruled that a cemetery, even if privately owned is a public burial ground "whose operation for purposes of profit is offensive to public policy." Other rulings have affirmed that land acquired for cemetery purposes becomes entirely exempt from real estate taxes the moment it is acquired, even before a dead body is buried in it.

This traditional view of cemetery land proved a blessing to the land speculators who began to enter the field fifty years ago, and whose handiwork can now be seen on the outskirts of thousands of American communities.

The major premises which, evolved over the years, lie behind modern cemetery operation are all, on the face of it, sound and intelligent enough. Cemetery land is tax-free, which is as it should be, since in theory the land is not to be put to gainful use. Cheap land which for one reason or another does not easily lend itself to such needs of the living as housing and agriculture is commonly used for cemeteries. The purchase of a grave for future occupancy is, surely, a rational and sensible act, showing foresight and prudence on the part of the buyer who wishes to spare his family the trouble and expense of doing so when the need arises. Innovations which result in more economical upkeep of cemeteries, such as dispensing with upright tombstones to facilitate mechanical mowing, seem practical and commendable; so does the establishment of an endowment fund for the future upkeep of the cemetery.

Economies achieved by new and efficient operating methods, tax exemptions such as only schools and churches enjoy, dedication to "pious and public use"—these would all seem to point in the direction of continuously reducing the cost of burial. The opposite has been the case. The cost of burial has soared, at a rate outstripping even the rise in undertakers' charges. The winning combination that has transformed the modern cemetery into a wildly profitable commercial venture is precisely its tax-free status, the adaptability of cheap land to its purposes, the almost unlimited possibilities of subdividing the land, the availability for reinvestment of huge "perpetual care" resources, and the introduction of "pre-need" installment selling. Given these propitious conditions, there is really no end to the creative ideas that can be put to work by the cemetery promoter.

A very creative idea for cemeteries is to establish them as nonprofit corporations. In California and in many other states virtually all commercial cemeteries enjoy this privilege. At first glance it would seem an act of purest altruism that somebody should go to all the trouble, at absolutely no profit to himself, to start a cemetery wherein his fellow man may be laid to eternal rest. A second glance discloses that the nonprofit aspect removes the necessity to pay income tax on grave sales. And a really close look discloses that the profits that are now routinely extracted by the promoters of "nonprofit" cemeteries are spectacular beyond the dreams of the most avaricious real estate subdivider.

There is nothing actually illegal about the operation. It works like this: Foreverness Lawn Memory Gardens, Inc. is organized as a nonprofit cemetery corporation, closely controlled by the promoters. Foreverness owns not a scrap of land. The acreage it will use for burial plots is owned by the promoters, either in their own names or, more commonly, in the name of a closely held land company. They enter into a contract with themselves—that is, the land company has a contract with Foreverness which provides that Foreverness will operate the cemetery and sell the graves, the promoters to receive for each grave sold 50 per cent of the selling price, and for each mausoleum crypt, 60 per cent. Since Foreverness out of its half of the income must bear all of the cemetery's operating, sales and maintenance costs, there is little danger that it will lose its chaste nonprofit character. The promoters, for their part, rake in hundreds of thousands of dollars per acre for their low-cost land.*

Modern transportation has made it possible for the cemetery, like the supermarket, to be at some distance from commercial centers and high-priced residential sections; therefore land for the vast new "park" cemeteries can often be acquired for a modest cash outlay—sometimes for as little as $300 an acre, more commonly for $500-$1,500 an acre. (Sometimes, of course, particularly when a mausoleum sales program is planned, the promoters will go higher. Recently a California cemetery announced the purchase of "100 acres of ocean view property" for a reported $5,000 an acre, for the development of "patio style" mausoleum crypts.)

Having acquired his tax-free, bargain land, the cemeterian (as he likes to be called) starts to get his property ready for occupancy. It is here that creativity begins to come into play.

A real estate promoter who subdivides land for live occupancy may be quite pleased if he can break an acre of land into 50-by-100-foot lots suitable for resale to people who can afford to buy and build. He counts himself lucky if he can squeeze six such lots out of an acre. But consider the cemetery promoter, who routinely breaks his acreage into easy-to-own little packages measuring 8 feet by 3 feet, 1,500 or better to the acre, each parcel guaranteed tax-exempt.

Fifteen hundred burial spaces per acre is an estimate that errs on the conservative side, and would today be considered old-fashioned. For one thing, it allows space for the accommodation of the now outmoded headstone, and it allows 15 per cent for drives, walks and little spaces between graves so that the fastidious or reverent may avoid stepping on the graves to get from one to another. The modern "lawn type" cemetery, the most creative idea of all, utilizes all this wasted space by simply eliminating footpaths between graves (the paths of glory

*See Chapter Notes.

now lead but to the gift shop and museum) and by banning tombstones altogether, thus making possible unbroken rows of snugly packed 7-by-3-foot graves. The tombstone is replaced by standard bronze markers set flush with the ground—a creative idea which a) enables the cemetery owners to appropriate from the sale of the plaques profits that formerly went to the monument makers for tombstones and b) by opening up the area to huge power mowers,* eliminates all need for hand-trimming of grave plots and saves 75 per cent of the maintenance cost.

To these innovations cemeteries now add a further refinement: the sale of nice, cozy "companion spaces" for occupancy by husband and wife. The advantage to the promoters is that the companions will repose one above the other in a single grave space, dug "double depth," to use the trade expression. One Los Angeles "lawn type" cemetery gives this estimate of its land use:

Adult graves	1,815 per acre
Additional graves, made available by reserving one-half of each acre for double-depth interments	907
Babyland (three in the space occupied by one adult)	120
Total number of graves	2,842 per acre

Another, also in Los Angeles, projects 3,177 "plantings" per acre in land used for ground burial.

It must not be thought that this sort of overcrowding is always the most profitable use of cemetery land. As in the conventional real estate transaction, it is more profitable to offer variety, something to suit every purse and give rein to every social aspiration, and cemetery land, like real estate for the living, is priced according to desirability. There are "view lots" and "garden locations" for those who aspire to be housed among the comfortably

*Rose Hills (Los Angeles) Memorial Park boasts "the world's largest lawnmower."

well-to-do; nice roomy "memorial estates" for the really rich; crowded, plainer quarters for those accustomed to tract housing. Neighborhoods develop here too along the lines of status and prestige, as well as along religious lines; lodges and clubs are represented by sections set aside for Masons, Lions, veterans' organizations, and the like.

Prevailing prejudices in the land of the living are mirrored in the land of the dead, and racial segregation as practiced in cemetery land parallels that which prevails aboveground. As court decisions force changes aboveground, the cemetery falls back accordingly. The cemetery salesman questioned on this controversial matter will hint, just as the owner of a housing tract might, that the cemetery has managed to get around the court decisions. I asked a Forest Lawn salesman about this and he told me, "We used to have a clause against colored but there's no restriction any more against Negroes being buried here. There are none here, though," he hastened to assure me. "I guess they feel more comfortable among their own people." Familiar refrain! But a Negro from a wealthy Los Angeles family told me, "What they don't know won't hurt them. Why, an aunt of mine is in a crypt there. She's got one of those fifteen-thousand-dollar jobs, right in with the best families, but then of course she had been passing for white for twenty years before she died."

The latest trend in cemetery development is upward expansion—the community mausoleum. Here indeed is a breakthrough in the space barrier. There may be limits to how deep one can conveniently dig to bury the dead, but in building for aboveground entombment the sky is literally the limit, and 10,000 mausoleum spaces to an acre is a most realistic yield. Referred to disparagingly by cemetery men of twenty years ago as "tenement mausoleums," these are now very In, and are an enormously lucrative proposition. Structurally and functionally they lend themselves ideally to the simplest form of block construction, for they consist merely of tier upon tier of cubicles made of reinforced concrete faced with a veneer of marble or granite. Crypt is stacked upon crypt—

six or seven high is currently the vogue—two deep, on either side of a visitors' corridor. The most advantageous size for crypts, it says in *Concept,* is 32 inches wide, 25 inches high, and 90 inches long.

The cost of a single mausoleum crypt in any of the promotional cemeteries is upwards of $600, compared with beginning prices of $150 to $300 for ground burial. The average mausoleum sale, nationally, is $720 for a single crypt.

The reader with a head for figures may find it interesting to compare the cost of housing for the dead with the cost of housing for the living. The size of a single crypt is approximately 42 cubic feet. At $720 per crypt, this works out to $17 per cubic foot. A small five-room house (the "compact bungalow, dandy five, two bedrooms, electric kitchen, 1½ baths, suitable for couple and one child" of the real estate ads) may have 1,200 square feet of floor space and be 9 feet high, for a total of 10,800 cubic feet. Such a house sells for about $15,000 in most parts of the country. At crypt rates, this house would fetch $183,600.

One large mausoleum construction firm suggests putting a whole acre into crypts, and offers the most alluring figures on property potential to be realized from the crypt-filled acre: potential gross sales, $4,308,000; net potential, $2,808,000.

All of the clever planning to extract the maximum use from each acre of land would avail little if the cemetery promoter then had to sit back and wait upon the haphazard whim of the Grim Reaper. With the death rate at its present low level, he might have to wait a very long time indeed to begin to realize profit on his investment. This barrier has been brilliantly surmounted in recent years by the introduction of the massive "pre-need" sales campaign, employing squads of door-to-door salesmen. One of the most successful devices in the history of merchandising, pre-need selling is the key to the runaway growth of the modern cemetery business.

The rate at which Americans are being sold cemetery

space for future occupancy is staggering. In 1960 pre-need sales of graves and crypts outnumbered "at-need" sales by four to one. In that year, of the 1.7 million who died in the United States, more than half had previously bought their graves; and more than three million burial spaces were bought by living Americans.

As pre-need sales continue to zoom, it cannot be long before every living American will own a grave, or at least have contracted to pay for one on the installment plan. Perhaps it is this prospect of a saturated market that spurs competing promoters in the race to get there first, to range ever farther in extending their chains of cemeteries to take in even the remotest hamlet. Only this can account for the prodigious rate at which cemetery development and mausoleum construction have been piling up in the last few years. No community is too small to attract the attention of the promoters: *Concept* cites the case of a town with a population of less than 750 where a successful 288-crypt mausoleum has been established. A mausoleum building firm reported construction of a 336-crypt "indoor-outdoor" mausoleum in Reserve, Louisiana, which at that time had a population of 1,126.

The flavor, the tempo and the scope of this activity may be sampled by scanning the brief announcements columns of *Concept*. Here are some of the developments reported in a single month:

Louisburg, N.C.—Development of new perpetual care cemetery, to be known as Highland Memory Gardens, has recently begun here. . . . It will serve all of Franklin County and is situated on a plateau of 30 rolling acres. Highland Memory Gardens is being handled by United Cemetery Consultants Inc., of Raleigh, N.C., making a total of 7 properties now handled by United.

Santa Ana, Calif.—Pacific View Memorial Park has purchased 100 acres of ocean view property for a reported $500,000. . . . The cemetery expansion program includes three mausoleums and a new chapel.

Seattle, Wash.—A $400.000 two-story addition to Acacia Mausoleum will be completed by June 15, 1962. . . . The interior is finished in French and Italian marble. An interior garden will have an illuminated fountain as its focal point.

Hillsboro, Ore.—Valley Memorial Park is planing to extend its present mausoleum with a 328-crypt addition. The addition will be known as Lilac Corridor.

From the point of view of the cemetery promoter, the special attraction of pre-need selling is its self-financing feature. With little or no cash, he acquires an option on some rural acreage and has it zoned for cemetery use. He has a landscape architect supply him with sketches picturing verdant terraces, splashing fountains, tall cypresses and blooming shrubs, and broad avenues converging on an imposing central "feature" (a word used throughout the trade for "statue"), usually in a religious motif. These can be ordered by catalogue number; popular models this year are The Good Shepherd, Model 221-Z, list price to the cemetery, $1,395; Christus, $850; Sermon on the Mount, $795; Last Supper, $1,795. He gets plans and drawings of his mausoleum-to-be from one of the national organizations that specialize in this form of construction. He then contracts with a sales organization that makes a specialty of pre-need selling to handle his sales, and he is in business.

The money comes rolling in—if ready cash is needed by the salesmen, they customarily discount their week's bag of pre-need installment contracts at the bank—and up to this point not a spadeful of dirt has been turned at the Beautiful Memory Garden; not a cement slab has been poured at the site of Sweet Repose Mausoleum. It is standard practice in this business not to start construction until at least one-third of all the projected burial and crypt space has been sold. Since this amount is far more than will ever be spent on development and construction, the buyers of these little burial spaces will have furnished the promoter, in advance, with all the capial he will need, and a handsome advance profit as well.

Explaining to cemeterians the advantages of employing aggressive sales promotion organizations to handle their pre-need programs, Mr. Chester A. Brown, president of the Central Sales and Service Company, spoke of the spectacular price increases that could be obtained by the right kind of selling. He illustrated his point with some examples from his own experience. At one cemetery where lots had been selling for $150, his company moved in, raised the price to $380, and racked up sales of $250,000 in two years. At another, lots were selling for $200 and his company succeeded in running the price up to $330.

It is not as hard as one might think to extract these prices from the public, because pre-need payments are customarily made in painless installments over a long period of time. The cemetery owner can, after all, afford to offer generous terms. Unlike any other commodity offered for sale on the installment plan, this one remains always in the seller's possession, and its use may not be called for until many years after it has been paid for in full. "Sunset View's 'Before Need' ownership plan offers the opportunity for purchasing family lots in monthly installments so small that they are hardly noticeable," says a circular mailed to me by a local cemetery. Sunset View's graves run $175 to $500 (plus an interment fee of $235.58); mausoleum crypts sell from $690 to $1,300 for a single, $1,360 to $2,150 for a double.

Pre-need selling is a costly proposition, and it is the customer, of course, who ultimately foots the bill. The sales organization usually works on a 50 per cent commission; the individual salesman gets 20 per cent to 40 per cent of the selling price. "In most cemeteries which have prearrangement sales programs, four to ten times more is spent for direct selling than is spent for the total cost of planning, development and landscaping," complains a cemetery architect.

The "space and bronze deal," as it is called by the door-to-door sales specialists, is exciting, heady work, full of the romance of a new Gold Rush and the conquest of new frontiers. The exuberant buoyancy, the spirit of confidence, the zeal and joie de vivre reflected in the soaring prose of *Concept* and the *American Cemetery* are in marked contrast to the embattled gloom, the righteous martyrdom, that stalks the pages of the undertaker's trade magazines.

There are thrilling success stories, such as that of Mililani ("meaning 'Gates of Heaven' in Hawaiian") Memorial Park near Honolulu, where an all-time high of $1,090,408 in installment sales was chalked up in a four-week period. Literally chalked up; *The Journal of Creative Ideas* has a picture of the ecstatically grinning vice-president and sales director before a huge blackboard, something like a tote board, showing "This Month at a Glance." On it are listed the Big Four salesmen, the Little Four, and the Midgets, with the numbers of "units" sold by each and their cash totals.

The gleeful sales director of Mililani, Mr. J. Calvin Harberts, is cover boy in another issue of *Concept,* and deservedly so, for he typifies the new look in cemetery leadership. Fifty years ago, before the advent of the commercial cemetery, the principal cemetery executive was the superintendent or head groundkeeper. Today, the unassuming fellow who kept up the cemetery grounds has been supplanted in place of first importance by a more dashing breed—the "specialty salesman." "Specialty salesman" is the selling fraternity's generic name for a specialist in door-to-door installment selling of a single, usually high-priced item not available in stores. Mr. Harberts is such a salesman.

Having made a fortune in real estate immediately after World War II, Mr. Harberts moved into the garbage-disposal-unit and food-freezer business; "he hired and trained a staff of 175 top-flight professional salesmen and laid the groundwork for today's success in the cemetery field." Many of his garbage-disposal and freezer boys later joined him in the Mililani venture, where some of them earned as much as $3,850 in commissions in a single week. "These men could sell anything they wanted, anywhere they wanted to do it," says *Concept*; perhaps in this case, without even revising their sales pitch too drastically, since the freezer men were dealing once again, by coincidence, in a rectangular product, measuring about 7 by 3 feet, geared to long-term preservation.

The lure of the space and bronze deal is attracting salesmen from many fields—"book men" (the door-to-door encyclopedia salesmen), appliance men, auto salesmen, insurance salesmen; yet *Concept* reports there is still a shortage. The classified pages of *American Cemetery* are loaded with "Salesmen Wanted" advertisements offering more than just fabulous earnings: "Salesman: Spend Your Summer in Maine and Make Money Too—There is Fishing, Hunting, Boating in VACATION LAND—Phone, Write or Wire, Gracelawn Memorial Park and Mausoleum"; "Perfect All Year Selling Climate—Join the Migration to San Diego in Southern California—The Most Perfect Climate in the country, both to lie in and to sell in—high commissions, bonuses,—a place where you'll enjoy working, El Camino Memorial Park." "Restlawn Memorial Park is designed with the Salesman in mind. Full commission paid every Wednesday, plus bonus for every $10,000 written. Area has not been scratched. Late model automobile, neatness, sincerity and truth a must."

Once the salesman is hired, he becomes a Memorial Counselor, and in this capacity must quickly acquire a few new postures. An executive of the California Interment Association sees the Memorial Counselor as walking a sort of tightrope: "Exploitation of cemetery sales achievements must assume the proper place in the delicate balance of ethical cemetery practices and the natural American drive to achieve the strongest possible business posture."

Luckily it only takes about a week for an experienced man to acquire the right amount of sincerity and truth at a school for Memorial Counselors. The trainee is "schooled in the best methods of gaining access into a home. He must be in a problem solving frame of mind, and must be one who has come to render a service and not one who has come to sell something. During the week he is reviewed constantly on trial closes and answering objections." At the end of the week the student is presented with his certificate as "Professional Memorial Consultant."

In a typical sales argument taught at the school, the salesman shows the prospect some pictures of a bottle of milk, labeled "1935—8¢ quart," "1962—28¢ quart," "1972—58¢ quart (?)." This plants the idea of inflation in the prospect's mind. Now for the "trial close":

Mr. Jones, if something should happen to me in the years to come, my wife, bless her heart, would feel inclined to go out and emotionally overspend. She would use money I left for her comfort and protection and buy cemetery property at its then INFLATED price to show her love for me. That's why I have tied her hands and protected her against her own affection and the rolling surge of INFLATION. This protection is possible only by acting now. I'm sure we husbands all agree on this point, don't we?

And another:

Mr. and Mrs. Jones, our birth certificate is a purchase contract for our cemetery property. We *must* have a place to be buried. Furthermore the laws of all 50 states confirmed the sale. We *must* be buried in a duly approved cemetery.* The only choice left to us is which of the *two* prices we desire to pay. If we *wait* we pay the *inflated* price—all cash—yes we buy an emergency. If we act *now* we stop inflation—under this program we even roll the price back. As good businessmen, we know which makes more sense, don't we?

Why do the customers buy? The aura of genteel respectability conferred by ownership of cemetery property (often, the only piece of real estate the prospect will ever own), the wisdom and economy of advance planning for a contingency that must inevitably arise, are powerful argu-

*Not true. In all but four states cremated ashes may be buried on private property or scattered.

ments. It sounds good, but the "economy" is a myth and the "wisdom" a snare. The customer in the pre-need era pays far more for burial than he would have in pre-pre-need days. Fifty years ago, while there was no pre-need selling, there was a certain amount of pre-need buying (a most important distinction) generally by those solid citizens, staid families of substantial means, who were accustomed in this as in other matters to planning in advance. Acquisition of a "family plot" was not a costly transaction; if a family paid $100 for a four-grave plot, it was paying a lot. Single graves ran from $1 to $20. Even today, people who live in communities that have not yet been invaded by the commercial pre-needers can buy from municipal, denominational or other noncommercial cemeteries burial space either in advance or when death occurs at a fraction of what they would have to pay a commercial solicitor.

Frequently people do not know of the existence in their community of a publicly owned cemetery; and few take the trouble to go there to make advance arrangements. Those who do so are prosaically just buying a grave, whereas the stay-at-homes, who wait for the Memorial Counselor to call, get so much *more* for their money: "Ideally a couple in their early years of married life will benefit by making arrangements at that time, affording them protection and economic benefits when they need it most and often creating a psychological bond that may enrich their marital relationship," says the Interment Association of America.

The pre-need sales program lends itself to endless variation and elaboration. Among the selling aids available is the M.I. Salesfilm Kit (M.I. stands for Memorial Impulse), films to be shown in the prospect's home. The Radio Bible Players of Hollywood offer a Bible drama recording; "Stress the Spiritual! Each Sunday in 1960 visit your best prospects in their homes. . . . Join the family circle . . . turn the pages of the family Bible and make their most-loved stories LIVE. Then, attention assured, tell your own story." Michigan Memorial Park, whose counselors offer prospects a free helicopter flight to the cemetery "as a routine part of their sales technique," is also credited with having pioneered the use of sound-color films to sell its grave and mausoleum facilities to prospects in their homes.

The advent of the mausoleum boom has added a new dimension to the pre-need sales rhetoric. "Talk Mausoleum!" urges *Concept;* and evaluating the results of a recent direct-mail campaign, it reports, "It was agreed that prestige and horror of ground burial motivated the bulk of replies."

Mausoleum advertising reaches back into history for its theme—Abraham's cave, the Pyramids, the tomb of King Mausolus, the Taj Mahal (usually referred to as "the $15,000,000 Taj Mahal"), the "$3,000,000 Lincoln Memorial," Grant's Tomb. *Concept* quotes Tressie Johnson of Texas ("she is a volume producer in mausoleum sales; sincerity plays a great part in her success") on how to make the most of the historical theme. She suggests mentioning the Taj Mahal, Napoleon, Lincoln, Grant and Lenin: "But what means even *more* to the family, tell them Jesus was supposed to have been placed in a rock tomb belonging to Joseph of Arimathea. They say, yes, that is right. . . ." To bridge the gap of centuries, to convey the idea that the mausoleum is actually the expression of an innate and universal drive, Dr. Frank Crane (the late syndicated homely philosopher) is often invoked, credited with the sonorous declaration, "Man is a tomb-building animal."

In real life, the brand-new mausoleums mushrooming in communities across the country do not look very much like the Taj Mahal. They look a good deal more like giant egg-crates, and the little receptacles have a certain sameness about them—which is not surprising, since they are identical. However, since purchasing power varies from customer to customer, and since those able to pay more should be given every opportunity to do so, distinction and desirability have been conferred on some of the receptacles by the magic of the sales talk.

Like uncounted millions of other Americans, I was visited last year by a cemetery "Memorial Counselor." He spread out for my delectation page after page of shiny color respresentations of rolling lawns, limpid pools, statues of the Good Shepherd, of sundry Apostles; "and here are some of our special Babyland features," he announced proudly, producing a folder of statues of toddlers and lambs. On each picture was printed in small letters "Artist's Conception."

"Can I go out and see it?" I asked.

"Well, there won't be anything much to see for a while yet; most of it is still in the planning stage. Here's how the mausoleum is going to look." He pulled out a folder showing "Preconstruction Corridor" in pink and gray marble, and "Sunshine Garden—An Innovation in Out-of-doors Memorial Construction" in cream and blue. It was gratifying to note that the brochure advertised, "Mausoleum staff to serve you every day of the year from sunrise to sunset," and particularly comforting (in view of the purpose of the property I was being offered) to learn that one's crypt would be "Judgement Proof."

From the counselor and his brochures I began to get an inkling of how the pricing is established; how liabilities can be transformed into assets, and economies, convenient for the cemetery promoters, made attractive. The crypts facing the corridor are called "mausoleum crypts." The ones facing outside, and forming in fact the outside wall of the structure, once less salable and therefore lower in price, are now called "garden crypts"—a stroke of creative genius—and often command even higher prices than the stuffy old indoor ones. "It's all part of the trend towards outdoor living," explained the counselor. The pavement of the corridors does not go to waste, either. A crypt below floor level has none of the associations of the bargain basement if it is labeled "Westminster Crypt" —on the contrary, it conjures up flattering thoughts of reposing eternally cheek by jowl with the great and famous. Likewise, the cost of a dividing wall between two crypts can be eliminated if they are advertised as "True

Companion Crypt—permits husband and wife to be entombed in a single chamber without any dividing wall to separate them. Here, husband and wife may truly be 'Together Forever.' "

"Then, the corridor crypts would all be one price, the garden crypts another, and so on?" I asked. Oh no, said the counselor, there's quite a difference. The corridor crypts vary considerably; the cheapest are the ones near the top. "And the most expensive?" "Heart level," he replied, tapping that organ with his right hand and giving one of his sincere looks.

Later, when I went to see the cemetery, I could see why the counselor was not too anxious to have prospects go out there. It was merely an expanse of dusty, dried-out California hillside, with a fine view of factories and warehouses of the industrial section below. The Lifetime Green artificial grass mats stacked near the office offered lurid contrast to the vistas of brown land on either side; the mausoleum was a stunted dwarf compared to the massive structure of the "artist's conception." The "features" were apparently also in the future, except for a rather forlorn-looking huge tin Bible at the entrance. A small slope, about the size of a town dweller's back garden, was already converted into graves; I counted seventeen of them, and six occupied crypts in the mausoleum. The Memorial Counselor had accurately told me that of 1,500 burial places sold, only twenty-three were actually in use.

The profit potential of a cemetery does not by any means end with the sale of burial space. Adjuncts of cemetery operation, such as the digging, planting, trimming and general maintenance of graves, which fifty years ago (before the advent of the commercial cemetery) were looked upon simply as chores to be handled by the groundkeeper or the sexton, are today systematically turned to good account. And there are today many extra profit items for the cemetery owner which played no part in cemetery operation or finance in the days before Forest Lawn became the arbiter of fashion in the burial world— the sale of vaults, bronze grave markers, flowers, postcards and statuary, and the collection, control and management of huge "perpetual care" funds.

A generation ago grave digging and markers were provided by cemeteries at a nominal cost. *Park and Cemetery* (now defunct), a fuddy-duddy forerunner of *Concept,* reported in 1921 that cemeteries in Seattle were charging $7 for opening and closing a grave.

Grave digging, now a mechanized operation which takes about 15 minutes, is currently priced at $70 to $130 in commercial cemeteries, usually much less in municipal cemeteries. A markup of three times the direct labor cost is about standard. Another profit item which the commercial cemetery tries to preempt for itself is the sale of cement vaults and grave liners. These are poured into forms on the premises and sell for $70 and up; the cost of production, one cemetery owner told me, is $5 to $10. There is little or no control over grave-digging and grave-lining charges in the United States, except in New York, where state regulation has recently been attempted.

Included in the $7 charge mentioned in *Park and Cemetery* for digging graves was a 15-by-7-inch cement grave marker ("made at the cemetery for 25¢ which covers both time and material"). The reporter discussed the advantages of such markers ("all graves are easy to find") but added wistfully, "Their disadvantage is that, while intended as temporary, they generally remain permanent. Because of the cement marker, Seattle is probably the poorest place for [bronze] marker business in the country."

The cement marker, once a threat to bronze sales, is no longer a problem. The commercial cemeteries, authorized by law to make their own rules, simply prohibit their use. The cemetery's specifications for the size, shape and installation of the bronze, granite, or granite-and-bronze markers which they now require are likely to be so stringent as to make it inconvenient to buy this commodity elsewhere, or to have it installed by an outside supplier. The ordinary bronze marker, inscribed with the name of the deceased and his dates of birth and demise, sells for

$75 to $180 for a single grave. The standard cemetery markup is 200 per cent.

In recent years a new type of sales organization has grown up that specializes in extracting a second harvest from areas already saturated with grave and mausoleum sales, a second pressing of the vintage, so to speak, by selling bronze markers "in advance of need" to people who have already purchased interment space. Although I find it hard to picture the customer placing the order for his own memorial ahead of time ("How shall I order the inscription? 'To My Dearly Beloved Self,' perhaps, or just simply 'Dear Me'?"), such sales are being made in substantial volume, and *Concept* reports that pre-need sales of bronze memorials in 1960 exceeded at-need sales by three to one, for an estimated revenue of over $140 million. The standard salesman's commission on bronze is 50 per cent.

The bronze deal, whether pre-, post- or at-need, can be greatly facilitated by the use of sales letters, which are followed up by telephone calls and personal visits from the Bronze Memorial Counselors. The Matthews Memorial Bronze Company has prepared dozens of suggested sales letters with which the cemetery can pepper lot holders at appropriate intervals:

Dear Friend,
The other day, we and our maintenance crews were out working the section of the cemetery where your family estate is located. Naturally, we couldn't help but notice that the graves were unmemorialized.
One of the workmen commented that an unmarked grave is a sad thing.

Some of the letters are geared to seasonal use: "Dear Friend, If Winter comes, can Spring be far behind?" . . . "Dear Friend, In a few weeks the forsythia and daffodils will raise their golden horns to the sky and trumpet in the warm winds of spring." . . . "Dear Friend, Soon the year will repeat its old story." . . . "Dear Friend, Soon Easter will be upon us once again." . . . "Dear Friend, The second Sunday in May is Mother's Day." . . . "Dear Friend, Does Memorial Day make you think about a drive in the country?" . . . "Dear Friend, Decoration Day is just a few short weeks away." . . . "Dear Friend, Once again Christmas is almost here." . . . After four or five paragraphs of trumpeting forsythia or happy Mom's Day visits, the point is made: "But if you want bronze memorialization by the holiday, you've got to act swiftly .You see, it takes many weeks to individually hand craft and deliver the memorial of your selection."

Just what happens to the money that is collected on the "pre-need bronze deal" is not quite clear. The preneed "space" buyer receives for his money a salable ownership interest in an existing bit of real estate, whereas the pre-need "bronze" buyer recieves only a certificate telling him that when he dies a piece of metal will be manufactured and set in his grave. The seller meantime— and it may be a very long time—has the use not only of the money paid for the memorial-to-be, but an additional sum which the purchaser has been obliged to pay for its perpetual care! The "bronze deal" is so new that regulatory laws that might give the buyer some measure of protection have not yet, in many states, had a chance to catch up with it. The Forward Research survey reports that only 14 per cent of the cemeteries polled have a merchandise trust set up for the protection of the pre-need bronze buyer.

Another idea now used by virtually all cemeteries is the "perpetual care fund." The uninitiated might expect that, having paid $600 to $3,000 for a crypt, or $150 to $1,500 for a grave, the costs of upkeep might be borne by the cemetery. Not at all. There is added to the cost of cemetery and mausoleum space a surcharge of 10 to 20 per cent for future care; some mausoleums charge as high as 25 per cent of the price of the crypt. Graves need tending, it is true, but the care that needs to be lavished on a cement crypt is somewhat hard to envisage. The monies so collected are kept by the cemetery owner, supposedly as an endowment fund to guarantee such care forever in the future, a promise palpably incapable of fulfillment. Nevertheless, the magic of pre-need selling has swelled these funds in many cases to huge proportions. More than a thousand cemeteries have perpetual care funds in excess of $100,000; more than fifty have over $1 million in the kitty. The money held in such funds in the United States totals over $1 billion.

The cemetery operators to whom these funds have been entrusted have not always been as scrupulously honest in their stewardship as one might hope. The itinerant promoter who moves his door-to-door sales crew into a community to saturate it with pre-need sales is hardly the type one would expect to sit around and wait for his sold-out cemetery to fill up, much less wait forever to lavish perpetual care upon it. And when he moves on to the next community, he has not always been able to resist the temptation to take the perpetual care fund with him—for safekeeping, of course—or at least to dip into it for a loan at low interest to purchase new cemetery property. After all, the money is there to be invested.

A fund of over $1 billion, available for investment at the discretion of cemetery owners, can serve as a powerful political weapon. Only in recent years, after the misappropriation of funds became a public scandal, did state legislatures begin to impose legal controls on the investment of cemetery trust funds. The potent cemetery lobby (it is the envy of the funeral directors, who carry less weight in the state legislatures) has contrived in most states to secure laws that are not unduly burdensome, and in some states the regulation of perpetual care funds is placed under the benign authority of a board composed entirely of cemetery owners.

The new merchandising approach does more than just step up sales. It solves in one stroke a number of problems that once vexed the cemetery promoter.

One such problem is competition from the thousands of municipally owned cemeteries that dot the country. Municipal cemeteries are operated as a public service, are often partially subsidized by public funds. Since they do not as a rule advertise, or send salesmen out on commission, they are able to offer cemetery space and services at moderate cost. For example, the average cost of a grave in Minnesota's 194 municipal cemeteries is $27.43—and this includes endowment care.

In 1935, 70 per cent of the cemeteries in the United States were publicly owned. By 1960, public ownership was down to 25 per cent. The high-priced pre-need cemeteries are driving out the low-priced municipal and church cemeteries, their only competition, in an apparent suspension of the ordinary laws of economics.

What happens when, for the first time, commercial cemeteries move into a community where there is already a municipal cemetery? A sales team blankets the community, sells pre-need lots at from three to ten times the price charged by the municipal cemetery, which has no advertising or pre-need promotion budget. The reaction of the city fathers is likely to be "Now that sufficient burial space is available from a private source, why spend money to operate a municipal cemetery?" or "Let's raise our rates and make it self-supporting—if they can do it, why can't we?" In the latter case, the municipal cemetery gets itself an advertising appropriation, perhaps hires a crew of pre-need salesmen, and up go the charges correspondingly.

Cemetery men have also found in pre-need selling a means of cutting themselves into the veterans' market, a source of business from which they were formerly excluded by Federal laws which give veterans and their wives the privilege of burial in national cemeteries without charge. The valuable burial privilege normally makes veterans' funerals especially lucrative for undertakers, who—since they stand to benefit from the savings made possible by the elimination of cemetery charges—are always quick to advise the veteran's bereaved family of the advantages of burial in a national cemetery. Pre-need selling enables the cemetery man to outflank the undertaker. He gets into the home first—years ahead of the undertaker, in fact—seduces the family with his pretty magic-lantern slides, and points out, truthfully enough, that the veteran's $250 burial allowance can be applied to the cost of the grave. Since death is not then impending, the veteran is not likely to be aware that by the same token the $250 will not then be available to apply against the undertaker's bill, nor is he likely to know that his wife, though not entitled to the $250 cash benefit upon her own death, does have the free burial privilege.

Mr. Chester A. Brown of Central Sales and Service Company who, according to *Concept,* has sold $10 million worth of lots and markers in the last fourteen years, makes this a prime argument in favor of aggressive pre-need selling: "It will eliminate the veteran and his wife (and remember, there are 40 million of them) from using the veteran cemetery or section without any cost."

Pre-need cemetery promoters, in considering whether a particular community is ripe for exploitation, are least of all concerned whether there is a deficiency of cemetery space. All they want and need to know is how often the town has been previously canvassed by pre-need salesmen; how many householders already own cemetery lots. Consequently duplication of cemetery facilities goes on apace. In recent hearings on a cemetery application in Los Angeles, there was testimony from numerous sources that there already existed sufficient cemetery facilities to handle all burials in the Los Angeles area for the next hundred years.

Having saturated a community with pre-need graves, crypts, vaults, memorials, and having established a perpetual care fund the control of which is firmly under his thumb, how next can the cemetery promoter cash in on his privileged position? It should surprise no one who has come this far that men of vision in the industry have already looked ahead and come up with the ultimate solution: a prepaid package that will include not only burial space and marker, but "casket," hearse, undertaking services and flower shop as well. Nor is this all. The really creative cemetery man is adding weddings to his list of services, pioneering with Easter sunrise programs, Christmas carol community sings, museums, art shows, lectures, tours for schoolchildren—anything to bring in the customers. For, as Mr. Donald F. Sager, executive secretary of the Interment Association of America, said, "The new concept of responsibility encompasses many services that make the symbols of death and gloom as outdated as the idea that the cemetery's sole function is that of a repository for the dead."

10

SHROUDLAND REVISITED

Nothing in Los Angeles gives me a finer thrill than Forest Lawn. . . . The followers of a triumphant Master should sleep in grounds more lovely than those where they have lived—a park so beautiful that it seems a bit above the level of this world, a first step up toward Heaven.
—BRUCE BARTON, quoted in
Art Guide to Forest Lawn

FOREST LAWN MEMORIAL-PARK of Southern California is the greatest nonprofit cemetery of them all; and without a doubt its creator—Hubert Eaton, the Dreamer, the Builder, inventor of the Memorial Impulse—is the dean of cemetery operators. He has probably had more influence on trends in the modern cemetery industry than any other human being. Mrs. Adela Rogers St. Johns, his official biographer, sees Forest Lawn as "the lengthened shadow of one man's genius." Even as she was writing those words, that long shadow was creeping over much of the cemetery land in the territorial United States; today it spans oceans, extending to Hawaii and even to Australia.

The Dreamer and his brainchild are already known to thousands of readers through *The Loved One*, by Evelyn Waugh—to whom *Mortuary Management* refers as "Evelyn (Bites-The-Hand-That-Feeds-Him) Waugh." If there are skeptics who think that Mr. Waugh may have been guilty of exaggeration, a visit to Forest Lawn should set their minds at rest.

I was among the one and a half million who passed through the entrance gates last year; the guidebook says they are the largest in the world, twice as wide and five feet higher than the ones at Buckingham Palace; and (presumably to warn anyone rash enough to try hefting one) adds that each weighs five thousand pounds.

It is all there, just as Mr. Waugh has described it, although in the intervening years since *The Loved One* was written, there have been many additions, so the overall impression is that today it far transcends his description.

There are the churches, ranging from wee to great, the Wee Kirk o' the Heather incongruously furnished with wall-to-wall carpeting, the Great Mausoleum Columbarium, primarily patriotic in theme, with its Memorial Court of Honor, Hall of History, Freedom Mausoleum and Court of Patriots. "Does one have to be a citizen or sign a loyalty oath to get into the Hall of Patriots?" I asked a guide. "No, ma'am!" was the answer. "Anyone can be buried there, as long as he's got the money to pay for it." (This is not strictly true; Forest Lawn refused Caryl Chessman's last remains "on moral grounds.")

There are statues, tons of them, some designed to tug at the heartstrings: "Little Duck Mother," "Little Pals," "Look, Mommy!", others with a different appeal, partially draped Venuses, seminude Enchantresses, the reproduction of Michelangelo's David, to which Forest Lawn has affixed a fig leaf, giving it a surprisingly indecent appearance.

Wandering through Whispering Pines, Everlasting Love, Kindly Light and Babyland, with its encircling heart-shaped motor road, I learned that each section of Forest Lawn is zoned and named according to price of burial plots. Medium-priced graves range from $434.50 in Haven of Peace to $599.50 in Triumphant Faith to $649.50 in Ascension. The cheapest is $308, in Brotherly Love—for even this commodity comes high at Forest Lawn. Ten per cent must be added to the price for Endowment Care, and $89 for opening and closing the grave, and $70-$145 for a vault. For those wishing something better (such as the Gardens of Memory, kept locked to the public but to which the property owner is given a Golden Key) there is almost no limit to the amount one can spend.

The present population of Forest Lawn is over 200,000, augmented by new arrivals at the rate of 6,500 a year. On all sides one may see the entire cycle of burial unfolding before one's eyes. There is a museum in Chicago containing a live exhibit of hatching chicks; the unhatched eggs are in one compartment, those barely chipped in another, next the emerging baby chicks and finally the fully hatched fledglings. The Forest Lawn scene is vaguely reminiscent of that exhibit. Here is a grass-green tarpaulin unobtrusively thrown over the blocked-out mound of earth removed to ready a grave site for a newcomer. Near it is a brilliant quilt of mixed orchids, gardenias, roses, lilies of the valley, signifying a very recent funeral. Farther on, gardeners are shoveling away the faded remains of a similar floral display, possibly three or more days old. Between these are scores of flat bronze memorial plaques bearing the names of the old residents. In the distance, the group of people entering one of the churches may be either a wedding party or a funeral party; it is hard to tell the difference at Forest Lawn.

Other sights to visit are the hourly showings of the Crucifixion ("largest oil painting in the world") and a stained-glass reproduction of The Last Supper. Mrs. St. Johns says of the Dreamer, "In Missouri-ese, he had always been a sucker for stained glass."

Behind the Hall of Crucifixion are the museum and gift shop. The purpose of the museum and the method used to assemble its contents are explained by Eaton in *Comemoral*. If a museum is established, people will become accustomed to visiting the cemetery for instruction, recreation and pleasure. A museum can be started on a very small—in fact, minimal—scale, perhaps to begin with in just one room with just one statue. Once started it will soon grow: "I speak from experience. People begin to donate things with their names attached, and bring their friends to see them on display." The results of this novel approach to museology is an odd assortment of knick-knacks—old coins, a bronze tablet inscribed with the Gettysburg Address, some suits of armor, Balinese carvings, Japanese scrolls, bits of jade, some letters by Longfellow, Dickens, etc., and lots more.

The museum received front-page publicity in the Los Angeles press in 1961 on the occasion of the Great Gem Robbery. With his enviable flair for showmanship, Dr. Eaton managed to turn the robbery and even the actual worthlessness of the "gems" to good account in a half-page advertisement in which he makes one of the most touching appeals ever addressed to a jewel thief: "We feel that you cannot be professional thieves, or you would have known that neither the black opal named 'The Pride of Australia' nor the antique necklace could be marketed commercially. These two are valuable principally for their worth as antiques. . . . The emerald and diamond necklace has small retail value today, because the cut of the stones has been obsolete for many years, and it would be difficult to sell it except as an antique." But it is when he speaks of the need to care for the black opal (named by *whom* "The Pride of Australia," one wonders) that he is at his most affecting: "We do hope that you bathe it every few weeks in glycerin to prevent it from shattering." Kidnappers! From the bottom of a mother's heart I beg you to give my baby his daily cod-liver oil.

A deeper purpose for the maintenance of a museum in a cemetery is also explained by Dr. Eaton: "It has long been the custom of museums to sell photographs, post cards, mementos, souvenirs, etc." The visitor is summoned to the gift shop ("while waiting for the next showing of the 'Crucifixion'") by one of those soft, deeply sincere voices which often boom out at one unexpectedly from the Forest Lawn loudspeaker system. Among the wares offered are salt and pepper shakers in the shape of some of the Forest Lawn statuary; the Builder's Creed, printed on a piece of varnished paper and affixed to a rustic-looking piece of wood; paper cutters, cups and saucers, platters decorated with views of the cemetery; view holders with colored views of the main attractions. There is a fold-out postcard with a long script message for the visitor rendered inarticulate by the wonders he has seen. It starts: "Dear ———, Forest Lawn Memorial-Park has proved an inspiring experience," and ends: "It was a visit we will long remember." There is a large plastic walnut with a mailing label on which is printed "Forest Lawn Memorial-Park In A Nut Shell! Open me like a real nut . . . squeeze my sides or pry me open with a knife." Inside is a miniature booklet with colored views of Forest Lawn. There is an ashtray of very shiny tin, stamped into the shape of overlapping twin hearts joined by a vermilion arrow. In one of the hearts is a raised picture of the entrance gates, done in brightest bronze and blue. In the other is depicted the Great Mausoleum, in bronze and scarlet with just a suggestion of trees in brilliant green. Atop the hearts is an intricate design of leaves and scrolls, in gold, green and red; crowning all is a coat of arms, a deer posed against a giant sunflower, and a scroll with the words JAMAIS ARRIÈRE. Never in Arrears, perhaps.

Forest Lawn pioneered the current trend for cemeteries to own their own mortuary and flower shop, for convenient, one-stop shopping. The mortuary "is of English Tudor design, inspired by Compton Wynyates in Warwickshire, England. Its Class I, steel-reinforced concrete construction is finished in stone, half-timber and brick," the guidebook says. There are 21 slumber rooms and a palatial casket room, in which the wares range from the much-advertised low of $145, through medium prices like $695 and $995, all the way up to $15,000.

The Forest Lawn board of trustees says of Hubert Eaton, "Today, Forest Lawn stands as an eloquent witness that the Builder kept faith with his soul." It is to the official biography of Eaton, and to his own writings, that we must turn for a closer glimpse of that soul.

If a goal of art is the achievement of a synthesis between style and subject matter, it must be conceded that *First*

Step Up Toward Heaven, the story of Dr. Eaton and
Forest Lawn by Adela Rogers St. Johns, is in its own
way a work of art. Mrs. St. Johns is best known as one
of the original sob sisters, a Hearst reporter in her youth,
later editor of *Photoplay,* the first Hollywood fan magazine.

Dr. Eaton, apparently born under whichever star it is
that guides a man to seek his fortune below the earth's
surface rather than above, started life as a mining engineer,
and in short order acquired a gold mine in Nevada. He
and his cousin Joe organized the Adaven Mining Company and built a company town named Bob. It was
here in Bob that Dr. Eaton ran slap-bang into his first
miracle—the first of many, it turns out. One night a group
of union organizers (or, in Mrs. St. Johns's words, "a gang
of desperadoes bent on murder") came threateningly up
the hill towards the mine—no doubt, Eaton thought,
armed with dynamite. " 'Unless God takes a hand,'
Hubert Eaton said, his voice cracking, 'there'll have to be
bloodshed.' The foreman beside him nodded grimly."

Just when all seemed lost, the strains of "Home, Sweet
Home" suddenly filled the night air. This proved to be too
much for the desperadoes; silently they slunk away back
down the hill. " 'Looks like He took a hand,' the foreman
said grimly, wiping the tears from his cheeks unashamed.
'We'd better give thanks, the way I see it,' Eaton said."

From then on, miracles dogged the footsteps of
Hubert Eaton. The next thing that happened to this Child
of Destiny was that his mine failed. "That night Hubert
Eaton spent longer on his knees, which he had been taught
was the proper way to say his prayers, than usual. Since
the earth was created for man's use, a man had a right to
ask God to help him locate the vein of gold that'd been in
his own mine." To no avail, however. Fortunately for
Eaton, Destiny had other plans for him this time. He had
lost a mere million in the mining venture, a trifle indeed
compared with what lay in store for him in future years as
he pursued his Dream. And it is to the site of the Dream
that we are now led.

The year was 1917; the place, a run-down, weed-infested cemetery called Forest Lawn. Hubert Eaton, as he stood regarding this scene, was trying to make up his mind whether or not to accept a job as manager of Forest Lawn. "If you suggest to Dr. Eaton, in his late seventies, that Destiny led him there, he will give you an I'm-from-Missouri look and say gruffly, 'There doesn't seem to be any other explanation, does there?' " In any event, he went back to his hotel room and there wrote out his vision of a future Forest Lawn: ". . . filled with towering trees, sweeping lawns, splashing fountains, singing birds, beautiful statues, cheerful flowers, noble memorial architecture . . . where memorialization of loved ones in sculptured marble and pictorial glass shall be encouraged. . . . This is the Builder's Dream; this is the Builder's Creed."

The Memorial-Park idea was born. Thus it has come about that today Forest Lawn is "a garden that seems next door to Paradise itself, an incredibly beautiful place, a place of infinite loveliness and eternal peace."

Dr. Eaton lives by certain moral precepts learned in childhood at his daddy's knee. They are: Perseverance Conquers All; A Place for Everything and Everything In Its Place; Anything That Is Worth Doing Is Worth Doing Well; and Let The Chips Fall Where They May. In the course of pursuing his Dream, he also developed a sort of informal business partnership with God. For, "unless God *was* with him, this was a pretty lonesome business." As he told a Rotary Club meeting, "Christ in Business is the greatest thing that can happen to business. We must in return give business to carry on for Christ." In his own bluff, Missouri way he interprets the New Testament, including his Partner in his plans at every turn: "No, he could not see anything in the Teaching against abundance. . . . Everybody wasn't called upon to don the brown robe and sandals of St. Francis."

Eaton's search for art treasures with which to adorn Forest Lawn led him to Europe on several occasions, and was frequently aided by divine intervention. There was some difficulty getting permission from the Vatican authorities to have a copy made of Michelangelo's Moses, but "Man who could tell the Red Sea to stand still so the Children of Israel could get across ahead of the Egyptians, ought not to have any trouble getting his statue reproduced," said Eaton, and "Of course, a lot of it was prayer. But I figure we got at least an assist from Moses." The firing of the stained-glass reproduction of "The Last Supper" gave some trouble, but " 'Nonsense and balderdash!' Hubert Eaton shouted. 'Of course God wants it finished.' " And finished it was.

If much of the Forest Lawn statuary looks like the sort of thing one might win in a shooting gallery, there's a reason for that, too. Some of it *was* bought at fairs—over the objection of the board of directors, but "as [Eaton] became a benevolent and paternalistic dictator and despot over his Dream Come True, he always met opposition with a gay and somehow endearing determination to win."

While the Builder's soul is something of an open book, facts about the temporal aspects of the Dream—how the "nonprofit" association works, the amount of money involved, how it is distributed—are harder to come by. Forest Lawn executives have shown a marked disinclination to discuss the financial side of the operations. Such reticence, understandable in the world of business, seems out of keeping with the nonprofit, tax-exempt status of Forest Lawn Memorial-Parks (there are now three of them in Southern California) which, declares the Dreamer, "are builded . . . for the living sacredly to enjoy and be benefited and comforted by."

There are some, however, cynical enough to assert that Eaton's cemeteries are builded for profit, and the occasional glimpses of the financial structure of Forest Lawn afforded by disclosures made in legal proceedings in which it is from time to time embroiled, support the view that the memorial parks are, for Eaton, a fantastically profitable form of real estate development.

The United States Board of Tax Appeals, in a 1941 decision, describes the advent of Hubert Eaton to Forest Lawn more prosaically than does Mrs. St. Johns. He was hired in 1912 not as manager but as sales agent for "before-need" sales of cemetery lots. Before he arrived, most of the sales had been made at the time of death— "at need"—and total sales had amounted to only $28,-000 in the previous year. Eaton's door-to-door selling efforts on behalf of that mean, ugly little cemetery upped sales by 250 per cent—and this was five years pre-Dream.

By 1937 annual sales of cemetery space had passed the $1 million mark, and sales of other commodities and services (flowers, postcards, urns, bronze tablets and undertaking services) added another $800,000. By 1959 the annual sales exceeded $7 million, of which over $4 million represented sale of cemetery space.

What happens to all this money? Is it really all plowed back for beautification of the Park? If so, it would pay for an awful lot of fertilizer and statuary.

The Forest Lawn *Art Guide* poses this question: "Again and again people ask: How can Forest Lawn afford to assemble and maintain all of these treasures in such a beautiful place, and open it freely for all to see and enjoy? How can it be that resting places sharing all this loveliness are well within the means of everyone?" The answer is inscribed on a sign by the steps to the Hall of the Crucifixion: "Forest Lawn Memorial-Park is operated by a non-profit association. Excess income, over expenses, must be expended only for the improvement of Forest Lawn."

Well, yes. Only the operative phrase there is "over expenses."

Forest Lawn Memorial-Park Association, Inc., the nonprofit cemetery corporation, is the sun around which cluster a galaxy of Eaton-controlled commercial corporations and holding companies. One of these, Forest Lawn Company, a Nevada corporation, is a land company. Another, a holding company, owns over 99 per cent of the land company's stock; one is a life insurance company (recently sold); one is a mortgage and loan company. To the nonprofit corporation, owning no land, is entrusted the actual operation of the cemetery—the mortuary, the flower shop, the sale of graves, crypts, vaults, statuary, postcards, souvenirs. Discreetly behind the scenes is Eaton's land company, skimming off 50 per cent of the proceeds of sales of lots, plots and graves, and 60 per cent of the gross on all sales of niches, crypts, vaults and other mausoleum space (exclusive of sums collected for endowment care).

It seems curious that the additional land that is needed from time to time for expansion of the existing "Parks" and the development of new ones is not acquired by the cemetery directly. This would save for the beautification of the cemeteries and the ennoblement of mankind the middle-man's profit that is now taken by the land company. Direct purchase of land by the cemetery company would result in substantial tax savings as well, since the land which is taxable in the hands of the land company would be tax-exempt if owned by the nonprofit cemetery. More curious still is the fact that the land company buys and develops the land with money which it borrows from the cemetery at only 3 per cent interest. As of 1959, Eaton's land company had borrowed over $5,000,000 from the nonprofit company at this exceptionally favorable rate.

All in all, Eaton's commercial companies seem to come off astonishingly well in their dealings with the friendly Memorial-Park company. In a stupendous display of Christ-in-businessmanship his land company in 1959 sold the Wee Kirk o' the Heather and two other churches to the nonprofit company for 18 times their depreciated cost, thereby realizing a bonnie profit of over $1 million. To ease the pain of the capital gains tax on this transaction, the Memorial-Park is paying the purchase price, plus 4 per cent interest, in installments of $100,000 per year.

As Mrs. St. Johns says of Dr. Hubert Eaton, "He was a businessman-idealist with an inspiration, whose plan's greatness lay in its simplicity."

The Dreamer is not through yet. In 1954, he announced his discovery of the Memorial Impulse. He says he might have called this force of nature the Memorial Instinct, but preferred to defer to "psychologists and scientists" who feel the term "instinct" is imprecise. The Memorial Impulse is a primary urge founded in man's biological nature and it gives rise to the desire to build (as one might have already guessed), *memorials*. It is also an indispensable factor in the growth of any civilization.

There are a number of ways to turn the Memorial Impulse, "as old as love and just as deathless," to cash account. "Let every salesman's motto be: *Accent the spiritual!*" says the Dreamer, and, "It is the salesman's duty to measure the force of the Memorial Impulse in his client and to persuade him to live up to that noble urge in accordance with his means. . . . Most important of all, every salesman should understand that if properly inspired the Memorial Impulse will do more for him than he ever did for himself, but let your financial desire be tempered with the morality of the Memorial Impulse."

The Memorial Impulse can also be channeled to remedy what was perhaps a tactical error in the early days of the Dream, insistence upon the use of small, uniform bronze grave markers.

Eaton says that while there is universal agreement that the elimination of tombstones was a good thing, nevertheless the tombstones did serve a purpose: they were a "great assist" to the Memorial Impulse. The "great assist" that was unwittingly discarded, we learn, is the good old epitaph. There just isn't room for it on the 12-by-24-inch bronze tablets currently in fashion. True, the little markers permit of vast almost unbroken areas of grass—the "sweeping lawns" of the original Builder's Creed—but since bronze markers are priced by the square inch, more or less, their size also limits the amount that can be charged for them. Now that the Impulse has been discovered, this can be corrected, and the epitaph is slated for a comeback that may radically alter the appearance of the memorial park, transforming its sweeping green lawns into seas of bronze. Eaton suggests that cemetery owners should be thinking in terms of "ever-larger" bronze tablets, big enough in fact to contain complete epitaphs and historical data—big enough to cover the entire grave! This, he says, would be a most "convenient outlet" for the client's Memorial Impulse.

Yet there are other outlets, which as a practical matter must be reckoned with. The Memorial Impulse does not always find expression in grave-sized bronze tablets, or even in the purchase of "private statuary memorials that have passed the artistic qualifications of Forest Lawn." There is the irksome problem posed by the people, particularly among the well-to-do, who express the Impulse through endowment of institutions—hospitals, libraries, museums and the like, thereby bypassing the cemetery. It is with these people in mind that the Dreamer springs his master idea. Could not the cemetery men take into custody all these manifestations of the Impulse, in fact corral them, and confine them within the precincts of the cemetery itself?

Dr. Eaton thinks this can be done. He foresees the day when foundations great and small will have their administrative offices actually housed within the cemetery grounds: "I have named this conception of the cemetery of the future the *Comemoral* (Co-mem-O-RAL—a coined word containing within itself the essence of commemoration and memorial)."

The amount of nonprofit that could be realized through such a tax-free Comemo*ral* is only hinted at: "Because their very essence is of the Memorial Impulse, the 'living memorial' will eventually have it stipulated in its original plan that the Comemoral must be given its proper share of funds to be used as care endowment."

Chips may yet be falling at an ever-increasing rate into the coffers of the nation's cemeteries if this new Dream ever gets off the ground.

11

CREMATION

Cremation is not an end in itself, but the process which prepares the human remains for inurnment in a beautiful and everlasting memorial.
— Chapel of the Chimes booklet, endorsed by
Cremation Association of America

A COMMON REACTION of people who learn for the first time some of the facts and figures connected with the American way of death is to say, "None of that for me! I'm going to beat this racket. I just want to be cremated, and avoid all the fuss and expense."

Cremation sounds like a simple, tidy solution to the disposal of the dead. It is available in most parts of the United States and (although frowned on by Catholics and some branches of the Jewish faith) is sanctioned by the majority religions. It appeals to the nature lover and the poetic-minded, who visualize their mortal remains scattered over sunny hillside or remote seashore. It is applauded by rationalists, people concerned with sanitation, land conservation and population statistics, and by those who would like to see an end to all the malarkey that surrounds the usual kind of funeral. It has appeal for the economy-minded; logically, one would think the expense would be but a tiny fraction of that incurred by earth burial. Many people are under the vague impression that the undertaker can be bypassed altogether, and embalming dispensed with; that the crematorium will, no doubt, arrange to place the body in a suitable container, and consign it to the flames; that the only expense incurred will be the crematorium's charge, something under $100.

It is true that in most countries where cremation is on the increase, the objectives of economy and simplicity are well served. In England, for example, where the number of cremations rose from 3 in 1885 to 107,159 in 1951 and today is the mode of disposal of 35 per cent of the dead, the cost is in the neighborhood of $10. Specifications for the coffin to be used are of the simplest, "easily combustible wood, not painted or varnished"; to facilitate scattering the ashes they are "removed from the cremator, and after cooling pulverized to a fine texture." The ultimate disposition of 90 per cent of English cremated remains is scattering, or "strewing," as the clergy prefer to call it. Sometimes the ashes are scattered over the ocean or from a plane over the countryside; more often, by a crematory attendant, in a Garden of Remembrance, consecrated ground specially set aside for the purpose. Most crematoria and cemeteries maintain such a garden; in some there is a nominal charge of about $1.50. The practice of scattering was formally approved by the Church of England in 1944.

The vogue for cremation is a very recent development in England. The cremation "movement" was initiated there in the nineteenth century. Its adherents included many distinguished physicians and chemists; intellectuals; radicals and reformers; a few members of the aristocracy. Among the organizers of the first Cremation Society in 1874 were Sir Henry Thompson, Bart., Surgeon to the Queen; Anthony Trollope, Spencer Wells, Millais, the Dukes of Bedford and Westminster. Naturally, that thorny old critic of the status quo, George Bernard Shaw, was strongly in favor of cremation, and he sums up the argument for it with his usual pithiness: "Dead bodies can be cremated. All of them ought to be; for earth burial, a horrible practice, will some day be prohibited by law, not only because it is hideously unaesthetic, but because the dead would crowd the living off the earth if it could be carried out to its end of preserving our bodies for their resurrection on an imaginary day of judgment (in sober fact, every day is a day of judgment)."

There were at first strong objections to cremation from some of the clergy, who thought that it would interfere with the resurrection of the body; this point was neatly disposed of by Lord Shaftesbury when he asked, "What would in such a case become of the Blessed Martyrs?" In the 1870s and 1880s, cremation advocates campaigned on a number of fronts for legality and public acceptance of the practice. They published expository material urging support for their cause; they experimented with various types of furnaces; they went so far as to cremate each other in defiance of the authorities, thus subjecting themselves to public censure and even to criminal prosecution. It was not until 1884 that they won a court decision declaring cremation to be a legal procedure, but there was still much opposition from church and public; police protection was sometimes necessary when cremation was to take place. In short, acceptance of cremation as a sensible and also a respectable disposition of the human dead was only won as the result of a hard-fought, uphill struggle.

The early partisans of cremation, willing to flout the law and risk imprisonment to simplify and rationalize disposal of the dead, would whirl in their urns could they but see what has become of their favorite cause today in America. For cremation, like every other aspect of the disposal of the dead, has long since been taken over by the funeral industry, which prescribes the procedures to be followed and establishes its own regulations to which the customers must adhere. Therefore, he who seeks to avoid the purchase of a casket, embalming and the full treatment will not succeed by the mere fact of choosing cremation rather than burial. Also, he is much more likely to end up in an urn housed in a niche in an elaborate "columbarium," complete with Perpetual Care, than to be scattered or privately buried in some favorite country spot.

"If you can't lick 'em, join 'em" would seem to sum up the funeral industry's attitude to cremation. There is a Cremation Association of America, but it has no resemblance to its English predecessor. It is in fact merely an association of persons, principally cemetery operators, who are in the cremation business. Simplicity and economy are not their goals; far from it. The philosophical outlook of the Association is expounded in some material issued by the Education and Information Committee:

Q. Is a funeral director necessary?
A. His services are exactly the same as for other forms of care, and his services are needed for the first call, embalming, casket selection and conduct of the service.
Q. What kind of casket is best for cremation?
A. Inasmuch as the casket serves its primary purpose in creating a memory picture at the time of the funeral service, this is a matter for each family to decide. In general, it is recommended that the casket be the same as for any other form of interment.
Q. What is done with cremated remains?
A. Cremation is not disposition; it is only a method for preparing the remains for memorialization. They are still human remains, and should be placed in a dedicated place such as a columbarium, mausoleum or other place where they will receive continuing care.

Administered by the cemetery interests, cremation has become just another way of making a buck, principally through the sale of the niche and urn plus "perpetual care" for the ashes. Cemetery men are most reluctant to relinquish the ashes for any other form of disposition; one told me rather plaintively, "If everyone wanted to take the ashes away and scatter them or bury them privately, we'd soon be out of business." The crematoria, competing for the good will of the undertakers upon whom they depend for business, naturally play along with them in the matter of building up their services and merchandise.

Arguments for and against cremation were discussed at a recent convention of the National Association of Cemeteries, to which were invited top officials of the Cremation Association of America. The theme of the meeting was "Profit Through Cremation Without a Crematory." A pro-cremation speaker pointed out that although few cemeteries have their own crematoria, "their operators can derive substantial profit if they accent the memorialization aspects of cremation. . . . Actually, in fact, most of the inquiries the C.A.A. receives come from cemetery men whose main feeling is that they're not so much interested in who sells the razor as in who sells the blades." The C.A.A., he said, is "endeavoring to show the cemetery men in an economic sense just what we show the public in a spiritual sense: that cremation is by no means the end-all." Another spoke of the space-saving aspects: "Within a given area for interment spaces, for example, the cemetery can sell a greater number of spaces for cremated remains than for regular caskets. The greater number of smaller sales within that given area can make up the difference, and then some. That of course means profit. . . . Land purchase costs can be avoided. So can expensive and controversial battles with public bodies on rezoning."

Arguments against cremation were advanced by a veteran sales director for one of Los Angeles's largest cemeteries, which operates its own crematory. He cited figures on costs in the Los Angeles area to support his point that cremation is a demonstrably cheaper process than ground burial, even when the cost of the niche and urn is figured in, and therefore much less profitable. The cost of cremation averages $60 (although the public authorities charge only $15 at the county's retort); containers for cremated remains average $55; interment spaces for the containers average only $85 as against an average $325 for regular graves. He said the most expensive space for a container in a columbarium is about $250, whereas the most expensive grave is about $1,000. "The economics of pro-cremation arguments are very questionable to me," he said. "A big volume of cremations, at a lower price for each, may total up to a profit exceeding that from a small volume of regular burials. But you work harder and there certainly is a shocking overhead in administration."

In spite of the admonitions of the Cremation Association, it remains true that families who choose cremation also tend to choose cheaper and less elaborate caskets. This may be because those who favor cremation incline in all matters towards rationality; it may be because of a rather natural disinclination to pay a lot of money for an embalmed and bronze-encased memory picture that is to be burned up in a few days. It is not surprising that there has always been a strong current of opposition to cremation among the undertakers, who are painfully aware of the financial hazards it presents to their end of the funeral business. As one wrote, "Cremations in volume will ruin any funeral director's business. We cremate quite a few cases, and no matter how you figure it, we make a reasonable margin of profit only on about 6 per cent of the cases we cremate."

Characteristically, they seek to counter the trend towards cremation by playing on the emotions of the survivors, portraying the procedure as hideous and horror-filled. A funeral director, writing in *Mortuary Management,* describes how this can be done: "When anybody asks me about cremation, I simply tell them the truth: that it can be the cheapest way of disposing of a body, but that anyone who had ever witnessed a cremation wouldn't cremate a pet dog. I drop it right there, unless they ask me why I say that, and then I give them a blow-by-blow description of what happens in the retort. About four out of five back off immediately, and express no further interest in cremation!"

Those with a direct financial stake in cremation, the owners of crematoria and the niche and urn salesmen, do not, of course, see it this way. On the contrary, they wax lyrical over "the clean, beautiful method of resolution by incandescence rather than the unspeakable horrors of decay . . . we think of our loved one as in his ethereal body, as 'robed in his garments of light,' " and so on. Above all, they vie with each other in the matter of tender concern for the remains. An advertisement for calcination, a new process in which the action of inert heat is employed, stresses, "No flame. The more *kindly* way." Once the body has been reduced to ashes, whether by kindly calcination or just plain cremation, the solicitude of the cemeterians for the continuing welfare of these ashes knows no bounds. "In its niche, the urn holding the snow-white fragments of the earthly garment, which for a time clothed the soul of the loved one, is safe from the driving rains of autumn and the snows of winter," says a crematorium brochure.

The Forest Lawn "Art Guide" has a good deal to say about the proper care of cremated ashes, and contains many a warning to those who might contemplate either scattering them, keeping them at home, or privately burying them. It reads in part like a Declaration of Principles for a Society for the Prevention of Cruelty to Cremated Remains: "Only by crushing or grinding can these hard, white bone-shapes be reduced to fine grit or ash, a practice as horrifying as any wilful mutilation. It is lack of understanding of this, and of the true nature of cremated remains, that has led to the deplorable vogue for 'scattering.' . . . In the past and in areas where protective legislation has not been enacted, receptacles containing cremated remains have sometimes been kept in homes, and have been lost through fire [!], burglary, or other unforeseen occurrences, resulting in lasting remorse. Even more regrettable are the results of the practice known as 'scattering.' Recognizable fragments of the human frame that come hurtling out of the skies, wash ashore on beaches, or roll about underfoot in gardens and parks appall the strangers who encounter them, and cause lifelong heartache to those who have had any share in such disposition of a loved one's remains." Follows, of course, a description of the niches for sale at Forest Lawn, marble-front, bronze-front or glass-faced, "designed to hold a bronze urn of artistic design."

The cemetery and columbarium people will, understandably, go to all sorts of lengths to nip in the bud any trend towards the English practice of scattering. Their first concern is to make sure that the ashes are not reduced to scatterable proportions; a simple matter of failing to apply enough heat during the cremation to completely destroy the bony structure (thus guaranteeing that "recognizable fragments of the human frame" will appear among the ashes) and of failing to pulverize the ashes as recommended by English cremation authorities. Their second concern is with the aforementioned "protective legislation," by which is meant legislation "protecting" the cremated remains from the next of kin of those decedents who have expressly directed that their ashes be scattered or privately buried.

California is one of four states in which cemetery lobbyists have succeeded in passing such legislation. (The others are Alaska, Indiana and Washington.) California is, from the point of view of the niche-and-urn business, a key state, for there is a very marked regional factor in the incidence of cremation in the United States. In 1960 almost half of the total number of cremations in this country—28,000 out of 59,000—took place in Pacific coast states. In California one out of six decedents is cremated, and the proportion is higher in the big cities.

The law in California does not contain an explicit prohibition against scattering or private burial of the ashes. It works like this: After a decedent has been cremated, the next of kin may arrange for removal of the ashes from the crematory, but only by designating a recognized cemetery or columbarium to which he wishes them shipped. Removal of the ashes for any other disposition is a misdemeanor, punishable by fine or imprisonment; if two or more persons participate in the removal, they could be prosecuted for conspiracy, a felony. If the next of kin fails to designate a cemetery or coumbarium, the crematory customarily begins to charge a monthly storage rate for the ashes of $1.50. If he demands that the ashes be turned over to him, he will be told by the cremator that this is "against the law." However if he protests loudly enough, the crematorium will almost certainly give in and hand over the ashes (thus presumably becoming a party to the felonious conspiracy) because the last thing the cemetery interests want is a legal test case on this question.

This peculiar piece of legislation, on the statute books since 1939, went unchallenged until 1961, when an amendment to the law was introduced by State Senator Fred Farr of Carmel and Assemblyman Nicholas Petris, which would permit the next of kin to obtain possession of cremated remains for private burial or scattering. The hearings that ensued were instructive because they demonstrated beyond question the enormous power of the cemetery interests and their ability to influence legislation in the face of reason, popular demand and expert testimony.

Both Mr. Farr and Mr. Petris received an unprecedented flow of mail from constituents in support of their amendment. Many of the letters were from people who had first-hand experience with the problem of trying to rescue ashes of relatives from the tenacious cemetery. One correspondent related a conversation he had had with a cemetery salesman: "This man, a professional hard-sell artist, said that their groups had it fixed so the bill would be tabled in committee, and added that if for some unknown reason the bill did slip by, it would not do the slightest good because the crematories would hand back the skull and bones intact to the customer and tell him to scatter them. He said the cemeteries were not in business to scatter ashes to the winds, and that they would lick this bill hands down."

On the eve of the hearing, Senator Farr learned that the lobbyists were indeed circulating among the legislators photographs purportedly of cremated remains, displaying knucklebones, bits of shin and other unappetizing remnants. These, they claimed, would become commonplace features of the California landscape if the proposed bill should pass.

The following morning, three stalwart matrons, supporters of the Farr-Petris amendment, appeared at the entrance to the State Capitol in Sacramento. They were carrying an odd assortment of objects. One had a large box, inscribed CREMATED REMAINS OF MR. ————, another carried an old-fashioned coffee-bean grinder, and the third wielded a claw hammer. A guard stopped them, and asked the lady with the claw hammer, "What are you taking that in for?" "To open this box of the cremated remains of Mr. ————," she answered. "And what's the coffee grinder for?" asked the astonished guard. "To grind up the cremated remains of Mr. ————," explained one of the ladies helpfully. The guard, open-mouthed, let them pass.

Senator Farr's purpose was a visual demonstration. On opening the box, he found not the gruesome hunks of human bone shown in the photographs but a grayish compound of fine and coarse ash, most of it the consistency of cornmeal, in which were contained some brittle bone fragments up to three inches in length. These he proceeded to put through the coffee grinder, preparing several trayfuls as evidence for other members of the committee. The San Francisco *Chronicle* reported, "As he passed the small box of ashes around to committee members, some of the dust of 'John Doe' wafted from the box, hung in the air for a few seconds, then settled on the highly polished table."

Senator Farr's demonstration succeeded in demolishing the first major argument of opponents of his amendment. With equal ease, he laid waste to their two remaining contentions: that scattering human ashes would endanger the public health, and that to permit dispersion of the remains would hamper crime detection in cases of suspected poisoning. A public health officer testified that human ashes are sterile and could not possibly create a public health problem. A pathologist said, "Many romantic stories tell of conviction following analysis of cremation ashes, but no documented case of this type exists. Anyone claiming such should be required to produce proof, which

I hold cannot be done. The only time that proper medi-
colegal post-mortem examination can be done is prior to
cremation. Such ashes have no importance in law enforce-
ment or crime detection."

Yet, when all the dust had settled, the bill was shelved by
a vote of 4 to 3, and referred to a committee for a
two-year study. In spite of the efforts of the sponsors,
the study was never made. Mr. Nicholas Petris declared
the measure lost because of a combination of fear,
superstition and enormous lobby pressure. He added
that he personally abhors cremation—the very thought
makes him shudder; furthermore it is contrary to the
doctrine of the Greek Orthodox Church to which he
belongs. But, he said, he intends to disinter this bill
anyway, because of the civil liberties issue involved; the
law as it now stands robs Californians of the right to arrange for such disposition as they see fit of their own
mortal remains.

At this writing, the final outcome of the legislation is
unknown. It can be predicted with certainty that the
cemetery interests will fight long and hard to maintain
their self-conferred role of protectors of the defenseless
little packages of human ash.

12

WHAT THE PUBLIC WANTS

The funeral service profession exists only because it has received the approval of the public. . . . Present methods, facilities and merchandise exist because the public has found in them values it has been willing to pay for in spite of the necessary sacrifice of other things. . . .

Are these values real? Do they spring from higher and finer motives? Do they lift and inspire? Are they worth what they cost? The answer is found in the reactions of the public. If the public accepts these things, prefers these things, the answer is in the affirmative.

> —*Psychology of Funeral Service*, by
> EDWARD A. MARTIN, B.A., Mortician.

THE THEME that the American public, rather than the funeral industry, is responsible for our funeral practices, because it demands "the best" in embalming and merchandise for the dead, is one often expounded by funeral men. "We are merely giving the public what it wants," they say.

This is an interesting thought. It is a little hard to conceive of how this public demand is expressed and made known in practice to the seller of funeral service. Does the surviving spouse, for example, go into the funeral establishment and say, "I want to be sure my wife is thoroughly disinfected and preserved. Her casket must be both comfortable and eternally durable. And—oh yes, do be sure her burial footwear is really practical"?

Perhaps it does not happen just like that. Yet it has been known to happen, and in fairness to the undertaking trade, an example should be given of a case in which the

funeral buyer, of sound mind and deeply aware of his own
desires, wanted and demanded the best.

The case involves Mr. August Chelini, fifty-seven-year-
old mechanic, sometime scrap dealer and garage owner.
His monthly earnings averaged $300 to $400. Mr.
Chelini, an only child, lived with his aged mother, who
died in 1943 at the age of ninety-nine years and seven
months. It then became incumbent upon Mr. Chelini to
arrange for the funeral, which he did by calling in Mr.
Silvio Nieri, an undertaker and family friend.

What developed is best recounted by quoting from the
transcript of the case of August Chelini, plaintiff, versus
Silvio Nieri, defendant, in the Superior Court of San
Mateo County, California.

Mr. August Chelini comes to life for us in the pages of a
court reporter's typescript. We learn to know his hopes and
fears, something of his history, something of his philosophy, his way of life, his motives and methods. He was
in some respects an undertaker's dream person, a
materialization of that man of sentiment and true feeling
for the dead so often encountered in funeral trade
magazines. Only the fact that he was suing an undertaker
for $50,000 casts a slight shadow.

The case opens with the arrival of Mr. Nieri at the
Chelini home. Mr. Melvin Belli, counsel for the plaintiff,
is examining:

Q. [Mr. Belli] When he came to the house, did you have a
   conversation with him?
A. [Mr. Chelini] Well, he come in and he asked me if he
   should move the body, and I told him I wanted to talk
   things over with him first.
Q. Did you have a conversation there?
A. So I talked to him out in the kitchen, and explained to
   him what I wanted, and the conversation was that I told
   him what my mother requested.
Q. What did you tell him in this regard?
A. Well, I told him that my mother wanted to be buried
   where there was no ants or any bugs could get at her.
Q. Had your mother made that request?

A. She made that request.

Q. By the way, was your mother of sound mentality at the time?

A. Oh, yes, very sound. Pretty bright.

Q. Did you tell him anything else?

A. Well, I told him that she had $1500 of her own money, and that I intended to put all that into her funeral, and she had other moneys coming, and I wanted a hermetically sealed casket because—

Q. You told him that, that you wanted—

A. I told him I wanted the best kind of embalming, and I wanted her put in a hermetically sealed casket.

Q. Did you know what a hermetically sealed casket was at that time?

A. Well, I know that it was a casket that no air or no water could get into.

Q. All right, did you tell him anything else?

A. I told him that is what I wanted. I didn't care what the cost was going to be, but I did have the $1500 on hand that belonged to her, and these other moneys were coming in that I could put into it later.

Q. All right. Did you tell him anything else at that time?

A. Also told him that I was anticipating making a lead box to eventually put her in, after the war was over; that lead couldn't be had at that time, and I am a mechanic. I intended to construct a lead box.

Q. You were going to do it yourself?

A. Yes, I have a sample of the box, the design of it, and I told him that I was going to figure to put her in a crypt until the war was over, and so that I could get the necessary things, and put her away in accordance with her wishes.

Q. By the way, you lived with your mother all her life?

A. There was times she lived out in South City, but we were with her pretty near every day.

Q. So, after you told him that you were going to make this lead coffin, after the war, did you have any further conversation with him?

A. Well, we talked about the embalming, how long he could preserve it, he says, "Practically forever," he says, "We got a new method of embalming that we will put on her, and she will keep almost forever."

Q. Pardon me. Go ahead.

A. I says, "That is a pretty long period, isn't it?" Well, he says, "They embalmed Caruso, and they embalmed Lincoln, that way, and they have these big candles near Caruso, and we have a new method of embalming. We have a new method of embalming. We can do a first-class job, and she will keep almost forever." . . .

Q. Then, the next day, did you have another conversation with him?

A. Then the next day he told me that I would have to come down to his establishment, and pick out a casket. . . .

Q. And you went down there?

A. My wife and I went down there.

Q. And when you got down there, did you have a further conversation with him?

A. Well, yes, he took me down in the basement there where he had all these caskets, and he told me to look them all over, and we picked out what we thought was the best casket in the house. . . . First I looked around, and my wife looked around. We both decided on the same casket. So, I asked him if that was a hermetically sealed job, he says, "Oh, yes, that is the finest thing there is, that is a bronze casket." . . . He told me this was a casket, it was a bronze casket, and was a hermetically sealed casket, and he said that that is the finest thing that is made, and he says, "This is pre-war stuff," and he says, "As a matter of fact, this is—I am going to keep one of these myself, in case anything happens to me, I am going to be buried in one of these myself." . . . He quoted me a price, then he says, "Well, that will be $875, that will include everything, everything in connection with the whole funeral," he says, "That will be completely everything in connection with the whole funeral, $875."

Q. Yes.

A. So, from what he told me, this casket was the best—it seemed very reasonable, so I told him that we would select that.

(Later that day, Chelini's mother was brought back to his house.)

Q. Was there any conversation in the house?

A. Well, by the time I got there, she was up there, the wife and I decided to put her in the dining room, originally, and when I got up there, he had her in the living room.

Q. Did you have some conversation with him at that time?

A. So, he said, "Well, I think it will be better to have her here, because there is a window here, she'll get lots of air." . . . He said he would have to put this body here in the front room on account of the window was here.

Q. Yes.

A. And he said it would be better to have a breeze, a flow of fresh air come in there.

Q. All right, did you have a conversation about the funeral with him to hurry over this?

A. Let's see. I don't think there was very much spoken about the funeral right then. I was feeling pretty bad. He spoke of this new embalming. He picked up her cheeks and skin on her and showed me how nice it was, pliable, it was—

Q. Did he tell you that that was a new method of embalming?

A. Yes, and her cheek was very pliable, her skin was especially.

Q. Is that what he said?

A. Well, that is the way he said that is the way it felt, and he told me that is a new type of embalming that they have, pliable. . . .

Q. All right, then you had a discussion with him at that time about paying him the money?

A. I asked him how much it was. He says, "it was $875." So I says, "Well, I want mother's ring put back on her finger," I says, "when she is removed from the crypt to her final resting place. I want that ring put back on her finger," and I says, "I want some little slippers put on her that I can't get at this time," I says, "I want her all straightened up, and cleaned off nice," and I says "I will add another $25 for that service, for doing that," so he says, "All right," he says, "if that is the way you want it, we will do it. I would have done it for nothing," so I gave him that extra check for $25. . . . Oh, I also reminded him to be sure that when they put her finally into the cemetery, to see that she was properly secured, and he says, "Don't worry about it," he says, "I will see that everything is done properly." So, he took the check, and I asked him if he would go out and have a little drink with me, which he consented to, and which we did, in the kitchen.

(Probably, seldom was a little drink more needed than at that moment and by these principals. The scene now shifts to Cypress Lawn Cemetery):

Q. Did you go out there when your mother was taken out there?
A. Yes, I went out to the funeral, and she had the services there. Why, she left here on one of those little roller affairs, and we all walked out. Mr. Nieri—I came out to the car and asked him if he would go in there and see that she was properly adjusted from any shifting, or anything, and make sure that she was well sealed in, so he went in there, and he come out, and I asked him, I says, "Did you get her all sealed in nice? Did you straighten her all up nice?" He says, "Don't be worrying about that, Gus," he says, "I will take care of everything."

Mr. Chelini was, it appears, the exceptional—nay, perfect—funeral customer. Not only did he gladly and freely choose the most expensive funeral available in the Nieri establishment; he also contracted for a $1,100 crypt in the Cypress Lawn mausoleum. He appreciated and endorsed every aspect of the funeral industry's concept of the sort of care that should be accorded the dead. An ardent admirer of the embalmer's art, he insisted on the finest receptacle in which to display it; indeed, he thought $875 a very reasonable price and repeatedly intimated his willingness to go higher.

At first glance, it seems like a frightful stroke of bad luck that Mr. Chelini, of all people, should be in court charging negligence and fraud against his erstwhile friend the undertaker, asserting that "the remains of the said Caroline Chelini were permitted to and did develop into a rotted, decomposed and insect and worm infested mess." Yet the inner logic of the situation is perhaps such that *only* a person of Mr. Chelini's persuasion in these matters would ever find himself in a position to make such a charge; for who else would be interested in ascertaining the condition of a human body after its interment?

It was not until two months after the funeral that Mr.

express wishes of the deceased as to the mode of his funeral must be observed. What happens then, he then asked, if the deceased has left instructions for a very simple funeral, but the survivors insist on something more elaborate? The funeral director answered with rare candor, "Well, at a time like that, who are you going to listen to?"

Odds are that the undertaker will be the arbiter of what is a "suitable" funeral, that a decedent's own wishes in this regard may not be the final word. Even if he is the President of the United States.

Franklin D. Roosevelt left extremely detailed and explicit instructions for his funeral "in the event of my death in office as President of the United States." The instructions were contained in a four-page penciled document dated December 6, 1937, early in his second term, and were addressed to his eldest son James.

The instructions included these directions:

"That a service of the utmost simplicity be held in the East Room of the White House.

"That there be no lying in state anywhere.

"That a gun-carriage and not a hearse be used throughout.

"That the casket be of absolute simplicity, dark wood, that the body be not embalmed or hermetically sealed, and that the grave be not lined with brick, cement, or stones."

Regarding the latter instruction, James Roosevelt writes, "So far as we can learn, he never had discussed this with anyone. Knowing Father, we can only speculate that he regarded the embalming procedure as a distasteful invasion of privacy, and that perhaps he had an inner yearning to follow the traditional funeral liturgy, 'Earth to earth, ashes to ashes, dust to dust, in sure and certain hope of the Resurrection. . . .'"

Nobody in the Roosevelt household knew of the existence of this document. It was found in his private safe, a few days after his burial. It is a common occurrence that when death comes unexpectedly to the ordinary home, burial instructions are found too late tucked away in a safe-deposit box or contained in a will which is not read until after the funeral; it seems ironic that the same mischance could occur in the White House itself. Furthermore, White House aides charged with arranging details of the funeral seem to have been as much at a loss, and as tractable in the hands of the undertaker, as any average citizen faced with the same situation.

News of Roosevelt's death, flashed around the world on April 12, 1945, meant many things to many people. To millions of Americans it signified the sudden and disastrous loss of the most commanding figure of the century and with him the disappearance of an era. To Mr. Fred W. Patterson, Atlanta undertaker, at home enjoying an after-dinner pipe that evening when his phone rang, it was (in the words of *The Southern Funeral Director*) "THE CALL—probably the biggest and most important ever experienced by a contemporary funeral director."

The Call was placed by Mr. William D. Hassett, White House aide who was with Roosevelt in Warm Springs, Georgia, at the time of his death. He was charged by Mrs. Roosevelt with the task of buying a coffin; being entirely without experience in such matters, he consulted Miss Grace Tully, F.D.R.'s secretary, and Dr. Howard G. Bruenn, who had attended the President in his last moments. Both were sure that Mr. Roosevelt would have wanted something simple and dignified, possibly a solid mahogany casket with copper lining similar to the one used for the President's mother.

From accounts of the placing of the order for the solid mahogany casket, it appears there was more than one telephone conversation between Patterson, the undertaker, and the harassed Presidential assistants. The following account of Hassett's conversation is given by Bernard Asbell: "Hassett said he wanted a solid mahogany casket with a copper lining. Patterson told him that copper linings had disappeared early in the war. He did have, however, a plain mahogany one, but—Hassett broke in to ask if it were at least six feet four inches long. Patterson said it was—but it was already sold. It was to be shipped the

next day to New Jersey to accommodate another undertaker. He added that he had a fine bronze-colored copper
model that would—Hassett, in his gentle but most firm
Vermont manner, said he wanted the mahogany brought
at once to Warm Springs. Patterson asked if he could
bring both. Perhaps, on reconsideration, they would
choose the bronze-colored copper one. Hassett said he
could."

Patterson, writing in *The Southern Funeral Director*,
describes a further conversation about the coffin, this time
with Dr. Bruenn: "After he [Dr. Bruenn] consulted with
William D. Hassett, the President's secretary, he requested that only the mahogany be brought; but on my
request, in the event a change was desired, we were allowed to bring, in addition, the copper deposit."

Mr. Patterson's very understandable desire to acquit
himself creditably and with honor in this situation comes
through strongly between the lines. There he was, caught
in the spotlight, before his colleagues and before the nation. He must have suffered a nasty moment before permission was granted to bring both caskets to the Little
White House.

Patterson and his assistants drove to Warm Springs
with two hearses, one containing the plain mahogany
casket, the other the "fine bronze-colored copper model,"
a National Seamless Copper Deposit No. 21200. Patterson
relates how the question of which casket to use was finally
resolved: "After Mrs. Roosevelt arrived at 11:25 and had
seen the President's remains, a conference was held as to
funeral arrangements. Dr. Bruenn was asked what they
wished to do about the casket. He consulted Admiral
McIntire who came with Mrs. Roosevelt. In the conversation, the Admiral was heard to use the word 'bronze' and
as the copper deposit had a bronze finish, of course that
was the casket to be used."

Did the Presidential aides feel that one had been put
over on them, albeit discreetly? We do not know.

In one important respect, Mr. Roosevelt's instructions
were observed: there was no lying in state. Mrs. Roosevelt

felt sure that he would not have wished it. She said, "We have talked often, when there had been a funeral at the Capitol in which a man had lain in state and the crowds had gone by the open coffin, of how much we disliked the practice; and we had made up our minds that we would never allow it."

Failure to carry out certain of his other instructions can only be laid to the unlucky circumstance that they were found too late. It is, however, interesting to compare President Roosevelt's words with accounts given by participants in the funeral:

MR. ROOSEVELT: " . . . the body be not embalmed"

MR. FRED PATTERSON: "All three assistants worked incessantly five hours to give the President the proper appearance, and to be certain of proper preservation. . . . We had a difficult case, did our best and believe that we pleased everyone in every respect. . . . Saturday morning Mr. William Gawler (a Washington undertaker) phoned me stating that the tissues were firm, complexion was fine and those who saw him remarked, 'He looks like his old self again and much younger.' "

MR. ROOSEVELT: "the body . . . be not hermetically sealed"

MR. WILLIAM GAWLER: "The casket was closed and the inner top bolted down at 8:30 P.M. Saturday night. The outer top was sealed with cement."

MR. ROOSEVELT: ". . . the grave be not lined with brick, cement, or stones."

MR. JAMES ROOSEVELT: "The casket was placed in a cement vault."

MR. ROOSEVELT: "That a gun-carriage and not a hearse be used throughout."

MR. PATTERSON: "As the caisson did not arrive at the last minute the casket was taken in our Sayers and Scoville Cadillac hearse."

Note: Three months after publication of the original edition of *The American Way of Death* it became once more the unhappy task of the widow of the President of the United States to supervise arrangements for his funeral. It is not the intention here to give a detailed account of John F. Kennedy's funeral, about which millions of words have been written and which was seen on television by the entire nation. But it is perhaps worth noting that in some important particulars, the conduct of the Kennedy funeral represented a departure from the prevailing funerary practices fostered by the American death industries.

There were no flowers by request of the Kennedy family. At no point did a Cadillac hearse intrude; the coffin was transported by gun-carriage. Although a bronze coffin was supplied in Dallas, according to Mortuary Management the President was actually buried in a wooden coffin, an aspect that other news media seem to have entirely missed. The coffin was closed throughout the ceremonies and was entirely covered by the American flag. The severity of these arrangements undoubtedly enhanced the solemnity of the proceedings and underlined, for the millions who watched, the sense of somber tragedy occasioned by the assassination.

The United Press International comments as follows on the closed coffin:

"When Mrs. Jacqueline Kennedy decided that President Kennedy's casket would remain closed while his body lay in state, she acted as many religious leaders wish that all bereaved families would do.

"Opposition to the custom of 'viewing the remains' has been growing in recent years among Roman Catholic and Protestant clergy.

"They feel that it is pagan, rather than Christian, to focus attention on the corpse. In Christian faith, the body is only the outworn shell of a spirit which continues to live eternally.

"Priests and pastors who share this view hold that a closed casket minimizes morbid concentration on the corpse, and makes it easier for the Christian funeral rites to get across the point that it is the soul that matters."

13

FASHIONS IN FUNERALS

. . . disposal of the dead falls rather into a class with fashions, than with either customs or folkways on the one hand, or institutions on the other . . . social practices of disposing of the dead are of a kind with fashions of dress, luxury and etiquette.

"Disposal of the Dead" by A. L. KROEBER.
American Anthropologist (New Series)
Volume 29:3, July-September, 1927

One of the interesting things about burial practices is that they provide many a clue to the customs and society of the living. The very word "antiquarian" conjures up the picture of a mild-eyed historian groping about amidst old tombstones, copying down epitaphs with their folksy inscriptions and irregular spelling, extrapolating from these a picture of the quaint people and homey ways of yore. There is unconscious wit: the widow's epitaph to her husband, "Rest in peace—until we meet again." There is gay inventiveness:

> Here lie I, Master Elginbrod.
> Have mercy on my soul, O God,
> As I would have if I were God
> And thou wert Master Elginbrod.

There is pathos: "I will awake, O Christ, when thou callest

me, but let me sleep awhile—for I am very weary." And bathos: " 'Tis but the casket that lies here; the gem that fills it sparkles yet."

For the study of prehistory, archeologists rely heavily on what they can find in and around tombs, graves, monuments; and from the tools, jewels, household articles, symbols found with the dead, they reconstruct whole civilizations, infer entire systems of religious and ethical beliefs.

Inevitably some go-ahead team of thirtieth-century archeologists will labor to reconstruct our present-day level of civilization from a study of our burial practices. It is depressing to think of them digging and poking about in our new crop of Forest Lawns, the shouts of discovery as they come upon the mass-produced granite horrors, the repetitive flat bronze markers (the legends, like greeting cards and singing telegrams, chosen from an approved list maintained at the cemetery office) and, under the ground, the stamped-out metal casket shells resembling nothing so much as those bronzed and silvered souvenirs for sale at airport gift shops. Prying further, they would find reposing in each of these on a comfortable mattress of innerspring or foam rubber construction a standardized, rouged or suntanned specimen of Homo sapiens, U.S.A., attired in business suit or flowing negligée according to sex. Our archeologists would puzzle exceedingly over the inner meaning of the tenement mausoleums with their six or seven tiers of adjoining crypt spaces. Were the tenants of these, they might wonder, engaged in some ritual act of contemplation, surprised by sudden disaster? Busily scribbling notes, they would describe the companion his-and-her vaults for husband and wife, and the approved inscription on these: "TOGETHER FOREVER." For purposes of comparison they might recall the words of Andrew Marvell, a poet from an earlier culture, who thus addressed his coy mistress:

> The grave's a fine and private place,
> But none, I think, do there embrace.

They might rashly conclude that twentieth-century America was a nation of abjectly imitative conformists, devoted to machine-made gadgetry and mass-produced art of a debased quality; that its dominant theology was a weird mixture of primitive superstitions, superficial attitudes towards death, overlaid with a distinct tendency towards necrophilism. . . .

Where did our burial practices come from? There is little scholarship on the subject. Thousands of books have been written describing, cataloguing, theorizing about the funeral procedures of ancient and modern peoples from Aztecs to Zulus; but about contemporary American burial practices almost nothing has been written.

The National Funeral Directors Association, aware of this omission and anxious to correct it, recently commissioned two writers, Robert W. Habenstein and William M. Lamers, to explore the subject and to come up with some answers. The resulting studies, *The History of American Funeral Directing* and *Funeral Customs the World Over,* bear the imprint of the National Funeral Directors Association and are the subject of a continuing promotion campaign by that organization: "Buy one for each clergyman in your community!" "Place them in your libraries!" are the slogans. The campaign has had some success. In fact, in most libraries these volumes sponsored by the undertaking trade are the only ones to be found on the subject of the American funeral.

The official historians of American undertaking describe the origin of our burial practices as follows:

"As a result of a long slow development, with its roots deep in the history of Western civilization, it is the common American mind today that the dead merit professional funeral services from a lay occupational group. These services include embalming, the preparation of the body for final viewing, a waiting period between death and disposition, the use for everyone of a casket that is attractive and protects the remains, a dignified and ceremonious service with consideration for the feelings of the bereaved, and an expression of the individual and group beliefs. . . ." Elsewhere they assert: "The roots of American funeral behavior extend back in a direct line several thousand years to early Judaeo-Christian beliefs as to the nature of God, man and the hereafter. . . . Despite the antiquity of these roots their importance as regards the treatment of the dead in the world that commonly calls itself Christian today cannot be overemphasized."

In two misinformation-packed paragraphs, we are assured not only that American funerals are based on hallowed custom and tradition, but that they conform to long-held religious doctrine. There is more than a hint of warning in these words for the would-be funeral reformer; he who would be bold enough to make light of or tamper with the fundamental beliefs and ancient traditions of a society in so sensitive an area as behavior towards its dead, had better think twice.

A "long, slow development with its roots deep in the history of Western civilization," or a short, fast sprint with its roots deep in money-making? A brief look backward would seem to establish that there is no resemblance between the funeral practices of today and those of even fifty to one hundred years ago, and that there is nothing in the "history of Western civilization" to support the thesis of continuity and gradual development of funeral customs. On the contrary, the salient features of the contemporary American funeral (beautification of the corpse, metal casket and vault, banks of store-bought flowers, ubiquitous offices of the "funeral director") are all of very recent vintage in this country, and each has been methodically designed and tailored to extract maximum profit for the trade.

Nor can responsibilty for the twentieth-century American funeral be laid to the door of "Judaeo-Christian beliefs." The major Western faiths have remarkably little to say about how funerals should be conducted. Such doctrinal statements as have been enunciated concerning disposal of the dead invariably stress simplicity, the equality of all men in death, emphasis on the spiritual aspects rather than on the physical remains.

The Roman Catholic Church requires that the following simple instructions be observed: "1) That the body be decently laid out; 2) that lights be placed beside the body; 3) that a cross be laid upon the breast, or failing that, the hands laid on the breast in the form of a cross; 4) that the body be sprinkled with holy water and incense at stated times; 5) that it be buried in consecrated ground." The Jewish religion specifically prohibits display in connection with funerals: "It is strictly ordained that there must be no adornment of the plain wooden coffin used by the Jew, nor may flowers be placed inside or outside. Plumes, velvet palls and the like are strictly prohibited, and all show and display of wealth discouraged; moreover, the synagogue holds itself responsible for the arrangements for burial, dispensing with the services of the Dismal Trade." In Israel today, uncoffined burial is the rule, and the deceased is returned to the earth in a simple shroud. The Church of England Book of Common Prayer, written several centuries before burial receptacles came into general use, makes no mention of coffins in connection with the funeral service, but rather speaks throughout of the "corpse" or the "body."

What of embalming, the pivotal aspect of the American funeral? The "roots" of this procedure have indeed leaped oceans and traversed centuries in the most unrootlike fashion. It has had a checkered history, the highlights of which deserve some consideration since embalming is (as one mortuary textbook writer puts it) "the very foundation of modern mortuary service—the factor which has made the elaborate funeral home and lucrative funeral service possible."

True, the practice of preserving dead bodies with chemicals, decorating them with paint and powder and arranging them for a public showing has its origin in antiquity—but not in Judaeo-Christian antiquity. This incongruous behavior towards the human dead originated with the pagan Egyptians and reached its high point in the second millennium B.C. Thereafter, embalming suffered a decline from which it did not recover until it was made part of the standard funeral service in twentieth-century America.

While the actual *mode* of preservation and the materials used differed in ancient Egypt from those used in contemporary America, there are many striking similarities in the kind of care lavished upon the dead. There, as here, the goal was to outmaneuver the Grim Reaper as far as possible.

The Egyptian method of embalming as described by Herodotus sounds like a rather crude exercise in human taxidermy. The entrails and brain were removed, the body scoured with palm wine and purified with spices. After being soaked for seventy days in a saline solution the corpse was washed and wrapped in strips of fine linen, then placed in a "wooden case of human shape" which in turn was put in a sepulchral chamber.

Restorative art was by no means unknown in ancient Egypt. The Greek historian Diodorus Siculus wrote: "Having treated [the corpse], they restore it to the relatives with every member of the body preserved so perfectly that even the eyelashes and eyebrows remain, the whole appearance of the body being unchangeable, and the cast of the features recognizable. . . . They present an example of a kind of inverted necromancy." The Egyptians had no Post Mortem Restoration Bra; instead they stuffed and modeled the breasts, refashioning the nipples from copper buttons. They fixed the body while still plastic in the desired attitude; they painted it with red ochre for men and yellow for women; they emphasized the details of the face with paint; they supplemented the natural hair with a wig; they tinted the nails with henna. A mummy of the XVIIIth Dynasty has even been found wearing some practical burial footwear—sandals made of mud, with metal soles and gilded straps.

Egyptian preoccupation with preservation of the body after death stemmed from the belief that the departed spirit would one day return to inhabit the earthly body; that if the body perished, the soul would eventually perish too. Yet although embalming was available to all who could pay the price, it was by no means so universally employed in ancient Egypt as it is today in the U.S.A. The ordinary peasant was not embalmed at all; yet, curiously enough, his corpse comes down to us through the ages as well preserved as those of his disemboweled and richly aromatic betters, for it has been established that the unusually dry climate and the absence of bacteria in the sand and air, rather than the materials used in embalming, are what account for the Egyptian mummies' marvelous state of preservation.

The Greeks, knowing the uses of both, were no more likely to occupy themselves with the preservation of dead flesh than they were to bury good wine for the comfort of dead bodies. They cremated their dead, for the most part, believing in the power of flame to set free the soul. The glorious period that conventional historians call the Golden Age of Greece is for historians of embalming the beginning of the Dark Ages.

The Jews frowned upon embalming, as did the early Christians, who regarded it as a pagan custom. Saint Anthony, in the third century, denounced the practice as sinful. His impassioned plea, recorded by Athanasius, might well be echoed by the American of today who would like to avoid being transformed by the embalmer's art and displayed in a funeral home:

"And if your minds are set upon me, and ye remember me as a father, permit no man to take my body and carry it into Egypt, lest, according to the custom which they have, they embalm me and lay me up in their houses, for it was [to avoid] this that I came into this desert. And ye know that I have continually made exhortation concerning this thing and begged that it should not be done, and ye well know how much I have blamed those who observed this custom. Dig a grave then, and bury me therein, and hide my body under the earth, and let these my words be observed carefully by you, and tell ye no man where ye lay me. . . ."

Mummification of the dead in Egypt was gradually abandoned after a large part of the population was converted to Christianity.

The eclipse of embalming was never quite total, however. The death of a monarch, since it is the occasion for a transfer of power, calls for demonstration, and it has throughout history been found politically expedient to provide visible evidence of death by exposing the body to public view. So embalming, of sorts, was used in Rome, and later throughout Europe, but only for the great and near-great, and by the very rich as a form of pretentiousness.

Alexander the Great is said to have been preserved in wax and honey; Charlemagne was embalmed and, dressed in imperial robes, placed in a sitting position in his tomb. Canute, too, was embalmed, and after him many an English monarch. Lord Nelson, as befits a hero, was returned to England from Trafalgar in a barrel of brandy. Queen Elizabeth, by her own wish, was not embalmed. Developments beyond her control caused her sealed, lead-lined coffin to lie in Whitehall for an unconscionable thirty-four days before interment. During this time, reports one of the ladies-in-waiting who sat as watchers, the body "burst with such a crack that it splitted the wood, lead, and cerecloth; whereupon the next day she was fain to be new trimmed up."

Although embalming as a trade or cult was not resumed until this century, there prospered in every age charlatans and eccentrics who claimed to have rediscovered the lost art of the Egyptians or who offered new and improved pickling methods of their own invention. These were joined, in the eighteenth century, by French and English experimenters spurred by a quite different motive—the need for more efficient methods of preserving cadavers for anatomical studies.

The physicians, surgeons, chemists and apothecaries who engaged in anatomical research were from time to time sought out by private necrophiles who enlisted their services to preserve dead friends and relations. There are many examples of this curious practice of which perhaps the most interesting is the task performed by Dr. William Hunter, the celebrated eighteenth-century anatomist. Dr.

Hunter was anyway something of a card. He once explained his aversion to contradiction by pointing out that being accustomed to the "passive submission of dead bodies," he could no longer easily tolerate having his will crossed; a sentiment echoed by Evelyn Waugh's mortuary cosmetician: "I was just glad to serve people that couldn't talk back."

In 1775, Dr. Hunter and a colleague embalmed the wife of Martin Van Butchell, quack doctor and "super dentist," the point being that Mrs. Van Butchell's marriage settlement stipulated that her husband should have control of her fortune "as long as she remained above ground." The embalming was a great success. The "preserved lady" (as curious sightseers came to call her) was dressed in a fine linen gown, placed in a glass-topped case and kept in the drawing room, where Van Butchell introduced her to all comers as his "dear departed." So popular was the preserved lady that Van Butchell was obliged to insert a newspaper notice limiting her visiting hours to "any day between Nine and One, Sundays excepted." When Van Butchell remarried several years later, his new wife raised strong objections to the presence of the Dear Departed in her front parlor, and insisted upon her removal. Thereafter the Dear Departed was housed in the museum of the Royal College of Surgeons.*

The two widely divergent interests which spurred the early embalmers—scientific inquiry, and the fascination and financial reward of turning cadavers into a sort of ornamental keepsake—were to achieve a happy union under the guiding hand of a rare nineteenth-century character, "Dr." Thomas Holmes. He was the first to advance from what one funeral trade writer jocularly calls the "Glacier Age"—when preservation on ice was the

*While on a recent visit to London, I applied to the Royal College of Surgeons of England for permission to see Mrs. Van Butchell. I received this reply from the office of the curator: "While it is true that the late Mrs. Martin Van Butchell once occupied a place of honour in the historical collection of this College, it is regretted that she was finally cremated along with so much valuable material in the destruction of the College in May, 1941, at the height of the London blitz."

undertakers' rule—and is often affectionately referred to by present-day funeral men as "the father of American embalming." Holmes was the first to popularize the idea of preserving the dead on a mass scale, and the first American to get rich from this novel occupation.

Holmes developed a passionate interest in cadavers early in life (it was in fact the reason for his expulsion from medical school; he was forever carelessly leaving them around in inappropriate places) and when the Civil War started, he saw his great opportunity. He rushed to the front and started embalming like mad, charging the families of the dead soldiers $100 for his labors. Some four years and 4,028 embalmed soldiers later (his own figure), Holmes returned to Brooklyn a rich man.

The "use for everyone of a casket that is attractive and protects the remains" (*attractive* seems an odd word here) is a new concept in this century, and one that took some ingenuity to put across. Surprisingly enough, even the widespread use of any sort of burial receptacle is a fairly new development in Western culture, dating back less than two hundred years. Until the eighteenth century few people except the very rich were buried in coffins. The "casket," and particularly the metal casket, is a phenomenon of modern America, unknown in past days and in other parts of the world.

As might be expected, with the development of industrial technique in the nineteenth century, coffin designers soared to marvelous heights. They experimented with glass, cement, celluloid, papier-mâché, India rubber; they invented Rube Goldberg contraptions called "life signals"—complicated arrangements of wires and bells designed to set off an alarm if the occupant of the coffin should have been inadvertently buried alive.

The newfangled invention of metal coffins in the nineteenth century did not go unchallenged. An admonition on the subject was delivered by Lord Stowell, Judge of the Consistory Court of London, who in 1820 was called upon to decide a case felicitously titled Gilbert vs. Buzzard.

At issue was the right to bury a corpse in a newly patented iron coffin. The church wardens protested that if parishioners were to get into the habit of burying their dead in coffins made proof against normal decay, in a few generations there would be no burial space left.

Said Lord Stowell, "The rule of law which says that a man has a right to be buried in his own churchyard is to be found, most certainly, in many of our authoritative text writers; but it is not quite so easy to find the rule which gives him the rights of burying a large chest or trunk in company with himself." He spoke approvingly of attempts to abolish use of sepulchral chests "on the physical ground that the dissolution of bodies would be accelerated and the dangerous virulence of the fermentation disarmed by a speedy absorption of the noxious particles into the surrounding soil."

The inexorable upward thrust towards perfection in metal caskets was not, however, destined to be halted by judicial logic. Just one hundred years after the decision in Gilbert vs. Buzzard, a triumph of the first magnitude was recorded by the D. H. Hill Casket Company of Chicago, and described in their 1920 *Catalogue of Funeral Merchandise*: "A STUDY IN BRONZE: When Robert Fulton said he could propel a boat by steam his friends were sure he was mentally deranged—that it could not be done. When Benjamin Franklin said he could draw electricity from the clouds his acquaintances thought he was crazy— that it could not be done. When our designing and manufacturing departments said they could and would produce a CAST BRONZE CASKET that would be the peer of anything yet developed, their friends and associates shook their heads sympathetically, feeling that it would be a hopeless task. All three visions have come to be realities—the steamboat, electricity, and the Hilco Peerless Cast Bronze Burial Receptacle."

The production of ever more solid and durable metal caskets has soared in this century, their long-lasting and even "eternal" qualities have become matter of pride and self-congratulation throughout the industry—and this in one area of manufacture where built-in obsolescence might seem (as Lord Stowell pointed out) to present certain advantages. As we have seen, the sales of metal caskets now exceed sales of the old-fashioned wooden types. A brand-new tradition has been established; how deep are the roots, Messrs. Habenstein and Lamers?

Mourning symbols have run the gamut. In medieval England and in colonial America, the skull and crossbones was the favored symbol, making its appearance on everything connected with death from tombstone to funeral pall to coffinmaker's sign. Funerary extravagance took the form of elaborate mourning clothes, the hiring of mutes (or paid mourners), tremendous feasting sometimes of many days' duration, and gifts to the living, who were showered with rings, scarves, needlework, books and, most customarily, gloves.

Funeral flowers, today the major mourning symbol and a huge item of national expenditure, did not make their appearance in England or America until after the middle of the nineteenth century, and only then over the opposition of church leaders.

From colonial days until the nineteenth century, the American funeral was almost exclusively a family affair, in the sense that the family and close friends performed most of the duties in connection with the dead body itself. It was they who washed and laid out the body, draped it in a winding sheet, and ordered the coffin from the local carpenter. It was they who carried the coffin on foot from the home to the church and thence to the graveyard, and who frequently—unless the church sexton was available—dug the grave. Funeral services were held in the church over the pall-covered bier, and a brief committal prayer was said at the graveside. Between the death and the funeral, the body lay in the family parlor where the mourners took turns watching over it, the practical reason for this being the ever-present possibility that signs of life might be observed.

The first undertakers were drawn mainly from three occupations, all concerned with some aspect of burial:

the livery stable keeper, who provided the hearse and funeral carriages, the carpenter or cabinetmaker who made the coffins, and the sexton, who was generally in charge of bell-tolling and grave-digging. In some of the larger cities midwives and nurses advertised their services as occupational layers out of the dead, and were so listed in city directories. The undertaker's job was primarily custodial. It included supplying the coffin from a catalogue or from his own establishment, arranging to bring folding chairs (if the service was to be held in the home, which was often the case), taking charge of the pallbearers, supervising the removal of the coffin and loading it into the hearse, and in general doing the necessary chores until the body was finally lowered into the grave.

Shortly before the turn of the century, the undertaker conferred upon himself the title of "funeral director." From that time on, possibly inspired by his own semantics, he began to *direct funerals,* and quietly to impose a character of his own on the mode of disposal of the dead.

Some of the changes that were in store are fore-shadowed in *The Modern Funeral* by W. P. Hohenschuh, published in 1900. Hohenschuh may have been the first to put into words a major assumption that lies behind modern funeral practices: "There is nothing too good for the dead," he declares. He goes on to advise, "The friends want the best that they can afford. . . . A number of manufacturers have set an excellent example by fitting up magnificent showrooms, to which funeral directors can take their customers, and show them the finest goods made. It is an education for all parties concerned. . . . It is to be commended." Hohenschuh's injunctions about funeral salesmanship, although vastly elaborated over the years, remain basic: "Boxes must be shown to sell them. By having an ordinary pine box next to one that is prepared, the difference is more readily seen than could be explained, and a better price can be obtained for the latter." And on collections he warns, "Grief soon subsides, and the older the bill gets, the harder it is to collect."

In 1900 embalming was still the exception rather than

the rule and was still generally done in the home—although Hohenschuh mentions a new trend making its appearance in California, that of taking the body to the funeral parlor after death for dressing and embalming. He proposes an ingenious approach to selling the public on embalming: "It may be suggested that bodies should be embalmed in winter as well as in summer. It may be a little difficult to have people accept this idea, but after having tried it a few times, and people realize the comfort to themselves in having the body in a warm room, this preventing them against colds, besides the sentimental feeling against having the body in a cold room, it is an easy matter to make the custom general." However, the most profitable aspect of the modern funeral—that of preparing the body for the public gaze—seems to have escaped this astute practitioner, for he opposes the open casket at the funeral service, and remarks, "There is no doubt that most people view the dead out of curiosity."

It was still a far cry from these early, hesitant steps of the emerging funeral industry to the full-fledged burlesque it has become.

14

FUNERALS IN ENGLAND

*A public exhibition of an embalmed body, as that of Lenin
in Moscow, would [in England] presumably be dealt with
as a revolting spectacle and therefore a public nuisance.*
　　　　　　　　　　—ALFRED FELLOWS, *The Law of Burial*

AMERICAN funeral directors often say, "England is about
fifty years behind us." To the English, this might sound
like a veiled note of warning; does it mean, for example,
that fifty years from now much of England's green and
pleasant land will have been converted into Memory
Gardens of Eternal Peace? From Sherwood Forest to
Forest Lawn in one easy step? It requires more than a
little imagination to visualize a bluff English squire and his
hard-riding, rugged-faced lady transformed into Beautiful
Memory Pictures, their erstwhile stony and disapproving
features remolded by the hand of a Restorative Artist
into unfamiliar expressions of benign sweetness. Would
their caskets be named (like the American "Valley
Forge") after famous battles—"Battle of Britain," in
delectable shades of Royal Air Force blue, or "Flodden
Field," with an archery motif? Or perhaps (like the
American "Colonial Classic") after periods in English

197

history: the Restoration Rolick, The Crusader, Knighthood in Flower, the Victorian Voluptuous with overstuffed horsehair interior made expressly to simulate the finest drawing-room furniture of the period? Would the squire and his wife be decked out as for the Royal Enclosure at Ascot, he in top hat and cutaway, she in trailing flowered chiffon, or more simply in Harris tweeds complemented by Practical Burial Gum Boots?

There has been heard in America a singing radio commercial whose words, set to the tune of "Rock of Ages," go like this:

> Chambers' caskets are just fine,
> Made of sandalwood and pine.
> If your loved ones have to go
> Call Columbus 690.
> If your loved ones pass away,
> Have them pass the Chambers way.
> Chambers' customers all sing:
> "Death, oh death, where is thy sting?"

This might be going a little too far for England, even fifty years hence; but it would be rash to underestimate the penetrating power of American enterprise. Jingles like this may one day be beamed on commercial telly and adorn billboards in the countryside: "Repose with your mate/ Near the bones of the great/ By appointment, I ween/ To H. M. the Queen."—Westminster Memory Gardens, Ltd. Or, "Your Heart in the Highlands—Forever!"—Happy Hebridean Haven, Ltd.

Fanciful, perhaps; yet perhaps also the English would be well advised to note that American missionary schemes to "civilize" English funerals are already under way, and some headway has been recorded.

As early as 1926, a member of National Selected Morticians reported to his colleagues on what had most impressed him on a vist to England: "I spent a day in Liverpool with a fine gentleman, one of the very best. They know very little about our embalming in any other

part of the world, outside of America. They are going to.
England has been agitating the matter. I take one of their
journals, and they commenced agitating it a couple of
years ago. I think if we could send some missionaries
over there, we would do them a world of good. . . .
Of course, I do not look upon Canada as a foreign country
at all. . . . I really think there is quite a strong tendency
in Canada to perform their work similar to the way we
perform ours. Of course you have all read probably quite
recently—that is comparatively recently—how the health
officer in Canada thinks that our system is all bosh, and
that we do not do anything in the way of sanitation and
all that sort of thing. But I think there are a large number
of practitioners in Canada who follow our plan."

Just recently, Mr. Bruce Hotchkiss, vice-president of
the N.F.D.A., told me that great strides are being made in
England towards the adoption of American funeral
practices. I was asking him for some specific information
about Grief Therapy; whether, for example, there is
evidence that there is more mental disorder resulting from
bereavement in England, where the dead are not ordinarily
embalmed, restored and viewed, than in the United States.
We had the following discussion:

MR. HOTCHKISS: Well, I'd question your statement they don't
view bodies in England. I've just been there, within the
last two years. I was there in 1960, and I disagree with
your statements which I have heard, that in England the
body just seems to disappear—
ME: Oh no, I never said that. You're going a bit too far.
MR. HOTCHKISS: They are, they are viewing the remains in
England now.
ME: But I was speaking of the restored and embalmed re-
mains. Are they?
MR. HOTCHKISS: Yes, yes, I have been through their establish-
ments, and they *are* embalming, and they *do* view them.
Yes, indeed. Incidentally they have some very fine mor-
tuaries.
ME: Oh, do they? They're coming up, eh?
MR. HOTCHKISS: Luscious names, too; Barons of Rygate. . . .

Finding out about funerals in England is, if anything, an even harder job than in America. The trade associations are not anxious to correspond on the subject. I wrote to one of them, with a long list of questions, and got in reply a printed postcard: "I have the pleasure to acknowledge receipt of your communication which is receiving attention," followed by a profound silence.

It is of little use to ask English friends to describe the procedures in a typical funeral, because so few have been to one. Whereas Americans flock to the funeral of a co-worker, a neighbor or a casual acquaintance, in England only the closest relations go; consequently many people, even those of middle age, have never actually seen a funeral. Some are, perhaps understandably, reluctant to make inquiries. One friend wrote, "I have not yet been to call at ———— Undertakers, although I walk past there every day; I fear I have the superstitious feeling of an old horse passing the knacker's yard."

Another friend spent some time with a country undertaker, and sent a full report: "First and foremost, he said—and this is borne out by my own feelings and the experience of everybody I have asked—that we aren't even on the fringe of imitating Americans yet, and there will have to be a big change in the psychology of everybody concerned before we do. This at least is one area where there's no attempt to produce a milk-and-water copy of the American original. The undertaker is quite definitely regarded as a tradesman—no cachet attached to the job whatsoever; and in the country he is almost invariably the local builder as well. About embalming, the local man said he's only had to embalm one corpse in ten years (the family was abroad and the funeral had to be delayed ten days), and there's not the slightest indication that it is likely to grow in popularity. The whole mentality of burying here is that the dead should be disposed of with quiet respectability and the minimum of fuss and publicity. Decent and quiet, you might say."

Evidently something was wrong somewhere; had not Mr. Hotchkiss told me that they *are* embalming, and they *do* view them, yes indeed? Was the thin edge of the wedge somewhere being inserted unknown to the English public and unknown even to sections of the trade?

Further investigation convinced me that there are contradictory forces at work. There are those within the trade who are envious of their American counterparts, who would love nothing better than to transplant the American way in England's unreceptive soil. They find themselves, however, up against the relentless English common sense and preference for the ordinary way of doing things. An English undertaker, speaking at a Dallas meeting of the National Selected Morticians, explained the difficulty: "The chief reason why our average is low is the very fact that I have tried to tell you about the British character—their desire for moderation. In our own selection room we display a full range of hardwood caskets, oak, walnut, and mahogany. Yet of the clients who can afford the best, 90 per cent would choose the traditional coffin. They would say of the caskets, 'Very beautiful, but too big, too elaborate! We will have an oak coffin like we had for grandfather!' This a problem that has concerned me for many years. . . . I must tell you, also, that our presentation must be accomplished without the use of cosmetics. Heavy cosmetizing would bring the strongest complaints from our clients. They tell us quite firmly, 'I don't want Mother touched up!'" He does, however, mention "an aspect of American funeral service which appears to be more readily accepted by our British public. All over the country funeral directors are building funeral homes, putting in private chapels and rest rooms.* They are not comparable with the beautiful buildings I have already seen this last week, but, nevertheless, our men have recognized the need and are now beginning to provide the facilities."

The English trade publications *The Funeral Director* and *Funeral Service Journal* reflect in their pages a predominantly traditional approach, with occasional reveal-

*Semantics Note: In England, "rest room" means room in which to rest.

ing flashes of possible changes on the way. Their very titles, which must have, to the English ear, an unfamiliar transatlantic ring, tell us something; yet unlike the American funeral magazines, they are modest in format and sparsely illustrated.

The advertisements for the most part call a coffin a coffin, a hearse a hearse and a shroud a shroud; there is "Coffinex Aqueous Emulsion, supersedes the old method of applying boiling pitch and wax, which was both laborious and uneconomical" (an improvement we can, surely, applaud); but "casket" is by no means unknown; there is "Casketite Bitumen Emulsion, for simpler, more economical sealing of caskets and coffins." Social events for English undertakers as reported in these journals have not yet reached the Vaultburger Barbecue stage, they adhere rather to traditional English ideas of what constitutes jolly good entertainment; we are told that "in April a number of members and their ladies attended a performance of 'The Iron Hand' given at H. M. Prison, Sudbury." The editorial writers tend towards conservatism. One of them, describing an American funeral director who distributes "packs of quite good quality playing cards which, on the back, carry an advertisement for so-and-so's funeral home," comments that he "would not like to see such advertising in this country." Yet there are also reprints from American magazines: how to use the telephone ("never use the personal pronoun 'I,' always use 'we', speak with warmth in your voice, clearly and with sincere friendliness"); how to set up a casket selection room, and the like—but they do not seem to have altered the basically English character of these journals.

There is a study course available, a fairly comprehensive text of some 75 mimeographed pages, prepared by members of the trade for the "voluntary examination in funeral directing." Since there is no law in England requiring licensure of undertakers, the study course and examination are in effect an exercise in self-improvement rather than, as in America, a legal requirement.

The study course, like the trade publications, is a

strange mixture of old and new concepts about the disposal of the dead, English and American terminology, the traditional English approach combined with aspects of the American Way.

How refreshing to read, for example, that "it is not the function of the funeral director to become the family sympathizer but rather to offer helpful advice." And that while it is permissible to let the family know that a private chapel is available on the premises for the service, it is "very wrong to be over-persuasive in this matter"; that if they are regular church attenders, "it is certainly good practice to suggest that the Service be held in their own church. This is appreciated by the family and the Clergy." Equally permissive—in contrast to the attitude of the American burial industry—is the position on cremated remains ("Cremains" has not yet found its way across the Atlantic): this is a "matter for the family to decide. The majority seem to prefer the scattering of the Cremated Remains in the Garden of Remembrance attached to all Crematoria" or at some other spot of their choice. Sentimentality is positively discouraged. Discussing obituary notices, the study course cautions, "In some cases, one is requested to insert over-sentimental verses and all the Funeral Director's tact is called upon to dissuade them in their own interest."

Some agreeably down-to-earth advice is offered about the proper treatment of the corpse itself: "Dress in clean clothing—pyjamas, shirt or nightdress, etc. . . . Insert the laying-out board under the body. . . . DO NOT TIE THE BIG TOES TOGETHER. . . . IN NO CIRCUMSTANCES WHATSOEVER SHOULD THE ARMS AND HANDS BE SECURED BY POSITIONING THEM UNDER THE BUTTOCKS. . . . DO NOT PLACE PENNIES OR WET PACKS OVER THE EYES."

However, there are indications that a new day may soon dawn for the dead in England. A large portion of the course is devoted to the importance of embalming and how to sell it to a reluctant client, apparently best accomplished by not being quite frank with him. The words "hygienic treatment," it is suggested, should be used in discussing the subject with the client: "By this, of course, you mean modern arterial embalming, but funeral directors are generally agreed that in the early stages of the arrangement, the use of the word 'embalming' is best avoided. . . . Although some funeral directors boldly speak of 'embalming' the majority consider it preferable to describe the treatment by some such term as 'Temporary Preservation,' 'Sanitary Treatment,' or 'Hygienic Treatment.' In this way it is felt that there is less likelihood of associating the modern science with that of the ancient Egyptians."

The familiar justifications are offered for what one English authority has called "the meaningless practice of embalming": it delays decomposition, it promotes public health, it restores a lifelike appearance. "The change effected is truly remarkable—gone is the deathly pallor . . . instead the family sees a life-like presentation of their loved one appearing as though peacefully sleeping. This result is a source of great comfort and has a decided psychologic value." Furthermore, the family may have "open casket or coffin at all times until closed for the Funeral."

It is to the growing army of embalmers that we must turn for enlightenment on progress in introducing American funeral practices into England. Most English people are astonished to learn that embalming is sharply on the increase there. The British Institute of Embalmers claims over 1,000 members. The uphill nature of their efforts to ply their trade can be inferred from an official statement issued by the Institute: "Two primary factors have retarded the progress. Primarily the fact that customs die hard in this country and in no case is this more evident than in funerals. The introduction of any new methods, apparatus or merchandise was treated with suspicion, not only by the mourners but often by the priest or minister conducting the funeral service. . . . Up to the present moment there has been little governmental support or recognition of the science. With exceptions, the medical profession ignore it. . . ."

Hard is the lot of the really go-ahead embalmer in England. There is the unaccommodating English law, which requires that a death certificate be obtained and the death properly registered before the embalmer can get going. No chance there of getting started, as recommended in America, before life is completely extinct. There is the difficulty of obtaining American embalming products because the necessary license to import them may be refused by H. M. Treasury; there is the opposition of the medical profession. Above all, there is the resistance of the survivors.

An English contributor to the American *Professional Embalmer* describes some of the roadblocks he has encountered. The main trouble seems to be that "the open-casket is unknown in this country. . . . The coffin is invariably closed at the funeral service proper and, more important still, the funeral director is frequently instructed at the first call to close the coffin immediately the remains are placed in it. This lack of acceptance by the public of a fundamental American concept produces more than one difficulty for British embalmers; with no demand there can be no practice."

Because there is no demand, there is no incentive for manufacturers to experiment and improve embalming chemicals and other related products; "in short, it is a vicious circle." However, a few lucky English embalmers have partially resolved this aspect of the problem; they have American friends who, "when they visit on business or on holiday, bring with them a little wax and cosmetics." (One can imagine the cries of joy as the suitcases are opened.) The writer, while expressing his regret that these products are so little known to his English colleagues ("they fill a very pressing need"), describes his pleasure at receiving a supply of True-Cov and Rosatint. But, as he points out, "Even a warehouse full of restorative material and cosmetics will not convince the bereaved that to permit restorative work to be performed on their loved ones is to everyone's advantage; that is the task of the embalmer."

English doctors, we learn, are most uncooperative: "The medical profession in Great Britain exercise a power second to none. Despite the National Health Service, and statements to the contrary, as a pressure group they are supreme . . . they would oppose with all the power at their command any attempt to limit autopsies. Indeed, no group can show more rooted opposition to modern funeral service and embalming in particular than this one. They stand squarely behind the Cremation movement here, actively campaigning for it, doing all they can to reduce funeral service to little more than simple rubbish disposal." Not only that, but the doctors are often unkind to the embalmers: "Except between friends any request by a funeral director or an embalmer for cooperation on the part of an examining surgeon will be wasted; if anything more than an ill-mannered rebuff is received it will be calculated obstruction carried even to the lengths of deliberate mutilation."

With true British grit, the author ends on a note of hope for the future: "There can be no argument about it; in England the embalmer is out on his own and any progress he makes is over hard won ground. That does not mean that he is a quitter, however; far from it. At the moment satisfactory restoration is almost impossible to achieve but it will be achieved in the end, with help or without it, and no matter how far distant that end may be!" Rather bravely spoken, considering that achievement of the distant end apparently depends upon a complete reversal of the law, of public attitudes, and of views of the medical profession.

Some months after I had read about the ups and downs in the English undertaking trade, I had a chance to visit an English funeral establishment to check the vision against the reality. The very location of the one I visited, in changeless South London, seemed to foreshadow the attitudes I should find there. The West End may present a new façade from year to year, here an unfamiliar skyscraper under construction, there a block of service flats where before had stood the London mansion of some

Scottish laird, everywhere the bright awnings and colored tablecloths of the newly imported espresso houses. South London remains the same: the haberdashery and furniture displayed in shop windows might have been there for generations; the very buns in the cafés have a prewar flavor. "Clapham Road?" said the corner newspaper vendor whom I asked for directions. "Not far, just a nice twenty-minute walk; it's just round from where my aunt's lived for fifty years." Not the sort of place, I thought, where people would be amenable to newfangled methods in any phase of life, let alone death; and in a way I believe I was right.

Mr. Ashton, whose establishment in Clapham Road is easily the most imposing building in the vicinity, is in some respects far from being a typical English undertaker. Whereas most of his colleagues are very small operators indeed, and generally perform this work as a sideline to some other trade, Mr. Ashton is the owner of nine London branches with a total volume of around 1,200 funerals a year. Few English establishments can compare with this. Furthermore he is among the tiny minority in England who routinely embalm all comers, and who might therefore be expected to have absorbed at least some of the concomitant American approaches to the funeral. For these reasons, he seemed the ideal person from whom to seek clarification about likely trends in English funeral practices.

Mr. Ashton was a charming host. He led me through his entrance hall, conservatively decorated with neutral wallpaper and wine-red upholstered furniture, up the stairs to his private office where we chatted over a cup of tea. I wanted to know about his own firm; something about the funeral trade as a whole; and above all, the steps taken and procedures followed in the average English funeral.

Like a great many English undertaking concerns, Mr. Ashton's is an old established family firm. It has been in existence for a hundred and fifty years, and he is of the fourth generation in the business. There is a growing tendency, he explained, for large firms to take over smaller ones, and this is how he acquired the nine establishments, all located in South London. The smallest of these averages about 50 funerals a year, the largest, 300. The clientele is mostly middle and lower class, and comes mostly from South London. He runs his own coffin factory, in which he employs twelve factory hands, woodworkers who make the coffins. He also employs nine managers, nine drivers, an office staff of five, and three full-time embalmers. It takes four months to learn embalming, he told me; the minimum embalmer's wage is £12 a week (about $34) and "perks"—use of the car, etc. The managers do no embalming; their function is entirely separate.

There are in all Great Britain perhaps ten firms the size of Mr. Ashton's, in the larger cities such as Edinburgh, Glasgow, Cardiff, London. There are a total of 4,500 full-time funeral directors in the country—that is, one for every 11,000 of the population, compared with one for every 7,000 in America. About 3,000 of them are members of the National Association of Funeral Directors. In London, there are some 350 major firms, compared with 800 in New York, serving a population about the same size. The larger firms all make their own coffins. There are a few wholesale coffin companies, which in many instances also furnish cars, embalmers and all services for the smaller establishments.

Discussing the routines that follow between death and the funeral, Mr. Ashton positively exuded the no-nonsense, humbug-free attitudes so prized by this "nation of shopkeepers" in all their dealings, and in this particular calling so reassuring to find. I asked him what happens when a person dies at home in the middle of the night. American undertakers, to a man, take the greatest pride in rushing to the scene at no matter what hour; in fact, high on their list of "essential services"—and a major justification for their high charges—is maintenance of a 24-hour operation, their ability to remove the deceased any time of the day or night within minutes of death. "I'd send along in the morning," said Mr. Ashton. "Well, I mean unless the chap dies in the lavatory, or something, which did happen once, and then I had to go along at once, you see." He explained that they are prepared, and could come in the night if necessary, "but we certainly don't encourage it as long as the family is under control. Personally I'm all for a quiet life and a little peace, and anyway people are more intelligent about such things these days. They realize that nothing can be done until the morning." Death at home is anyway the exception. Eighty per cent of deaths occur in hospital. In that case a relative goes to the hospital and procures the death certificate, which the registrar must have before burial can be authorized. The practice of keeping the body at home until the funeral is losing favor. Before World War II, this was done in 90 per cent of cases, today in less than 10 per cent. The minority who prefer to keep their dead at home tend to be at the opposite ends of the social scale; the very poor ("poorer people are far more traditional") and the very rich, who are not only traditional but have more room in their houses. "The middle classes say, 'It's all unpleasant, let's get it over.' "

We went to look at Mr. Ashton's stock of caskets and coffins, which are kept in two small rooms. The caskets are styled somewhat after the American ones, only far less elaborate; all are made of wood. The use of metal for this purpose is almost unheard of. In fact the only difference between an English "casket" and a "coffin" is in the shape, the former being rectangular and the latter, tapered or "kite-shaped." The lids of all were shut. Feeling that I ought to make some remark, I murmured, "Lovely, lovely," which would have done nicely in America where the funeral men take enormous pride in their stock. "*I* think they're perfectly awful-looking things," commented Mr. Ashton cheerfully. He opened one: "Look at that frightful lacy stuff, and all that ghastly satin." He told me that there is practically no demand for the caskets; not more than a dozen a year are sold. We proceeded to another small room, containing five or six coffins. The cheapest are made of imported African hardwood or

English elm, chosen by the majority of Mr. Ashton's clients. Next in price is English oak, and most expensive, mahogany. Vaults, in the American sense of a metal or concrete container for the individual coffin, do not exist ("quite unnecessary," said Mr. Ashton), although sometimes a family vault of brick may be built to accommodate six or eight coffins. I asked whether without a vault earth might not tend to cave in as the coffin disintegrates. This apparently is not a problem, although it is customary to wait for six months for the ground to settle before putting up a gravestone, which is generally erected upon a concrete slab laid over the grave.

The majority of Mr. Ashton's funerals average about £50 ($140), to which must be added about half as much again for the additional expense of cemetery or crematorium fee, memorial stone and the like. The most expensive funeral offered in the ordinary course of his business is £100 ($280), and the most expensive one he remembers doing came to £300. Cremation costs about £4, and graves are from £15 up—"Londonwise, that is," said Mr. Ashton. Away from London the cost is lower. The great majority of cemeteries and many of the crematoria are municipally owned.

After the war, as an alternative to government control of funeral charges, an informal agreement was reached between the government and the National Association of Funeral Directors that a minimum-priced, simple funeral costing £20 would be made available to anybody requesting it. Specifications for the simple funeral drawn up by the N.A.F.D. include: "Elm or Scots Fir Coffin, suitably finished, soundly constructed from ¾" timber, waterproofed and upholstered with swansdown or good quality calico. Side sheets, Robe or Shroud. Fitted with electro brassed or nickle plated handles, inscribed or written name-plate, closing screws and, if usually fitted, lid ornaments, end rings and cords and tassels." Also: "Delivery of Coffin to house, Hearse and One Following Car to local Cemetery or Crematorium, Minimum of Four bearers, Attendance and Supervision."

The minimum has since risen to £33, exclusive of cemetery of crematorium charges. "Of course we do offer it, but I can't say we stress it," said Mr. Ashton in his practical way. "Wouldn't really pay us to do that, would it?" I noticed that the minimum-priced coffin was not displayed with the others, and here I thought I detected the introduction of a particularly obnoxious American practice; was the cheapest coffin being deliberately concealed from the public gaze? I asked where the coffin for the £33 funeral was kept, and Mr. Ashton said there were plenty of them in the factory. Hidden there from the customers? I asked. Of course not! The customers never come up here; very, very rarely does a person ask to *see* the coffins in the course of arranging a funeral. "You mean this isn't a selection room in the American sense—you don't bring them up here to choose?" "Good Lord, no!" said Mr. Ashton, rather reprovingly as though the very suggestion was in violation of decency and good taste. "People don't want to *look* at these dreadful things. I mean, why should they? All that is settled when we talk to the family in the office."

We next proceeded to the "rest rooms" where the deceased is laid out until the day of the funeral. They looked like cozy little sitting rooms, comfortably furnished with chairs and curtains. While they did not begin to approach the elegance of slumber rooms I have seen in the States, they were, I was told, exceptionally well appointed for England. I was curious to know to what extent survivors make use of these rooms. This varies quite a bit. A fair number never come at all. Generally, one or two of the immediate relatives, perhaps the widow supported by her grown-up son, come once to see the deceased; "It's a sort of identification. Having looked, and presumably approved, that's probably that." Occasionally the reverse is true; a small percentage come daily with fresh flowers. Among the poorer classes, the neighbors sometimes come.

The funeral is usually held in the crematorium or cemetery chapel; ("They all have these horrid little chapels

nowadays," said Mr. Ashton) although an effort is
being made by the Church of England to get the funeral
back to the church. The Ashton premises have one large
room which he was intending to convert into use for a
funeral chapel, but he found there was so little demand
for it that instead he uses it for a rest room. On an
average, a "car and a half," six to seven people attend the
funeral, although attendance varies tremendously; between
two and three hundred may show up for the funeral of a
prominent person. As in America, mourning is no longer
worn except by the very old, who still think it proper to
go out and buy "a bit of black" for the funeral. "Flower-
wise," said Mr. Ashton (once more springing this
incongruous Americanism), he estimates that there would
be an average of twenty floral pieces at an ordinary
funeral, costing between £2 and £3 apiece, for an average total of £60 to £70. Workers spend a lot more on
funeral flowers than do the middle classes; in fact the
latter tend to be more moderate in all ways.

If a country dweller happens to die in London, his body
is generally taken back to his home parish for burial. A
private motor hearse may be used, or the body may go by
train: "British Railways have a complete system, with
special carriages for this purpose. They come and fetch
the coffin and take it to the station in a hearse." I asked
whether embalming is required when a body is to be
shipped. "If it's to go by air, it's got to be embalmed, but
British Railways don't require it; they're not particularly
fussy."

An open-casket funeral is almost unheard of, said Mr.
Ashton. Such a thing would be considered so absolutely
weird, so contrary to good taste and proper behavior, so
shocking to the sensibilities of all concerned, that he thinks
it could never become a practice in England. He recalled
the funeral of a Polish worker whose family requested an
open casket: "The gravediggers objected very much to
this. Rather absurd of them, when you come to think of
what their job is, don't you know, but still they didn't see
why they should stand for having the thing *opened*."

Cosmetics are never used. "That sort of thing might go over in America, but really, I mean I don't think you could get the people here used to it. If I had to say, 'Come and see your *loved one,*' I honestly don't think I could keep a straight face." Mr. Ashton added that Evelyn Waugh's book *The Loved One* is one of his favorite novels, and that when it first came out he bought four copies for the amusement of his staff. But nevertheless, what about the adoption of certain American euphemisms—"funeral director" instead of "undertaker," for example? Mr. Ashton thought that was originally instituted to stop the music-hall jokes about the trade, and because "the word 'undertaker' doesn't mean anything." He said that doctors and officials continue to use "undertaker," although the telephone directory has recognized the new term and now has a listing for "funeral directors." He added that some practitioners prefer "funeral director" simply because "it sounds more chichi, but personally I don't mind." As to other euphemisms—avoidance of words which connote death, "space" for "grave," "expire" for "die," "Mr. Jones" for "corpse," and so on—he did not think these would catch on in England. "The attitude of the general public is, it's a practical thing—if you don't want to say anything about it, just don't mention it."

All of this led directly to the subject of embalming; if there is to be no viewing, why then embalm? Mainly, for the convenience of the funeral establishment personnel. There is an average lapse of four to six days in London between death and the funeral (it takes one full day to get a grave dug) and, said Mr. Ashton, "the unpleasantness can be simply appalling."

There is no restorative work done at Mr. Ashton's place, and no cosmetics are used. Although he embalms routinely, without seeking permission of the family, he has not had any complaints. Over the past ten years there have been perhaps three people who had specifically requested that there be no embalming: "When there's been a long series of operations before death, somebody may say, 'I don't want 'er cut abaht any more,' " he explained. He agreed that the argument that embalming benefits the public health by preventing spread of disease is not well founded: "We've tried to prove the disease factor, but we can't—we'll have to accept the pathologists' view on that."

The complicated procedures required by English law relating to obtaining the death certificate have often been condemned in American funeral circles; I wondered whether there were any efforts afoot by English undertakers to get the law changed. Quite abortively, said Mr. Ashton, there are attempts in that direction; in fact, he himself is a member of a Home Office "working party" initiated by the Cremation Authorities to simplify the law and speed up the process of getting the death certificate. "But I'm absolutely outnumbered on that," he said cheerfully. "The doctors are dead against it, because the embalming process can hide certain poisons, makes crime detection very difficult."

Having in mind the "do-it-yourself" efforts of certain American funeral reform groups, I asked whether in England it would be possible for a survivor to bypass the funeral establishment altogether and take the deceased directly to the crematorium. Such a thing actually did happen once in Mr. Ashton's experience. Two young men drove up in a Bedford van and said they wanted to buy a coffin. Mr. Ashton told them he didn't sell coffins, he sold funerals. The young men insisted they did not wish a funeral; their mother had died, they had procured a properly issued death certificate, they had been out to the Enfield Crematorium to make all arrangements, they intended to buy a coffin and take the mother out there themselves. "We chatted and chatted," Mr. Ashton recalled. "Finally I was convinced they were on the level, so I sold them a coffin. What could I do? They weren't doing anything wrong, there was nothing to stop them. But it really shook me. Afterwards I rang up the chap at the crematorium. I said, 'Did that shake you? It shook me.'"

My final question was about "pre-need" arrangements;

is there much buying and selling of graves and funeral service to those in the prime of life? Practically none, it seems. You can reserve a grave space, but it is almost never done. Once in a great while, said Mr. Ashton, some old lady may come round to his establishment, explain she is all alone in the world and feeling poorly, and ask him to take care of all arrangements when her day comes. "We just put her name in our N.Y.D. file," he said. "Meaning?" "Not Yet Dead, don't you know. But nine times out of ten she'll start feeling much better, might live another twenty years."

Throughout our discussion Mr. Ashton impressed me as a realistic businessman, a kindly and responsible person, straightforward and practical in his approach to his work, with a good dash of wit in his makeup. One cannot even quarrel with the innovations he has introduced; the pleasant appearance of his premises is undoubtedly an improvement over the forbidding London undertaking establishments of years ago. It reflects concern for the comfort of those he must deal with, but does not remotely approach the plush palaces of death to be found everywhere in America. Whatever one may think of his practice of embalming all, at least he advanced truthful and comprehensible reasons for so doing.

If Mr. Ashton is a typical representative of the English undertaking trade, traditional English attitudes towards the disposal of the dead may after all be safe from the innovators for some time to come.

15

THE NEWEST PROFESSION

Funeral directors are members of an exalted, almost sacred calling . . . the Executive Committee believed that a cut in prices would be suicidal, and notified the manufacturers that better goods, rather than lower prices, were needed. . . . A $1,000 prize was offered for the best appearing corpse after 60 days. . . . A resolution was passed requesting the newspapers in reporting the proceedings to refrain from flippancy.

Sunnyside,* 1885

THESE OBSERVATIONS are culled from an 1885 report describing the proceedings of one of the earliest National Funeral Directors Association conventions. Almost eighty years later, the problems they reflect continue to occupy the attention of the undertaking trade: how to be exalted, almost sacred, and at the same time be successful businessmen in a highly competitive situation; how to continually upgrade their peculiar product; how to establish successful relations with press and public.

The special public relations problem that dogs the undertaker has existed for all time, arising out of the very nature of his occupation. It is uphill work to present it attractively, but he tries, perhaps too hard. Of late years he has compounded his built-in dilemma by veering off in

---

*This journal later merged with *The Casket*. The result: *Casket and Sunnyside. Sunnyside* had for a time a short-lived competitor named *Shadyside*.

his own weird direction towards a cult of the dead unsanctioned by tradition, religion, or common sense. He has painted himself into a difficult corner. His major justifications for his practices fly in the face of reality, but he persists; the fantasy he has created, and in which he by now has so much cash invested, must somehow be made desirable to the buying public. And, like every other successful salesman, the funeral salesman must first and foremost believe in himself and his product.

He is in any case not just a funeral salesman. There is the creative aspect of his work, the aesthetically rewarding task of transforming the corpse into a Beautiful Memory Picture. Pride of craftsmanship, fascination with technique and continuous striving for improvement shine through all that he writes on this subject.

The sort of passionate devotion it is possible to develop for embalming, the true Art for Art's Sake approach, is captured in a testimonial letter published as part of an advertisement for Cosmetic Tru-Lanol Arterial Fluid. Like any other craftsman, the embalmer gets satisfaction from rising to a challenge and often hates to part with his finished product. The letter describes an unusually difficult case: "The subject . . . was a 69-year-old lady, 5'2" tall with 48" bust and 48" hips. Death was a sudden heart attack. She lay 40 hours in a heated apartment prior to being moved." The writer goes on to mention other inauspicious circumstances surrounding the case, such as a series of punctures made in the center of circulation by some bungler in the Medical Examiner's office. However, Tru-Lanol comes to the rescue: "Surface penetration was slow and even, with excellent cosmetic results. . . . By the fourth day, the swelling in the features was receding in a very uniform manner, and the cosmetic was still excellent. Honestly, I don't know of another fluid that would have done as good a job in this case, all things considered." He adds wistfully, "I wish I could have kept her for four more days." How poignant those last words! And, in a way, how very understandable.

Every craft develops its outstanding practitioners, those

who seem to live for the sake of their work. Such a one
is Elizabeth "Ma" Green, born in 1884, a true zealot of
funeral service. *Mortuary Management,* in a recent tribute
to this unusual woman, recalls that "Ma" got her start
in a life-long career of embalming as a teen-ager: "It was
during this early period of her life that she became interested in caring for the dead. As this interest increased, she
assisted the village undertaker in the care and preparation
of family friends who passed away." "Ma" never looked
back. By the early twenties she had become a licensed
embalmer, and later took a job as principal of an
embalming college. She has been in this work, woman and
girl, some sixty years: "It was obvious she had an almost
passionate devotion to the Profession."

Funeral people are always saying that "funerals are for
the living," yet there is occasional evidence that they
have developed an eerie affection, a genuine solicitude,
for the dead, in whose company they spend so much
time. It is as though they really attribute feelings to these
mute remains of humanity, much as a small child attributes
feelings to his Teddy bear, and that they are actually
concerned with the comfort and well-being of the bodies
entrusted to their care. A 1921 issue of *The Casket*
describes a chemical which "when sprayed into the mouth
of a cadaver, prevents and stops the development of
pyorrhea." An advertisement in the trade press for Flying
Tiger Airlines is headed THIS TIGER CARES: "This kind
of caring has made Flying Tigers the most experienced
air shipper of human remains. There's Tigers' exclusive
Human Remains log. . . ." In Massachusetts, proposed
legislation approved by the funeral industry would make
it an offense to "use profane, indecent or obscene
language in the presence of a dead body."

When the funeral practitioner puts pen to paper on
his favorite subject, the results are truly dreamy flights
of rhapsody. Mr. John H. Eckels says in his textbook,
Modern Mortuary Science, that "The American method
of arterial embalming . . . but adds another laurel to
the crown of inventiveness, ingenuity, and scientific re-

search which the world universally accords to us. . . . In fact, there is no profession on record which has made such rapid advancement in this country as embalming. . . . In summing up this whole situation, the funeral profession today is one of the most vital callings in the cause of humanity. Funeral directors are the advance guards of civilization. . . ." These vivid metaphors, these laurels, crowns and advance guards, express with peculiar appropriateness the modern undertaker's fond conception of his work and himself. How to generate equal enthusiasm in the minds of the public for the "funeral profession" is a more difficult problem.

Mr. Edward A. Martin, author of *Psychology of Funeral Service,* sees undertakers in a role "similar to that of a school teacher who knows and believes in his subject but who must find attractive ways to impress it indelibly upon his pupils. Our class consists of more than 150 million Americans, and the task of educating them is one that cannot be accomplished overnight." He adds, "Public opinion is based on the education of the public, which believes what it is told."

There is some evidence that while this great pedagogical process has taken hold most strongly among the funeral men themselves, it has left the public either apathetic or downright hostile. In other words, the funeral men live very largely in a dreamworld of their own making about the "acceptance" of their product in the public mind. They seem to feel that saying something often and loudly enough will somehow make it true. "Sentiment alone is the foundation of our profession!" they cry. "The new funeral director is a Doctor of Grief, or expert in returning abnormal minds to normal in the shortest possible time!"

But the public goes merrily on its way, thinking (when it thinks of the matter at all) that the moneymaking is the foundation of the funeral trade, that the matter of returning abnormal minds to normal is best left in the hands of trained psychiatrists, that it has neither been asked for nor has it voiced its approval of modern funeral practices.

There are really two parts to the particular selling job confronting the funeral industry. The first is that of convincing people of the correctness and essential Americanism of the kind of funeral the industry wants to sell; convincing them, too, that in funerary matters, there is an obligation to adhere closely to standards and procedures established by the funeral directors—who, after all, should know best about these things. The second is that of projecting an ever more exalted image of the purveyors of funerals.

Funeral men constantly seek to justify the style and cost of their product on the basis of "tradition," and on the basis of their theory that current funeral practices are a reflection of characteristically high American standards. The "tradition" theory is a hard one to put across, as we have seen; the facts tend to run in the opposite direction. Therefore certain incantations, Wise Sayings with the power of great inspiration, are frequently invoked to help along the process of indoctrination. There is one in particular which crops up regularly in mortuary circles: a quotation from Gladstone, who is reported to have said, "Show me the manner in which a nation or a community cares for its dead and I will measure with mathematical exactness the tender sympathies of its people, their respect for the law of the land and their loyalty to high ideals." One could wish he were with us in the twentieth century to apply his handy measuring tape to a calendar issued by the W. W. Chambers Mortuary. Over the legend "Beautiful Bodies by Chambers" appears an unusually well endowed, and completely naked, young lady. Another favorite soothsayer is Benjamin Franklin, who is roped in from time to time and quoted as having said, "To know the character of a community, I need only to visit its cemeteries." Wise old Ben! Could he but visit Forest Lawn today, he would have no need to go on to Los Angeles.

In their constant striving for better public relations, funeral men are hampered by their inability to agree on *what* they are, what weight should be given the various roles in which they see themselves, what aspect should be stressed both within the trade and to the public. Is the funeral director primarily merchant, embalmer, lay psychiatrist, or a combination of all these? The pronouncements of his leaders, association heads, writers of trade books and manuals, and other theoreticians of the industry betray the confusion that exists on this point.

"Embalming is the cornerstone upon which the funeral service profession was founded and it has remained so through the years. It is the only facet of service offered by our industry that is not wholly based upon sentiment, with all its attendant weaknesses," editorializes the *American Funeral Director*. The authoritative Messrs. Habenstein and Lamers see it differently. They are of the opinion that funeral service rests primarily on "the psychological skills in human relations necessary to the proper handling of the emotions and dispositions of the bereaved." Still another journal sees it this way: "Merchandising is the lifeblood of the funeral service business. . . ." And, in a laudable effort to reconcile some of these conflicting ideas, there is an article in the *American Funeral Director* headed "Practical Idealism in Funeral Directing," which declares, "The highest of ideals are worthless unless they are properly applied. The funeral director who thinks only in terms of serving would very likely find himself out of business in a year or less. . . . And if he were compelled to close up his establishment what possible use would be all his high ideals and his desire to serve?" And so the Practical Idealist comes back full circle to his role as merchant, to "costs, selling methods, the business end of his costs."

Funeral people are always telling each other about the importance of ethics (not just any old ethics but usually "the *highest* ethics"), sentiment, integrity, standards (again, "the highest"), moral responsibility, frankness, cooperation, character. They exhort each other to be sincere, friendly, dignified, prompt, courteous, calm, pleasant, kindly, sympathetic, good listeners; to speak good English; not to be crude; to join the Masons, Knights of Columbus, Chamber of Commerce, Boy Scouts, P.T.A.; to take part in the Community Chest drive; to be pleasant and fair-dealing with employees and clients alike; not to cuss their competitors; and, it goes without saying, so to conduct themselves that they will be above scandal or slander. In short, they long to be worthy of high regard, to be liked and understood, a most human longing.

Yet, just as one is beginning to think what dears they really are—for the prose is hypnotic by reason of its very repetitiveness—one's eye is caught by this sort of thing in *Mortuary Management:* "You must start treating a child's funeral, from the time of death to the time of burial, as a 'golden opportunity' for building good will and preserving sentiment, without which we wouldn't have any industry at all." Or this in the *National Funeral Service Journal:* "Buying habits are influenced largely by envy and environment. Don't ever overlook the importance of these two factors in estimating the purchasing possibilities or potential of any family. . . . Envy is essentially the same as pride. . . . It is the idea of keeping up with the Joneses. . . . Sometimes it is only necessary to say, '. . . Here is a casket similar to the one the Joneses selected' to insure a selection in a substantially profitable bracket."

Merchants of a rather grubby order, preying on grief, remorse and guilt of survivors, or trained professional men with high standards of ethical conduct?

The funeral men really would vastly prefer to fit the latter category. A discussion has raged for many years in funeral circles around this very question of "professionalism" versus a trade or business status, and the side that contends that undertaking is a profession is winning out in the National Funeral Directors Association.

Once again, it is apparently expected that the mere repetition of the statement will invest it with validity. Sample speeches are hopefully prepared and circulated among Association members: "I am not an undertaker. He served his purpose and passed out of the picture. I am a funeral director. I am a Doctor of Services. We are members of a profession, just as truly as the lawyer, the doctor or the minister."

The striving for "professionalism" is accompanied by a restless search for newer and grander-sounding titles; in 1959, the Commission on Mortuary Education proposed that the terms "funeral director" and "embalmer" should be replaced by the single title "funeral service practitioner." Probably this will happen, for the undertakers have been more successful in changing the language than in any other phase of their public relations work.

At a 1926 meeting of National Selected Morticians, a big step forward was reported by Mr. Hanson, the secretary: "You will be interested to know that some of your men on the Coast have succeeded in getting the classification in the telephone directory changed from 'Undertaker' to 'Funeral Director.' Somebody on the Coast did that last year. Now, I find out that the telephone directory people in Washington, who have the control of the entire Atlantic Seaboard, all the way down the line, are going to do the same thing in every one of our cities. We have gotten Rotary to consider, in their spring board meeting, a changing of the classification there for Rotary. It has been a dickens of a job, but I think it is going to go over."

The minutes of that 1926 meeting, a faded typescript housed in the National Foundation of Funeral Service in Evanston, Illinois, contain another fascinating semantics note. Mr. Hanson relates a little difficulty: "The word 'Morgue' has been used quite a good deal by some of the advertsing firms who advertise their morgue supplies. And so I did not know very much about the classification, but Mr. Patterson had compiled a very fine list of changed words, as he classified them, and so I went after this one advertising firm, to change their terminology and got myself into a little trouble. This one firm advertised their morgue table, which is your regular preparation room table, down in your preparation room, and I wrote to them and asked if they would not make the change and told them why. They wrote back a very nice letter and said,

'We appreciate your calling our attention to a mistake in advertising, we, after our next issue, will change it to embalming table,' which they did. So they call it an embalming table. And they came right back at me and said, 'Now, you have asked us to change that classification. Now, we want to know what we are going to call the table that we take into the home. We used to call that our embalming table.' The result was that I did not know what to call it, and we took it up at the Board meeting and we decided to give them the suggestion of calling it a preparation couch or a mortuary couch. That shows how the people who sell supplies are willing to cooperate with us in the changing of the terminology."

In 1951, *Mortuary Management* reported another example of successful pioneering on this front by National Selected Morticians: "Leave it to N.S.M. to come out with new names for old things. We've passed through the period of the 'back room,' the 'show room,' the 'sales room,' the 'casket display room,' the 'casket room.' Now N.S.M. offers you the 'selection room.' "

A 1949 press release issued by N.F.D.A. on a survey of public attitudes towards the funeral business hopefully asks, "Please Do Not Use the Term 'Undertaker' at the Head of This Story." As late as 1962, the *American Funeral Director* was moved to chide *The New York Times* for its "continued insistence upon using the relatively obsolete and meaningless words 'undertaker' and 'coffin' to the exclusion of the more generally accepted and meaningful ones, 'funeral director' and 'casket.' "

Funeralese has had its ups and downs. The word "morticians," first used in *Embalmers Monthly* for February, 1895, was barred by the *Chicago Tribune* in 1932, "not for lack of sympathy with the ambition of undertakers to be well regarded, but because of it. If they haven't the sense to save themselves from their own lexicographers, we shall not be guilty of abetting them in their folly." "Casket," dating from Civil War days, is denounced by Hawthorne: "a vile modern phrase which compels a person to shrink from the idea of being buried at all." Emily Post uses it, albeit reluctantly: "In spite of the fact that the word coffin is preferred by all people of fastidious taste and that the word casket is never under any circumstances used in the spoken language of these same people, it seems best to follow present-day commercial usage and admit the word casket to these pages."

A network of trade associations reflects the complexity of ambitions and viewpoints within the industry. While one undertaker may (and often does) belong to more than one association, and while the various associations may (and often do) join forces on a specific issue, the associations are not always in accord, for on many questions they represent conflicting economic interests.

The names of the associations are in some cases merely descriptive of the membership they represent: National Funeral Directors Association, Jewish Funeral Directors Association, Negro Funeral Directors Association. Others have chosen more imaginative and even lyrical names: Order of the Golden Rule, Guild of Ethical Practices, Preferred Funeral Directors International, National Association of Approved Morticians, Successful Mortuary Operators International, National Selected Morticians.

The associations with the high-sounding names generally limit membership to one funeral establishment to a community, to enable members to display the "Preferred," "Certified," "Selected," etc. insignia on their advertising material and letterheads. Since there are seven such organizations, it is not unusual to find communities where every undertaker in town belongs to one or the other. To the public, it might seem that to be Preferred, Approved, or Selected denotes some sort of official certification by an outside agency; actually the members Prefer, Approve and Select each other.

The National Selected Morticians is a go-ahead concern numbering among its 700 members some of the largest and most successful firms in the country. "You have to be sponsored by a member and you join by invitation," one of them explained to me.

While all the trade associations like to refer to undertaking as "the profession," their understanding of that term varies widely. N.S.M. seems to use it because it sounds nice, rather than for its full implications. The N.S.M. emphasis is on merchandising, sound business methods. They are in favor of prearranged, pre-financed funerals and price advertising, because their member establishments depend primarily on big volume.

Mr. Wilber Krieger, managing director of N.S.M., is also the director of the National Foundation of Funeral Service in Evanston. Here a school of management is maintained, where courses are offered in Advertising, Market Analysis, Credit and Collection, Ethical Practice, Letter Writing, Sales Techniques in Funeral Service, and so on. The Foundation is housed in a two-story ersatz-Colonial mansion. Among its facilities are a "selection room for Merchandising Research to improve merchandising, to demonstrate lighting (more than five different types in the room), to show arrangements and decoration through the 25-unit balanced line of caskets." The Avenue of Approach and Aisles of Resistance, Mr. Krieger's own brainchildren, are here laid out for all to see. There is also a Vault Selection Room "aimed at helping the funeral director create a 'Quality' atmosphere, conducive to better vault sales" and at showing him how to "increase his burial vault profits by encouraging better sales through better merchandising."

The oldest, largest and most influential of the funeral trade associations is the National Funeral Directors Association, founded in the eighties and today claiming more than 14,000 members. From the beginning, N.F.D.A. has campaigned for professional status; from the beginning their dilemma, still unresolved after the passage of years, was evident. The first code of ethics, adopted in 1884, says, "There is, perhaps, no profession, after that of the sacred ministry, in which a high-toned morality is more imperatively necessary than that of a funeral director's. High moral principles are his only safe guide." But a corollary objective of the organization—that of keeping prices pegged as high as possible—is expressed in a resolution passed in the previous year: "Resolved, that we, as funeral directors, condemn the manufacture of covered caskets at a less price than fifteen dollars for an adult size."

The National Funeral Directors Association services its affiliated state groups through bulletins, keeping watch on legislative developments, lobbying activities, advising member firms on methods of cost accounting and other business procedures. It conducts an annual convention with an average attendance of 4,000 at which casket manufacturers, burial clothing firms, vaultmen and embalming fluid supply houses exhibit their wares. It sends speakers to state conventions. It conducts surveys among its members on operating expenses, income, etc., as well as on such apparently far-afield subjects as reading habits—a 1958 survey reveals with pride that 56.7 per cent of funeral service personnel read "newspapers, trade journals, magazines and books," compared with only 40 per cent for the population as a whole.

The N.F.D.A. concerns itself deeply with public relations, and has issued a couple of films: *Funeral Service—A Part of the American Way* and *To Serve the Living,* prepared in conjunction with the Association of Better Business Bureaus, Inc. Two of the most important public relations aids, the use of which is constantly urged upon its members by the N.F.D.A., are a pamphlet, "Facts Every Family Should Know About Funerals and Interments," issued by the Association of Better Business Bureaus, and "Funeral Service Facts and Figures," issued annually by N.F.D.A.

The Association of Better Business Bureaus is held in high esteem by many people, who regard it as a watchdog organization designed to protect the public from unscrupulous and crooked businessmen. Its stamp of approval on the line of conduct of any enterprise is bound to allay doubts and suspend criticism. I was surprised to find how many of the "facts" every family should know had the familiar ring of N.F.D.A. propaganda, and that the pamphlet, which has been distributed by funeral directors in the hundreds of thousands, closely follows the N.F.D.A. line in all important respects. I asked the B.B.B. where they got the "facts" for the pamphlet; they replied, from the National Funeral Directors Association and other (unidentified) sources. For example, the "fact" given in the pamphlet that "there is an adequate service available in every funeral establishment for every purse and taste" is given "on the basis of information furnished by the N.F.D.A." The "fact" that "most funeral directors do not consider it ethical to advertise prices . . . and this view is shared by a majority of the public" is again "reporting the official position of the N.F.D.A."

"Funeral Service Facts and Figures" purports to be a statistical breakdown of expenses and income for funeral establishments throughout the United States. It is prepared annually by Mr. Eugene F. Foran, a graduate of Brown's Business College in bookkeeping and general business courses, and former executive secretary of the Wisconsin Funeral Directors Association. From it the N.F.D.A. extracts material for general press releases, and for pep talks to the membership. An economist to whom I showed the report and the questionnaire on which it is based clutched his head in despair; he pointed out that the figures are based on a sample in which only 3 per cent of the funeral establishments responded to a mailed questionnaire, that there is no way of knowing whether the responding firms are representative. This, it seems, is not the way reliable statistics are gathered. Reliable or not, they are very useful to N.F.D.A.; as the president of that organization pointed out in a letter to the membership, "Results of these studies recently were (1) referred to in discussions which led to last year's amendment to the Social Security Law, (2) were given to the *Reader's Digest* to counteract some figures in *Jubilee,* (3) proved to a powerful labor union their death benefit expenditures for funerals were close to average, (4) are being used in many states where welfare funeral legislation is being considered."

The Foran report could serve an even more important objective, that of establishing uniform price minimums. But such price-fixing would be a violation of the antitrust laws; so the report is prefaced with a statement: "The National Funeral Directors Association sponsored this study to give you statistics with which you can compare data from your funeral service operation. However, you should not take all or any of the findings of this survey as a suggestion for funeral service pricing in your establishment." This caveat is reminiscent of a legend printed in prominent letters on the wine bricks sold for a time during prohibition: "Do not under any circumstances place this brick in one gallon of water and let it stand at room temperature for one week, since this will cause it to turn into wine, an alcoholic beverage, the manufacture or possession of which is illegal."

The N.F.D.A. has also taken the lead in educational matters. For example, in 1963 it officially changed the name of those centers of higher learning which teach embalming from "embalming schools" to "colleges of mortuary science." In 1930, the N.F.D.A. established an academy of funerary erudition with the scholarly-sounding name Institute of Mortuary Research—the actual function of which was, according to the N.F.D.A.'s official historians, "to disseminate information favorable to organized funeral directing to the various media of communication . . . and to 'trouble-shoot' points of hostility and attacks on the occupation."

Throughout its history the N.F.D.A. has generally acted to boost the educational requirements for licensing of embalmers. The time required for completion of an embalming—or mortuary science—course has crept up by stages from six weeks in 1910 to about twelve months (it varies in different states) at the present time. This trend has not been without opposition in the industry, for the upgrading of the embalmer is likely to carry with it demands for higher wages. Fifteen states now require two years of college and three require one year in addition to "mortuary science" education as a prerequisite for licensure as an embalmer.

However, there are still some six or seven states that require no license at all for the embalmer's boss, the funeral director. And while most states do license funeral directors, all but a handful impose no educational requirements whatsoever. Funeral directors may qualify for a license to practice their trade without so much as a high school diploma. Just what meaning the term "profession" can have when applied to this calling is hard to conceive.

The N.F.D.A. itself sets no educational, moral or ethical standards for membership. In fact, the only personal qualification set forth in its constitution for membership in this "professional organization" is membership in "the white race."

A major reason for the existence of most professioanl organizations is the maintenance of standards of ethical practice among its members, and the disciplining of members who deviate from these standards. Here the N.F.D.A. is in some difficulty, because the practices that have led to the severest public criticism—tricky selling methods and over-charging—are nowhere condemned in its official policy pronouncements. On the contrary, members are more likely to be subjected to discipline, up to and including expulsion, for such offenses as advertising low-cost funerals. *Mortuary Management* comments on this difficulty: "[N.F.D.A.] has little or no control over who belongs. It has to accept any member of an affiliated state association, and that includes everyone from the 'desk and telephone' curbstoner to the 5,000 case a year corporationtion. . . . True, N.F.D.A. has a Code of Ethics. But there are no minimum standards for membership. . . . There is no restriction whatever on the curbstoner. Even an officer of the organization was not long ago peddling cast off preparation room supplies obtained from government surplus."

The N.F.D.A., not to be deterred by a little thing like the realities of a situation, in 1961 issued a ringing cry for professional status: "Before this decade is completed,

professionalism will be a standard for funeral service."
There is more behind this yearning than just the desire
for gentility and recognition. The achievement by undertakers of professional status would be a convenient way
to secure legal sanction for a ban on price advertising,
long an objective of the N.F.D.A. Restrictions on
advertising by businesses are almost invariably invalidated
by the courts on constitutional grounds. Members of the
learned professions, on the other hand, have codes of
ethics, recognized and enforced by law, which prohibit
advertising.

The great majority of undertakers, the low-volume men
whose hopelessly unwieldy method of operating makes
it necessary for them to charge high prices, are fighting for
"professional" status as a weapon against price advertising
and price cutting by their chain-store competitors. The
emerging giants, like Forest Lawn and Utter-McKinley
in California, Walter B. Cooke in New York, W.W.
Chambers in Washington, D.C., and Van Orsdel in Florida whose operating structure depends on ever-increasing
volume, are quite willing to be "businessmen" if this will
facilitate their drive to capture the market at the expense
of the little fellow.

This apparently highly theoretical difference of approach
(whether funeral directing is a business or a profession)
masks a real divergence of interest between the two types
of undertaker. The issue was joined, momentously, in a
recent court case in Florida. The funeral directors'
licensing board of that state had promulgated a regulation
prohibiting price advertising, and had tried to enforce it
by revoking the license of the Van Orsdel mortuaries. The
licensing board contended that funeral directing is a
business, that the advertising restriction was therefore in
restraint of trade.

The organizational split over the question of "professionalism" was expressed in the Van Orsdel case by the
opposing testimony of the heads of two powerful industry
groups. Howard Raether, executive secretary of N.F.D.A.
testified in support of the position that funeral directing

is a profession. Wilber Krieger, managing director of the National Selected Morticians, whose select membership numbers some of the largest establishments in the country, many of them price advertisers, took the opposite view. The newspapers entered the fray with editorial support for the right to advertise. Seldom have appeals to principle so transparently cloaked self-interest.

The outcome was never in doubt, however, and the "professionalists" were completely routed. The Florida District Court of Appeal, in its decision rendered in February, 1962, said, "Undertaking or mortuary practice is a business rather than a profession, and the fact that it is referred to in certain instances in the regulatory statute as a profession does not make it so. . . ."

Possibly the vast gap between desire and reality on this question of professionalism—the contradiction between the high-flown talk of Ethical Values and vexatious commercial necessities—accounts in good measure for the painful sensitivity to criticism evidenced by the funeral men. The slightest suggestion of opposition to any part of their operation, the slightest questioning of their sincerity, virtue and general uprightness, produces howls of anguish and brings them running like so many Brave Little Dutch Boys to plug the holes in the dike.

It is as though generations of music hall jokes, ribald cartoons, literary bons mots of which the undertaker is the butt had produced a deep-seated persecution complex, sometimes bordering on an industry-wide paranoia. The very titles of their speeches reveal this uneasy state of mind. Topics for addresses at a recent convention were: "What Are They Doing To Us?" and "You Are Probably Being Talked About Right Now."

In their relations with the community as a whole, the funeral men carry on a sort of weird shadowboxing, frequently wildly off the mark. There is an old act— possibly originated by the Marx brothers?—in which a bartender is trying to get rid of a bothersome fly. He goes after it with his bar towel, knocking down bottles as he swings; soon the bar is a shambles. Finally the fly settles on his nose and the bartender takes a last swipe, this time with a full bottle—and succeeds in knocking himself out while the fly unconcernedly buzzes off. The funeral industry's approach to public relations is frequently reminiscent of that bartender.

Enemies seem to lurk everywhere—among competitors, of course, but also among the clergy, the medical profession, the tissue banks, the cemetery people, the press. There is hardly an issue of the many funeral trade publications that does not reflect some aspect of this sense of bitter persecution, of being deeply misunderstood and cruelly maligned.

16

THE "NOSY" CLERGY

"To the avaricious churchman there must be provided proof that a funeral investment does not deprive either the church or its pastor of revenue." This extraordinary statement appeared in the *National Funeral Service Journal* for April, 1961, together with the opinion that the three most important reasons for the mounting rash of criticism of funeral service are "religion, avarice and a burning desire for social reform."

The same idea is expressed a little more fully in another issue of the same magazine: "The minister is perhaps our most serious problem, but the one most easily solved. Most religious leaders avoid interference. There are some, however . . . who feel that they must protect their parishioners' financial resources and direct them to a more 'worthy' cause. Some of these men, after finding more dimes than dollars in the collection plate, reach the point of frustration where they vent their unholy anger on the supposedly affluent funeral director."

These are salvos fired in a rather one-sided battle which rages from time to time between some of the clergy and some sections of the funeral industry—one-sided because, while the funeral men are always ready with dukes up to go on the offensive, the average minister is generally unaware that war has been declared.

The issue boils down to this: The funeral men resent the intrusion into their business of clergymen who take it upon themselves to steer parishioners in the direction of moderation in choice of casket and other matters pertaining to the production of the funeral. Many of the clergy, for their part, deplore what they regard as the growing usurpation of their role as counselors in a time of grief and need, and the growing distortion of what they view as an extremely important, solemn religious rite.

Not infrequently the controversy spills over into print. There is a considerable body of church literature on the subject: pamphlets, booklets and ecclesiastical magazine articles which explain the religious significance of the funeral as an expression of faith. These stress the importance of ministerial counsel at the time of death, the spiritual nature of the funeral service, the need to face realistically the facts of life and death, the advisability of giving some thought to the type of funeral desired before the need arises.

Sometimes the advice is taken a step further: "Consider the cost in the context of your stewardship. Thoughts of preservation of a body, coupled with the inflationary pressures of our time, have led some people to excessive expenditures for burial vaults and caskets. Yet, we know that the body shall return to the elements from which it came. . . . This means that we will be conservative in the purchase of casket, burial, and additional services, conserving frequently limited funds to meet the needs of the living. Let us recognize that ordinarily this would also be the desire of the deceased. . . ."

From the funeral director's point of view, these are

fighting words; bad enough on paper, but when followed up by the corporeal presence of a clergyman with the family at the crucial moment of the selection of a casket, they constitute a call to arms. "The man who has the clergyman making the selection for his families does have a nasty problem," wrote an undertaker.

The posing of this nasty problem in the pages of *Mortuary Management* produced some very down-to-earth advice, best relayed by quoting from the correspondence of the funeral directors who participated in the discussion:

There is one possible solution to the problem of ministers accompanying families to the casket display room in an attempt to persuade them to purchase a minimum funeral service. Have a card in each one of the caskets in the display room that indicates the total charge for a standard funeral service including the casket. This card should also clearly describe the casket construction. Then the funeral director should do a little "pre-selling" before taking the family to the showroom. . . . Take the family into the showroom, introduce them to a few caskets, showing them the price card and then say that you realize that the selection of a funeral service is a very intimate and personal thing which the family alone can do and that you want them to be able to do this without the influence of others. At this time, *invite the minister to join you in your office** while the family discusses the selection.

The scheme of separating the minister from the selecting group by "inviting him to join you in your office" is discussed more explicitly by the next writer:

We tell the family to go ahead and look over the caskets in the display room, and that the minister, if he has come with them, will join them later. We tell the minister that we have something we would like to talk to him about privately, and we've found that if we have some questions to ask him, he seems to be flattered that his advice is being sought, and we

*Italics in the original.

can keep him in the private office until the family has actually made its selection.

Just in case the point has not been thoroughly clarified, a third writer describes in further detail how best to lure the unsuspecting man of God from the side of his parishioners:

Ministers seem to be getting into the act more and more, and, in general, becoming more and more inimical to us. . . . We make a point of emphasizing, during our pre-selection period, the idea that making the selection is something that only the family can do. . . . We emphasize this very strongly, particularly if there is a minister around. Also, we make it a point to think up something to talk about, if the minister comes with the family . . . such as the new addition to the church property, their parking problem, the local Boys' Club in which they are interested, their golf game, politics (a red-hot subject in this part of the country, right now!) or anything else that will keep them occupied and happy while the family goes ahead with the selection.

A fourth writer throws in the sponge:

We have this same problem of nosy clergymen in our town, and I am convinced that there is nothing that can be done about the situation. We tried!

Compared with these views, those expressed by the clergy themselves are moderate and even tolerant. Their occasional criticism is mild and reserved. Some of the clergymen with whom I discussed the matter confessed to having been sorely tried from time to time in their dealings with the funeral men. Most of them—including the most outspoken foes of high-priced, showy funerals—made a sharp differentiation between the funeral price gouger and the "honest, ethical mortician." Others felt that the funeral director is in a sense the prisoner of his own wall-to-wall carpeting; that having installed all the expensive gadgetry and luxurious fittings, he is obliged to charge high prices in order to pay for the upkeep of his fancy establishment.

I sought to learn from a number of churchmen of different faiths something of ecclesiastic attitudes towards the funeral service. What are the actual ritualistic requirements, what is the status of the dead body, what the position on "viewing the remains," on the willing of the body for medical research? How closely does the sort of funeral generally provided today conform with the traditions of the church? What, if any, criticisms are there of today's typical funeral service? Should the clergyman participate with the family in making the actual arrangements for the funeral—should he go with them into the selection room? These were some of the questions I asked.

The Right Reverend James A. Pike, Bishop of the Episcopal Diocese of California, came out foursquare in favor of the "nosy" clergy. He urges that the pastor be called in *first*—that is, before the funeral director is consulted—when death occurs. The clergyman should accompany the family to the funeral parlor for the specific purpose of helping them to resist the pressures toward overspending. In any event, the casket, whether pine box or magnificent solid bronze, is, in the Episcopal Church, covered with a funeral pall during the service—"the point being to minimize the showpiece aspects. We feel that earthly remains are not to be made that much of." Although the clergy strongly favor moderation in funeral expense and simplicity of decor, individual freedom in the choice of a coffin is respected: "If people insist on doing something foolish in the matter of funeral expense, that's up to them, of course. What's sometimes wrong is the element of pride, apparently fostered in the advertising approach of some funeral directors. In terms of a remedy, a lot of teaching in advance is needed—the use and purpose of the funeral pall, and why it is our position that the casket should be closed during the service."

What about the practice of displaying the body in a slumber room at the mortuary before the funeral? "This might bring some comfort and peace to the relatives; one can see that the widow might wish a final glance at the deceased. This is a private affair, up to the family to decide." While Bishop Pike is neutral on the matter of the "open casket" beforehand, he is definitely opposed to it during and after the service. "This is not merely my personal view," he said. "Our tradition does not favor the 'viewing of the remains' after the service by those who have come. In other words, when the casket is closed after the preliminary period, it remains closed."

Theologically, Bishop Pike explained, the body has served its sacramental purpose, that of housing the personality of the individual, "which in life to come receives a new, appropriate means of expression and relationship." The remains are not the person, they are rather like discarded clothing; nevertheless, as the outward and visible sign of personality, they are to be treated with respect and reverence. In the same way, the presence of the casket at the funeral service has a symbolic function, much like that of a flag in a parade. There is no objection to cremation; on the contrary, most Protestant clergy think it a very good idea. The memorial service, at which the coffin is not present, is also quite permissible, and this practice is, in fact, on the increase.

Is there any contradiction between the reverent treatment of human remains and bequeathing those remains to medical schools for research purposes? "No, a positive, constructive use of the body for medical research is by no means irreverent. It is in fact a noble and fine thing for a person to make such provision in his will. We believe in the resurrection and the continuous personal life of the individual spirit, not of the earthly remains."

Speaking of the use of flowers at funerals, Bishop Pike explained that while people are free to have flowers sent, this is not encouraged. More and more frequently donations to charity in memory of the deceased are in order. "When many flowers are in fact sent, in many churches they are placed in the narthex or in the transept—except for flowers in the two vases at the altar."

Lastly, Bishop Pike emphasized that the proper place

for a religious funeral service is in church—and *not* in the "chapel" of a mortuary. Protestant ministers will officiate at the funerals of non-church members if asked to do so. Most churches make no charge whatsoever; some churches in the East do make a small charge to those who are not contributing members, "but it's chicken feed compared to the overall cost of the funeral." The family may want to give the verger $5 or $10 ("That's up to them") and the organist generally charges somewhere between $10 and $25. A cause of resentment among ministers, the Bishop said, is the frequent implication that they are being "hired" as "props" by the funeral director, who takes it upon himself to indicate to the family an appropriate amount for the minister's honorarium, then acts as go-between by adding this sum to his own bill, collects it from the family, and in due course passes it along to the minister.

In all of this, there is cold comfort indeed for the funeral director, who is most understandably anxious to put his entire range of goods and services fully at the disposal of the mourners. For, to what avail the art of the embalmer if his handiwork is to be concealed in a closed coffin? Of what use is the "copper casket of SEAMLESS construction, made without joints or seams of any kind," if its seamlessness and freedom from joints are hidden beneath a funeral pall? (Not to speak of the pity of so hiding the Monoseal Coronet, in which "the foot-end cap lining duplicates exactly the designs and materials used in the head-end caps.") What is to become of the "authentic Victorian style chapel, with its rheostat-controlled lighting, deep-piled wall-to-wall carpeting, cushioned pews, soft gold color scheme and Pilcher organ," if funeral services are to be conducted in—of all things—a *church?* And, if the family so desires, with no casket present at all? Lastly, if the minister is to be charged with counseling and comforting the bereaved family, what is then left of the funeral director's "professional" role of grief therapist?

Many of the views expressed by Bishop Pike were

echoed by a Jewish religious leader, Rabbi Sidney
Akselrad, of Temple Beth El, Berkeley, California. He
reminds his congregation that "in Jewish practice, simplicity is the rule. There's no need to go into debt over a
funeral. The Jewish tradition emphasizes a very simple
coffin." He spoke with approval of a Jewish custom in
pre-Hitler Germany; simple, identical coffins were stored
up for rich and poor alike "that there might be no
competition in death." Rabbi Akselrad advises his people
to call three or four funeral establishments: "Ask the cost,
don't be embarrassed to put the question to them." But
he finds that people on the whole do not like to go through
this kind of survey; in most cases, they pick one of the
four establishments he has suggested and settle for that
one.

Although the Jewish faith requires the presence of the
coffin during the funeral service, Rabbi Akselrad does
not, as a general rule, approve of the open-casket
ceremony: "I don't like the display; it's not very Jewish.
I don't like the parade to view the handiwork of the funeral
director, especially *after* the service, which should attempt
in some small way to bridge the gulf between life and
death; the viewing of the remains tends to reopen the
wound." However, like Bishop Pike, the Rabbi felt that
in some cases the immediate family might derive comfort
from looking on the face of the dead.

The elaborate use of flowers at funerals is also not in
keeping with Jewish tradition. Once, the flower people
sent a letter to Rabbi Akselrad complaining of his advice
that flowers be omitted and that instead contributions to
charity in memory of the deceased should be encouraged.
"The letter said, think of how many people in the flower
business would be thrown out of work if this were to
become the practice!" Of slumber room visiting, he
thought this was something of a social experience, where
people gather for a reunion—"So glad to see you" said
all around—but "sometimes the deceased is overlooked."

Rabbi Akselrad related one embarrassing experience
in which a widow begged him to accompany her to the

funeral establishment to help negotiate the price of the funeral. The funeral director quoted $500 as the most inexpensive funeral he offered. The rabbi demurred, saying that he had told the woman she could purchase one for under $400; upon which the funeral director tore up the price tag and said, "You can have this one for $400." Since that time Rabbi Akselrad, who does not like to see members of his congregation put in such a position, has been loath to get involved in the financial end of the funeral.

Not so Reverend Laurance Cross, pastor of the Berkeley Community Church of Berkeley, California. As one who has officiated at more than six thousand funerals, Mr. Cross is a veteran in dealing with undertakers of every kind.

He placed great emphasis on the importance of distinguishing between the fair-minded, ethical undertaker with a conscience and those who use "psychological pressure" to force up the price of a service. "You can't damn them all," he said. "It's not true to portray them as all of a kind." He told of several in his own community—"decent, sincere people, who pursue their work according to the highest ideals." Many of these would like to see far-reaching changes in the approach and practices of the industry; one almost suffered a nervous breakdown because of the sharp business dealings of his partner. "Unfortunately, though, of the two kinds of undertaker the expensive kind dominates," Mr. Cross said.

In relating one of his selection-room skirmishes, he took on aspects of an avenging angel with an Alabama accent—for he hails originally from that state.

The selection-room arrangement described by Mr. Cross had none of the subtleties of the Triangle Plan or the Keystone Approach. "First you come to a magnificent casket—it's like a pink show window. You'd think it was the Queen's jewels on display. The inside is made of beautiful satin, and it's set out on a thick white carpet. You walk along and come to the next one. That's another beauty, maybe in a different pastel shade. You see a few more, and then you come to the absolute end. There aren't any more. Those you have seen are priced around $1,095. For some reason they are all priced like that, in odd figures rather than a round sum. At this point, most people say, 'Well, that's more than I can afford, but he doesn't have any others—I guess I'll have to settle for one of these.' However, if the customer is mean enough to say, 'I haven't got $1,095, we'll have to take the body elsewhere,' then the funeral director opens a door you *never knew existed*."

Shifting angrily in his chair, Mr. Cross warmed to his theme. "You go into another room, where there are maybe half a dozen caskets priced around $895—in less attractive colors than the $1,095 beauties. That's where psychology comes in; the average person who has managed to avoid the $1,095 casket now feels that at least he has saved $200, and will agree to take one for $895. But if you're as mean as the devil, you may still insist that $895 is more than you were prepared to pay. So you go through the same procedure. The funeral director opens yet another door you never knew existed, and here are some priced around $695. If you are so mean that you still won't spend that much, you are led into the last room. The funeral director pulls down a thing that looks like an ironing board, and shows you an ugly casket, maybe purple in color, for $395. The cheap ones are purposely made up in hideous colors, and they have no handles, no lining. If you still won't buy that, you are taken from there through a concrete alleyway as dark as Egypt, you come to a garage where all the funeral cars are parked. There he throws down a picture of what he calls a 'china,' meaning the sort of box they used to bury Chinamen in, in the undertaker's way of talking. It's just six pieces of redwood nailed together."

"How much does he charge for that one?"

"He'll charge anything he can get out of you for it," said the Reverend Mr. Cross, giving that avenging angel look.*

---

*The type of casket arrangement described by Mr. Cross has been criticized by some industry leaders. Mr. Leon S. Utter, dean of the San

I asked Mr. Cross how the "expensive type" of undertaker decides in which room to start a person off; for surely even in the establishment he was describing, consistent overselling would result in a large number of uncollectable bills. In this matter, it seems, nothing is left to chance: "This type uses every intelligent way of judging what there is to judge." The undertaker generally offers to send a car for the person wishing to arrange a funeral, which provides an opportunity to size up the general class of the prospect's home and neighborhood. In the initial, or "arrangement," interview, held in the undertaker's private office before the casket selection, much information can be gleaned under the guise of obtaining necessary data for vital statistics and other records: Where was the deceased employed? What insurance policies did he carry? "And then they all know exactly what the CIO gives in death benefits, what the Pacific Gas and Electric Company allows, and so on. By the end of that interview, there's almost nothing about the financial standing of the customer that they *don't* know."

There is every evidence that the whole funeral industry lives in a state of perpetual exacerbation and alarm over this question of relations with the clergy. It crops up time and again as a subject for panel discussions at conventions: how to woo the clergy, how to fend them off, how to achieve some sort of peaceful coexistence. In 1959 a sociological study on the subject of clergy attitudes to funerals and funeral directors was conducted for the National Funeral Directors Association by Dr. Robert L. Fulton, University of Illinois sociologist.

The results of the survey proved to be something of a mixed bag. For one thing, the Catholics (slightly less than one-third of the total number of participants) tended to be considerably less critical of present-day funeral service

Francisco College of Mortuary Science, writes: "Let's get away from 'hidden merchandise.' They find these hidden rooms and sometimes it's mighty hard to get them back to the main display room. Put some of your better caskets into that hidden room, if you have one. They will find them." (*Mortuary Management's Idea Kit.*)

than the Protestants. Dr. Fulton ascribes the difference of opinion to an underlying difference of fundamental approach to funerals by Catholics and Protestants:

The Catholic priests of our study viewed the funeral as an instrument for prayer and the salvation of the soul. The funeral for them was a ceremony honoring both the memory and the body of the deceased. It was also for them a reminder for the bereaved to prepare for his own death.

The Protestant ministers of our sample, on the other hand, viewed the funeral in terms of the peace and understanding it brings the survivors. The purpose of the funeral, for them, was primarily to comfort the bereaved. It was also seen, of course, as a ceremony which serves to emphasize the hope of a future life.

Some of the tabulations appear to be contradictory, possibly betraying uncertainty in the minds of the participants. A majority of both groups thought the modern-day funeral adequate for its purposes; yet the majority of all the Protestant clergymen polled were also reported as thinking "changes *were* needed." Changes advocated by this majority (especially significant because they strike at the heart of the "standard" funeral service) included a discontinuance of "pagan display" such as the open casket and elaborate use of flowers; more stress on the religious aspect; emphasis on the meaning of death rather than its concealment; and (unkindest cut of all) less expensive funerals.

On the subject of exploitation of grief, it was estimated that a "hard core" of 23 per cent in each religious group believes the funeral director takes advantage of his position for personal gain.

In summing up, Dr. Fulton said:

The results of the survey leave no doubt as to the degree and extent of concern felt by clergymen for the American funeral program. Clergymen, and in particular Protestant clergymen, are gravely disturbed over those aspects of the funeral program which in their eyes are neither necessary nor proper.

The Fulton report was certainly no cause for celebration in funeral circles. Nevertheless some interpreted it optimistically; after all, a majority of all the clergy polled thought that incidents of exploitation of grief were isolated rather than general occurrences; after all, the hard core who believed the funeral industry takes advantage of the bereaved only amounted to 23 per cent. The relatively uncritical attitude of the Catholic clergy was seen as cause for self-congratulation—but not for long.

Shortly after the report was issued, there appeared a blistering article in *Jubilee,* a nationally distributed Roman Catholic monthly. The writers took note of clerical criticism: "Many funerals are not held in church at all, but in synthetic chapels where, in place of a priest, the funeral director administers empathy and semi-classical music." They condemned the prettying up of the body: "Modern embalming, featuring 'that alive look' has enabled corpses to look more and more like window-display mannequins, and visitation with them has become quite popular." They charged the undertakers with setting "a uniform tone which bemused mourners from coast to coast will abide by submissively, irrespective of their personal views on death," and with charging the poor exorbitant prices. "The whole industry," they concluded, "has been moving steadily beyond the reach of satire."

Troubles seldom come singly. The *Jubilee* piece was picked up by *Time* ("with its millions of readers!" wailed a funeral industry public relations man) and by the *Canadian Register,* official organ of the Catholic Church Extension Society. The latter ran a prominently featured editorial and a news story in which it advised readers to contact the Toronto Memorial Society, "a group of citizens who decided four years ago to encourage simplicity, dignity and moderate expense in funeral arrangements. It wishes to discourage 'money standard' thinking concerning funerals."

The funeral men reacted in character. Editorials denounced *Jubilee* as irresponsible, brazen, calumnious, false and malicious; they pointed the finger of scorn at the writers of the *Jubilee* piece "whose qualifications for discussing the subject were not given." They hinted that *Jubilee*, "a so-called Catholic magazine," was parading under false colors: "*Jubilee* is apparently a little known Catholic magazine that does not have approval and backing of the Roman Catholic hierarchy." "While billing itself as 'A Magazine of the Church and Her People,' *Jubilee* is not church-sponsored and does not carry the Imprimatur indicating official church sanction."

Worse was to follow. Mr. James O'Hagan, editor of *Canadian Funeral Service,* rose to the challenge. As reported by a colleague, in terms gently critical of O'Hagan's hasty action, "his Irish hackles were up and stirring when he came to all that criticism and the glowing recommendation for the Memorial Society. . . . And so, perhaps a little testily, he dashed off letters to several archbishops in Canada—asking whether they approved such comments in a Catholic newspaper." Mr. O'Hagan posed these questions to the archbishops: "Do you approve of the general statement of the editor of the *Canadian Register?* Do you approve of the *Canadian Register* advising Catholics to join the Toronto Memorial Society? Is it the official policy of the Catholic Church to approve 'cheaper' funerals simply to save money, no matter the loss to human dignity? Do you agree with the policy of any newspaper that fails to give a complete and truthful analysis of all aspects of any given question?"

A reply came from the Apostolic Delegate, Most Reverend Sebastiano Baggio. It dealt with the Catholic view of death and funerals in the most explicit terms, and left no doubt as to where the Church stands on these matters:

You have inquired whether or not I approve the general statement of the Editor as expressed in this editorial—and I must say that I do. The high cost of funerals is a fact that no one can deny—and the editor lays the blame for this at the door of the general public itself, in its worldly desire to make a showing before neighbours and friends.

This has set a pattern which even the poor are fearful to break for fear of comment. Rarely do funeral directors inquire about the means of the bereaved before encouraging them to have the best for their "loved one."

The Catholic Church has no policy concerning funeral directors—nor about the prices they charge. But the Church teaches the reality and real significance of death—it is a penalty for sin, but it is also the gateway to God in heaven. On Ash Wednesday, the Church's Liturgy crosses the foreheads of the faithful and reminds them, "Remember, man, that thou art dust and to dust thou shalt return." It is most salutary for Christians to look upon the face of death, which should not, therefore, be camouflaged by cosmetics or any other device. When "death" becomes a bad word, it is time for us to make a serious examination of our Christian convictions. . . .

Regarding "cheaper funerals" and the loss of human dignity, let me say this: contemporary English distinguishes between that which is inexpensive and that which is cheap, in the sense of being vulgar. Human dignity is never lost when man acts according to reason, with prudence and moderation, and thus according to his faith and his means. There is no loss in poverty that is unequalled by any other dignity of this earth—it was the only earthly dignity chosen by God for His Divine Son.

Thus for a poor man to choose an inexpensive funeral (if and when such is available) for a loved one is eminently dignified, for it is in keeping with faith, reason and common sense. When a poor man attempts to make a lavish display— with all the modern trappings of questionable taste—that is obviously beyond his means, it is then that he suffers a loss of dignity and has put on an expensive show that has been cheap and vulgar.

In view of the growing public sentiment, as evidenced by editorial comment in various publications, that the cost of dying is getting out of all proportion, it might be well for the association of Funeral Directors to make an "agonizing reappraisal" not only of price structures but also of pagan customs and trappings that have crept into the industry. The alternative may well be that Christian communities, in their dissatisfaction, will set up cooperatives to operate according to the dictates of Christian conscience and to their means. . . .

Such is the myopia of the funeral men that despite the forthright words of Archbishop Baggio, the editor of the *American Funeral Director* was in September, 1961, still writing about "distortions of the discredited *Jubilee* article." Distorting what, and discredited by whom, one wonders.

The Protestants and Catholics had been heard from. In early 1962, the Conservative United Synagogues of America were considering a proposal of their Committee on Funerals which would put funerals under synagogue control. The synagogue would negotiate the fee with the funeral director—$300 was the proposed limit—and would make all arrangements for burial. If cooperation was not forthcoming from existing funeral establishments, it was suggested that the synagogues should establish their own funeral facilities. Pine coffins with a black covering should be used by all members, the committee report declared; the use of vaults should be discouraged because they are not in keeping with the Jewish tradition. There should be no viewing and the coffin should not be opened; therefore fancy clothes for the deceased would be unnecessary.

Casket and Sunnyside reported, in March, 1962, "Counter measures are being taken by the Jewish Funeral Directors of America" and Awareness Meetings set "to arouse funeral directors to the dangers confronting them."

It should not be supposed from the foregoing that there are no clerical supporters of the funeral industry and its methods. An enthusiastic partisan of the funeral directors is Dr. William Clyd Donald II, pastor of Bethel Church in Detroit. He often speaks at their meetings and contributes to their journals. He is very keen on the idea of funeral directors being grief therapists, and in fact goes a step further; in his view, people do not merely come to them for the drear task of making necessary funeral arrangements—"When they come to you, first of all, they are actually seeking some answer to the meaning of life. They are also seeking to assert the individuality of the deceased."

Dr. Donald is heartily opposed to any effort on the part of a clergyman to intercede in the monetary transaction. The following exchange is reported in the official proceedings of the 76th Annual Convention of the National Funeral Directors' Association:

Mr. J.A. Walters, of the District of Columbia asked:

What would you recommend in a situation where the clergyman goes into your display room with the family and takes them right to the lowest priced unit that you have in the display room and tells them that is good enough? Particularly one time the family called up after they had been recommended by the minister to the lowest price unit and they said they would be interested in a solid mahogany casket but inasmuch as Rev. Blank had recommended this, they would probably use this instead of using the better unit. . . . And only yesterday the minister in question came in with another family and he said, "I understand you have something that you don't have in your display room here that is a little more reasonable and the next time I come in I would like to see that."

Answered the gentle minister of the gospel:

If I were a funeral director and Rev. Blank came in with a family and went over to the cheapest unit in the display room, I would suggest to the family they buy it for him and I would put him in it. (Laughter.)

17

PRESS AND PROTEST

For as long as anyone now alive can remember, our traditional American way of caring for and remembering the dead has been subjected to criticism.

—*American Funeral Director*
June 1961

To HEAR the funeral men complain about the bad press they get, one might think they are the target of a huge newspaper and magazine conspiracy to defame and slander them, to tease them and laugh at them, and eventually to ruin them.

Actually, they have not fared too badly. There have been in the last forty years perhaps half a dozen full-length, documented exposés of the funeral trade in national magazines of large circulation, occasional short items in *Time, Newsweek, Business Week* and the like, and a few feature stories in metropolitan newspapers.

Industry leaders spend an enormous amount of time worrrying over these articles. Criticism, and how to deal with it; projected magazine articles, and how to get them suppressed; threatened legislation, and how to forestall it; these are their major preoccupations. If all else fails, they snarl at the world from the pages of the funeral trade

press, like angry dogs behind a fence unable to get to
grips with the enemy.

Two articles, published a decade apart, caused particular
consternation and alarm within the industry: "The High
Cost of Dying" by Bill Davidson, which appeared in *Collier's* magazine in May, 1951, and "Can You Afford to
Die?" by Roul Tunley, in *The Saturday Evening Post*
of June 17, 1961.

The Davidson piece very nearly triggered a major
upset for the funeral industry, at least in California. It
was the most comprehensive statement on the industry that
had thus far appeared, it was detailed and well documented, and it made some very specific charges: "Even
this honest majority of undertakers is guilty of accepting
a mysterious, nation-wide fixing and raising of prices,"
and "The burial industry's great lobbying and political
strength enables it to cow a significant number of legislators and jurists and do pretty much as it pleases. . . .
The lobbying is spearheaded in the state legislatures by
associations of funeral directors and cemeteries."

The funeral press reacted, as usual, like a rather inefficient bull confronted with a red flag. In a brave attempt
at incisive sarcasm, *Mortuary Management* prefaced an
editorial: "Coal is black and dirty. A Collier is 'a vessel
for transporting coal'—Webster." The words "Shabby handling!" and "Dirty journalism!" reverberated through its
pages. Forest Lawn's spokesman, Ugene Blalock, called
it "an invitation to socialism." But what was to follow
required a subtler and more sophisticated approach than
mere angry denunciation.

Because the article dealt quite fully with funeral industry abuses in California, the legislature of that state
launched an official investigation of "Funeral Directors,
Embalmers, Morticians and Funeral Establishments." For
a while it looked as though real trouble was in store. The
resolution creating the investigating committee mentioned
"need for closer regulation" of funeral establishments and
"needed revision of laws" relating to the funeral business.
The funeral men were thrown into a state of alarm and

confusion; should they or shouldn't they answer the questionnaires sent out by the legislative committee? ("Don't be in too big a hurry to complete and send in your questionnaire," counseled *Mortuary Management*.) Should they or should they not cooperate with the committee's investigators?

This consternation in the ranks proved to have been unwarranted, for their interests were being more than adequately protected. The committee's report, when it finally appeared in June, 1953, over the signature of Assemblyman Clayton A. Dills, must have been cause for much rejoicing and self-congratulation in funeral circles. What a relief to read, after the months of nagging uncertainty, "The funeral industry of California is unsually well organized for the public interest. . . . Criticisms of retail prices overlook the high operating costs, many of which are mandatory under the public health laws, while others are required under social and religious custom and the stress of emotion. . . . It is the considered opinion of the committee that no further legislative action is needed in this matter."

The report has a strangely familiar ring to anybody versed in the thought processes and literary style of funeral directors. There are phrases that could have come directly out of the proceedings of a National Funeral Directors Association convention: "Embalming is first and foremost an essential public health measure. A concomitant function, which developed with the evolution of embalming and funeral directing as a distinct vocation, is to restore the features of the deceased to a serene and natural appearance. Both functions demand a high degree of professional skill based on specialized education and training." There is mention of the "evolution of the funeral director as a part of the American way of life"; there is praise for the funeral home with its "special features planned and furnished to provide facilities and conveniences to serve the living and reverently prepare the dead for burial." The Association of Better Business Bureaus pamphlet "Facts Every Family Should Know" (itself based on material furnished by the N.F.D.A.) is reproduced in its entirety as part of the report.

Was this report really written by a subcommittee of the California State Assembly? Apparently not. A more plausible explanation of how it came to be written is contained in a letter which came recently into my possession. The letter, dated July 24, 1953, is from J. Wilfred Corr, then Executive Secretary of the California Funeral Directors Association, and is addressed to Mr. Wilber M. Krieger, head of the National Selected Morticians:

DEAR MR. KRIEGER,

Thank you for your letter dated July 21 congratulating us on the Dills Committee Report and requesting 12 copies. The 12 copies of the report will be mailed to you under separate cover.

I want to correct a possible wrong impression as indicated in the first sentence of your letter. You congratulated us on "the very fine report that you have prepared and presented to the Dills Committee." Although this may be one hundred per cent correct, it should be presumed that this is a report of and by the Dills Committee, perhaps with some assistance.

Actually Warwick Carpenter and Don Welch wrote the report. I engineered the acceptance of the report by Dills and the actual filing of the report, which was interesting. One member of the committee actually read the report. He was the Assemblyman from Glendale* and Forest Lawn naturally wanted the report filed. He approved the report and his approval was acceptable to the others.

Sometime when we are in personal conversation, I would like to tell you more about the actual engineering of this affair. In the meantime, as you realize, the mechanics of this accomplishment should be kept confidential.

                          Cordially yours,
                          J. WILFRED CORR

Mr. J. Wilfred Corr is today the Executive Director of the American Institute of Funeral Directors. He contributes occasional articles to *Mortuary Management* in which

*Home of Forest Lawn Memorial-Park.

he likes to make ringing appeals for ever-higher ethical standards for funeral directors: "Perhaps we will live to see the triumph of ethical practices, born of American competition, fair dealing and common honesty." Mr. Donald Welch is one of California's most prosperous undertakers and the owner of a number of Southern California mortuaries. Mr. Warwick Carpenter is a market analyst who prepared the statistics on funeral costs used in the legislative committee report. According to *Mortuary Management*, the statistics were originally developed by Mr. Carpenter for Mr. Welch, "to illustrate an address he made before a national convention of funeral directors." *Mortuary Management* opines that Mr. Carpenter "performed a very helpful service to funeral directors in California now under investigation." The Assemblyman from Glendale who actually read the report was the Hon. H. Allen Smith, now a Congressman.

The report itself has since been liberally circulated by the undertakers, who rather naturally see it as a first-rate public relations aid.

The ten years following the *Collier's* article were relatively tranquil ones for the funeral industry, at least so far as the press was a matter of concern. Mr. Merle Welsh, president of the National Funeral Directors Association, was able to report to the 1959 convention: "By our constant vigil there is a lessening of the derogatory and sensational in written matter. Several articles of which we have been appraised of have either not been written or were watered down versions of that which they were originally intended."

A year later, *Casket and Sunnyside* made the same point: "For many years only a very few derogatory articles about funeral service have been printed in national publications. . . . Many times the information that an author is planning such an article is leaked to a state association officer or to N.F.D.A., so that the proper and accurate information may be given such writer without his asking for it. In practically all such instances, such proposed articles either never appear or appear without their 'sensational exposé,' entirely different articles than were at first planned."

The funeral men were far from easy in their minds, however, for a new peril was appearing on the horizon. Said Mr. Welsh, "I could speak for hours on the problems and rumors of problems besetting funeral service as a result of the times. . . . There are memorial societies and church groups trying to reform funeral practices. There are promoters telling funeral directors to take on a plan or plans or else. There are writers who would like to reduce the American funeral program to a $150 disposal plan. . . . While it is true we have patches of blue in our sky through which shines the light of professionality, there are also dark clouds involving crusades, promotions, unjustifiable attacks and designs to replace the American funeral program of to each his own with a $150 disposal plan."

There is a semifictional character, who often crops up in lawyers' talk, known as the "man of ordinary prudence." He is a person of common sense, able to look at transactions with a normal degree of sophistication, to put a reasonable interpretation on evidence, to apply rational standards to all sorts of situations. He has, down the ages, often given the undertakers trouble; but never, it would seem, so much trouble as he is giving them in America today. He is, in fact, their worst enemy.

It is he who grins out at the funeral men from the pages of magazines, frowns at them from the probate bench, speaks harshly of them from the pulpit or from the autopsist's disecting room. It is he who writes nasty letters to the newspapers about them, and derides them in private conversation. The burden of his criticism has changed little over the years. He thinks showy funerals are in bad taste and are a waste of money. He thinks some undertakers take advantage of the grief-stricken for financial gain. He thinks the poor and uneducated are especially vulnerable to this form of exploitation when a member of the family dies. Lately, he has begun to think that there are important uses to which a dead body could be put for the benefit of the living—medical research, eye banks, tissue banks and the like. More significantly, he is taking some practical measures to provide a rational alternative to the American way of death. Over the past few years, some 85 funeral societies (or memorial associations) have been established in the United States and Canada, devoted to the principle of "simple, dignified funerals at a reasonable cost."

This is, from the undertaker's point of view, a particularly vile form of sedition. The *National Funeral Service Journal* (April, 1961) denounces funeral society advocates as "The burial beatniks of contemporary America . . . far more dangerous than the average funeral director realizes, for they are fanatics; they are the paraders for human rights, the picketers of meetings and institutions that displease them, the shouters and hecklers and demonstrators for any number of causes." Whether the mild-mannered clergymen, professors and social workers who form the backbone of the funeral societies would recognize themselves in this word picture is uncertain, but it is a fairly typical funeral trade reaction to any suggested deviation from their established procedures.

The funeral society people were not the first critics of American funeral practices, nor are they indeed the harshest;* they were merely the first to think in terms of an organization through which an alternative to the "standard funeral" might be made available to the public. It is the organizational aspect that terrifies the undertakers, and that gives rise to purple passages in the trade press:

"An atomic attack on our Christian funeral customs . . ."

". . . hang over our heads like the fabled sword of Damocles."

"The Memorial Associations are like all the other selfish interest groups that infest the American way of life like so many weasels sucking away at the life blood of our basic economy."

*See Chapter Notes.

"Those who seek to destroy the very foundation of the American funeral program are making headway."

"What do we do about this menace? How do we fight it?"

"It poses a threat to religion itself."

"Those who promote it are in the same class with the demagogue, faddist, and do-gooder who from time to time in history has jumped on his horse and ridden off in different directions."

"Some telling blows have been struck directly at the heart of funeral service recently. So far we have been able to roll with the punch. But we must come back championing our heritage. We cannot throw in the towel or fight the way the enemy wants us to. To compromise or do what the opposition does is to lose forever the finest funeral standards in the world."

"The very concept of the memorial society is alien to every principle of the American way of life. Therefore, it must be opposed with every ounce of decency we can muster."

What, then, is the "concept of the memorial society" against which these ounces of decency must be mustered? It is set forth in a pamphlet issued by the Cooperative League of the U.S.A., titled "Memorial Associations, What They Are, How They Are Organized":

Memorial associations and their members seek modesty, simplicity and dignity in the final arrangements over which they have control. This concern for spiritual over material values has revealed that a "decent burial" or other arrangement need not be elaborate. . . . Some families wish to avoid funerals and burials altogether. They prefer cremation and a memorial service later, at which the life of the deceased and the spiritual aspects of death are emphasized, without an open casket and too many flowers.

Still others want to will their bodies to a medical school for teaching and research. They also may offer their eyes to an eye bank so the corneas may be transplanted and the blind may see.

Whether it's an unostentatious funeral, a simple burial, cremation, a memorial service, or a concern for medical science, these people want dignified and economical final arrangements. Accordingly they have organized several kinds of memorial associations in more than a dozen states and several Canadian provinces. . . .

Even for the person whose family wants the conventional funeral and burial, membership in a memorial association offers support and counsel in achieving simplicity, dignity, and economy in a service that centers not on public display of the body but on the meaning of death.

Above all, the memorial association provides the opportunity for individuals to have the kind of facilities and services they choose at what is perhaps the most mysterious moment of all.

With these modest objectives, a number of associations came into being in the late fifties. They were organized for the most part by Unitarians, Quakers and other Protestant church groups; they flourished best in the quiet backwaters of university towns; their recruits came from youngish, middle-income people in the academic and professional world rather than from the lower income brackets, or, as the *National Funeral Service Journal* put it, "The movement appeals most strongly to the visionary, ivory tower eggheads of the academic fraternity."

Some of the societies function as educational organizations and limit themselves to advocacy of "rationally preplanned final arrangements." Most, however, have gone a step further and through collective bargaining have secured contracts with one or more funeral establishments to supply the "simple funeral" for members at an agreed-on sum, generally around $100. There is some diversity of outlook in the societies: some emphasize cremation; others are more interested in educational programs advocating bequeathal of bodies to medical schools; still others stress freedom of choice in the matter of burials as their main concern.

All operate as nonprofit organizations, open to everybody, and all are run by unpaid boards of directors. Enrollment fees vary all the way from $2 for an individual "life membership" to $10 covering the whole family; a few groups collect annual dues. The money is used for administrative expenses, printings, mailings and the like, and in a few cases for newspaper advertising. As of 1961, only two of the groups employed paid office help, this on a part-time basis.

A major objective of all the societies is to smooth the path for the family that prefers to hold a memorial service, without the body present, instead of the "open-casket" funeral—and to guarantee that the family will not have to endure a painful clash with the undertaker in making such arrangements. The memorial service idea is most bitterly fought in the trade. With their usual flair for verbal invective, industry spokesman have coined a word for the memorial service: "disposal." "Point out that those who know say the disposal type service without the body present is not good for those who survive," says the President of National Funeral Directors Association. *Casket and Sunnyside's* expert on proper reverence writes, "The increasing support which members of the clergy have been giving to the memorial society movement stems in part from a lack of understanding on the clergy's behalf of what proper reverence for the dead really means to the living. They have little knowledge of the value of sentiment in the therapy of healing."

The idea the funeral industry wants to get across is that a memorial service without the body present is a heartless, cold affair, devoid of meaning for the survivors, in which the corpse has been treated as so much garbage. Actually, the character of a memorial service depends entirely upon the wishes of the family involved. It may be a private affair in a home (or in the chapel of the funeral establishment), or a regular church service conducted according to the custom of the particular denomination. The only distinguishing feature of a memorial service is the absence of the corpse and casket.

My husband recently attended a memorial service for a distinguished California jurist, a warmhearted, public-spirited man whose many affiliations included membership on the advisory board of the Bay Area Funeral Society; he had left instructions that his body was to be given to a medical school. This is how my husband described it to me:

"The service was held in a large Unitarian church. There were two or three hundred people seated when I entered, among them about twenty judges, a great many lawyers, Judge ———'s family sitting among them but up near the front. There were no decorations in the church except for a huge bowl of cut garden flowers in the center of the platform; there was not a single store-bought wreath. (the obituary notices had specified "donations to the Heart Fund preferred.") After some organ music, four men walked up to the platform. One I recognized as a Justice of the State Supreme Court, wearing his judicial robes. He rose first to speak, recalling his many years on the bench as a colleague of Judge ———, giving a warm and vivid personal view of the humane and dedicated, almost saintly character of this man whom he had learned to know and love. He was followed by a rabbi who spoke of the Judge's devoted participation in community welfare activities. There followed remarks by a Congregationalist minister and a Unitarian minister. There was no 'master of ceremonies,' no funeral director overseeing the procedure; there were no ushers in white gloves. When the last speaker had concluded, all four rose and descended from the platform, indicating that the service was over. There being no casket to 'view,' we in attendance filed directly out into the lobby."

The memorial societies might have gone on for years, their rate of growth dependent mainly on word-of-mouth advocacy in very limited circles, had it not been for Roul Tunley's "Can You Afford To Die?" in the June 17, 1961, issue of *The Saturday Evening Post*. This article provided an unlooked-for boost for the tiny memorial associations. With its appearance, the conflict between the funeral industry and the Man of Ordinary Prudence came into the open.

Tunley told the story of the Bay Area Funeral Society, describing its activities in these words: "San Franciscans have lately become witnesses to one of the most bizarre battles in the city's history—a struggle to undermine the funeral directors, or 'bier barons,' and topple the high cost of dying." He concluded that three choices confront the average citizen intent on making a simple, inexpensive exit from the world: "(1) You must make strict arrangements in advance for an austere funeral, a plan which may be upset by your survivors; or (2) you must join a co-operative enterprise like the Bay Area Funeral Society; or (3) you must will your body to some institution. If you do none of these things, statistics show that even the most scrupulous funeral director will probably hand your family a bill for at least $750—a figure that will get your body to the edge of the grave, but not into it. All in all, the final journey will probably be the most expensive ride you've ever taken."

Roul Tunley's article, though milder in tone and less sharply critical of the undertakers than the one in *Collier's*, represented, from the point of view of the industry, a far more potent threat, for it dealt with the kind of practical remedial action which people in any community could take. This put the cat amongst the pigeons. The "bizarre battle" was about to become positively outlandish.

Pandemonium broke loose in the industry, reflected in headlines which appeared in the trade press: SENTIMENT AND MEMORIALIZATION ARE TODAY IN GRAVE DANGER!, MIS-INFORMATION SPREAD AMONG FIFTEEN MILLION AMERICANS!, LORIMER WOULD DISOWN IT!, OR WE'LL ALL HANG SEPARATELY!, and my favorite, in *Mortuary Management*, THEY CAN AFFORD TO DIE!.

There was at first a strong tendency to panic. *Casket and Sunnyside* editorialized:

There is little doubt that funeral service today, beset by powerful adversaries, will buckle under the strain unless there is united action in a common cause by all groups of funeral

directors. If not, funeral service faces the danger of retro-
gressing to a point which we do not care to contemplate.

And the *American Funeral Director*:

Although articles critical of funeral practices have been
published many times before in magazines and newspapers,
there are aspects to this one which are especially disturbing. . . . The article is a persuasive sales talk for the memorial societies which today constitute one of the greatest
threats to the American ideals of memorialization.

And the President of N.F.D.A.:

. . . part of an organized move to abolish the American
funeral program.

From the cacophony of angry voices, a number of
distinct viewpoints could be discerned; differences of
opinion emerged as to the essential nature of the threat.

The editor of *Mortuary Management* wrote:

Offhand, it would appear that memorial societies have the
one aim of reducing the price of funerals. As you study it,
however, you begin to realize that it runs far deeper than
price alone. . . . The leaders in these memorial society
movements are not necessarily poor folk who cannot afford
a standard funeral. Many of them are educated people. Many
are both educated and of substantial means. Their objective
is only partly to force lower funeral prices. Equally strong is
the desire to change established customs. It can be focused
on funerals today and on something else tomorrow. The pro-
mulgations of these outfits hint at Communism and its
brother-in-arms, atheism.

The point that memorial society advocates are not only,
or even perhaps primarily, interested in funeral costs was
expanded by Mr. Sydney H. Heathwood, a public relations
specialist in the funeral field, credited by the *National
Funeral Service Journal* with having, years ago, "origi-

nated and developed the 'Memory Picture' concept which was adopted by the Joint Business Conference and became familiar to the whole profession." Mr. Heathwood sees "the continuing growth of *clerical* criticism" as the fundamental problem facing the funeral men, and says that as a consequence of it, "the past few months have marked a gathering storm—more dangerous, I believe, in its potential harm to the whole profession than anything before it of the kind."

What he finds particularly devastating in the *Post* article are the words of Dr. Josiah Bartlett, Unitarian minister and one of the organizers of the Bay Area Funeral Society: "My people are in increasing rebellion against the pagan atmosphere of the modern funeral. It is not so much the cost as the morbid sentimentality of dwelling on the physical remains," and "[The funeral societies] vowed to work together for simpler and more dignified funerals which are not a vain and wasteful expense and do not emphasize the mortal and material remains rather than the triumph of the human spirit." Mr. Heathwood, in an analysis of the article, concludes: "the criticism of modern funerary refinements is not—in essence—against the costs, as such. Rather, the central part of all the criticism is against the actual goods and services which comprise the modern funeral service." He dismisses as "woolly argument" the charges that "either the critical clergymen are hungry for the funeral director's fees—or their criticism shows that they are halfway communists or fellow-travelers."

The *National Funeral Service Journal,* too, was concerned that the memorial societies might become trend setters in funerary matters: "Unchecked in its early stages, this movement could spread to engulf much of the population, for current funeral customs are based largely on the herd instinct—the doing of a thing because all others do it and because it is the accepted thing to do." And again: "The only thing that will change the custom is for people to become convinced that 'it is the thing to do.' This is what must be guarded against; this is what must be prevented." And again:

The 'average' funeral sale is representative of the lowest point or price at which a client can make a selection without feeling cheap in the eyes of relatives or friends. The current average sale of five or six hundred dollars could easily be reduced considerably by the Memorial Society Movement, clergy criticism and other types of so-called reform. If others wear silk, you feel conspicuous in anything less costly; if others wear burlap, you would feel superior in gingham.

The cemeterians, watching from the sidelines, had some comments. *Concept* struck a discordant and unkind note:

While it is not necessary to be in agreement with the extremity of their protests, it seems significant that there are so many people who are protesting the costs of funeral services through these societies. Certainly there must be some reason for discontent and these people must feel that there is injustice in funeral prices. It is important that members of the cemetery industry realize this before rushing to the defense of the allied burial industries.

Turning the screw a notch, the writer adds, "The cemetery industry has found its answer to high cost through prearrangement."

But has it? Another cemetery writer patiently spelled out for his more complacent colleagues an obvious difficulty for the cemeteries, arising from the tendency of memorial societies to encourage their members to donate their earthly remains to medical science:

What most assuredly results is that the remains are disposed of in a manner other than interment. Consequently, it is axiomatic that these organizations pose a threat to the tradition of earth interment with which our profession is concerned. Memorial associations, therefore, cannot be ignored. I have found, however, that many of my fellow cemeterians are not too concerned over their growth, believing that they may affect others, but never us.

The *American Cemetery* agrees with this appraisal:

Although presently the focal point of their attack is funeral service, the philosophy of the movement is that current American funeral, burial and memorialization practices are largely pagan and wasteful; that they should be greatly simplified; and that regardless of a family's wealth and social position, only modest expenditures should be made for such purposes. If this point of view were to generally prevail, as well it might if not effectively countered, the future of everyone in this field would most certainly be seriously jeopardized.

So does Mr. Frederick Llewellyn, executive vice-president of Forest Lawn Memorial-Park, whose speech to the American Cemetery Association is reported in the *American Cemetery*:

In discussing this trend he mentioned funeral services with closed caskets and the 'please omit flowers' movement. Although these now only directly affect funeral directors, he said, they will ultimately affect cemeterians as well. Even now, he said, there is a trend toward purchasing fewer large burial estates, less expensive memorials and fewer family mausoleums.

He urged that cemeterians join with funeral directors, florists and others in the allied memorial fields in educating the general public, including clergymen and newspapermen, regarding the true meaning of memorialization, especially its religious significance.

The debate on how to handle the memorial society problem, what action to take, what stance to assume, reflects some basic differences of approach within the undertaking trade. *Casket and Sunnyside* calls repeatedly for united action:

We firmly believe that there is one best way to meet this threat as well as to counter the mushrooming growth of the memorial societies and the actual or threatened religious encroachments on our concept of funeral service. That is through the efforts of a highly skilled public relations firm to conduct an extensive public relations program on a national basis. Thus, purely unselfishly on our part, we have called on all funeral service and trade organizations to join in this common endeavor.

Mortuary Management advises lying low and saying little:

We think a serious mistake has been made in parading around over the nation the figures of N.F.D.A.'s economist, Eugene F. Foran. His average adult funeral service charge of $764* has been used for the purpose of telling the public that funerals are not too high. It is fine for the funeral director to possess this information for study but it is dangerous to spread it before the public. . . . Don't make the mistake of engaging in public arguments with memorial society representatives on television or radio to defend the present day American funeral program. That's like shooting craps with the other fellow's dice.

To the extreme annoyance of N.F.D.A. officials, the *Post* article was seized on by insurgents within the industry who had found price advertising and solicitation of prearranged funerals to be profitable. In defiance of N.F.D.A., some of these rushed into print with advertisements substantially agreeing with the *Post*, offering "dignified funerals from $150," and prearrangement programs. "Enemies from within!" cried the N.F.D.A. leadership, and a convention speaker, flourishing one of the advertisements, said, "The ad says that prearranging a funeral protects the family against sentimental overspending. Yes, there are funeral directors who go further than the most critical writers when they tell the world through their ads and brochures that the family must be protected against itself during the emotionally difficult funeral period."

The N.F.D.A.'s line is essentially to hold fast, to refuse

---

*Mortuary Management has erred here. The Foran Report (1961 edition) gives the figure $708.

to have anything to do with the memorial societies, above all to maintain price levels based on the Foran concept of "overhead per case." There are others who see it differently. Mr. Wilber Krieger of National Selected Morticians, while yielding to none in his opposition to the funeral societies, thinks that the industry has brought this development on itself by a lack of flexibility in "serving people as they wish to be served" and by a failure to meet a growing demand for prearranged and pre-financed funerals. In an address to the selected ones, he said "Please don't go out and start shouting before the world, 'My cost per funeral is XXX dollars.' Who cares? More funeral directors do more damage in the public mind by talking all the time about this cost-per-funeral fallacy. Who cares about your costs? . . . I am greatly disturbed at what I am seeing across the country. Where many funeral directors today are showing a minimum over $600, that is not defensible. When we talk about a realistic minimum, we mean a realistic minimum—$150."

If the funeral industry was astir over the *Post* article, no less so were the funeral societies—and particularly the Bay Area Funeral Society. The board members had naturally been pleased that the society was to be the subject of a national magazine article, and had expected there would be some response from readers. But they were completely unprepared for what followed. The headquarters of the Society, consisting of a desk and telephone in the building of the Berkeley Consumers Cooperative, was inundated with letters which poured in at the rate of a thousand a week. Volunteer crews were hastily assembled to help with the huge job of answering the letters and processing applications for membership. The editor of *The Saturday Evening Post* reported an equally astonishing flood of letters to the magazine. He commented, "The article seems to have touched a sensitive nerve." The three members of the Bay Area Society who were mentiond by name in the *Post*, Dr. Josiah Bartlett, Professor Griswold Morley and I, received several hundred letters apiece within the first few weeks; more than a year later, letters are still arriving, sometimes apologetically prefaced, "I only just read 'Can You Afford to Die?' in an old copy of the *Post* at my barber's. . . ."

Even more surprising than the quantity of letters was their quality. Those who are by the nature of their work on the receiving end of letters from the general public—newspaper editors, radio commentators and the like—have told me that a good percentage of the letter writers are crackpots of some kind, that all too seldom does the solid citizen trouble himself to set down his views on paper. The opposite was true of these letters. In tone, they ran the gamut, some bitter, some funny, some reflective; but they were almost without exception intelligent—in many cases deeply thought out—comments on a subject about which the writers obviously felt most strongly. They were indeed evidence of a widespread public revulsion against modern funerary practices the extent of which even the funeral society advocates had never fully realized. Another extraordinary thing about the hundreds of letters I received was that only one took the side of the funeral industry. It was full of invective, it bore no name, it was signed simply "An American Funeral Director." The Bay Area Funeral Society reported but three hostile letters out of the first 1,100.

Some of our correspondents had long since taken matters into their own hands. It seems that a variety of ingenious solutions to the problem are being tried. We learned of the "plain coffin" offered by the St. Leo Shop in Newport, Rhode Island: "For those who would not like to be caught dead in a plush-lined coffin, we offer the traditional plain box of pine, cedar or mahogany, with strong rope handles. Covered with cushions, it doubles as a storage chest and low seat, until needed for its ultimate purpose." And we learned of "the world's first do-it-yourself tombstone kit" offered by a South African inventor: "Selling for $26.50, it is expected to shock traditional monument makers, whose prices generally start at ten times this figure."

We learned of two burial committees connected with

Friends Meetings, one in Ohio, the other in Burnsville, North Carolina. When a member dies, the committee supplies a plain plywood box, places the body in it, and delivers it by station wagon to the crematory or medical school. The next of kin pays for the cost of the lumber in the box plus crematory charges and obituary notices. There is no charge for the committee's services, which include making the box. The total expense is generally under $100. The committee arranges for "help with the children or with food, a lift with the housework, hospitality for visiting relatives—a rallying of friends in a quiet coordinated way." A memorial service is held generally three or four days after death.

A unique do-it-yourself organization flourishes in Chico, California. Its members, in this little community of 15,000, number an amazing 3,000, many of them old-age pensioners. The Chico Christian Burial Society owns its own cemetery and its own refrigerated facilities where unembalmed bodies can be kept for as long as sixty days. The cost of a funeral is $200, which includes coffin, grave, and complete service. Payment is made in small monthly amounts, through a plan operated by the society, which provides funerals for all members, including those not fully paid up. The society, which operates without benefit of undertakers or undertaker's license, has survived a number of attacks. The casket manufacturers refused to furnish them with merchandise; the members responded by making their own coffins. Their right to conduct funerals without a funeral director's or embalmer's license was challenged in court on more than one occasion. The society's response, which proved successful on each occasion, was to point out that it was not engaged in the business of burial; that it was merely a community of neighbors who cooperatively bury each other when the need arises.

A letter from Mr. Irving Baldinger, vice-president of Retail, Wholesale and Department Store Union, Local 65, described the operation of his union's burial benefits program:

The Plan has made arrangements with several reputable funeral establishments in the city to provide a simple but dignified funeral service at a total rate of $175. This cost covers removal and preparation of the remains, a simple casket, use of chapel, hearse and one limousine. The Plan has also purchased sizable tracts of burial grounds in an established New York cemetery (Kensico, at Valhalla, New York). Part of these grounds are located in the Jewish section of Kensico, and the remainder in a non-sectarian section of the same cemetery. The average cost to the Plan for each grave in these grounds is $30. In addition the Plan pays a flat rate of $75 to the cemetery for the service of its crew when a burial takes place. The total cost is therefore $280 for all funeral and burial facilities and services.

When the Plan makes all arrangements, the costs are covered in full with no charge to the family, which may then use the union death benefit to tide it over its period of readjustment.

In the wake of the *Post* article, several other publications took up the subject of disposal of the dead, evoking in each instance spirited response from the funeral industry. The *Reader's Digest* of August, 1961, ran an article "Let the Dead Teach the Living," which pointed to a critical shortage of cadavers for anatomical study in medical schools. Said the *Reader's Digest,* "Every individual who bequeaths his remains to a medical school makes an important contribution to the advance of human knowledge." Said Mr. Howard C. Raether in a speech delivered to the N.F.D.A. convention: "The ultimate of all these programs is to give the entire body to medical science. With no body there is no funeral. If there are no funerals, there are no funeral directors. A word to the wise should be sufficient." Said the *National Funeral Service Journal,* "This is a practice that cannot openly be opposed without branding the funeral directors as being indifferent to the health and welfare of mankind. . . . The loss of a casket sale will create a financial blow in those cases where the body is contributed to a medical school. Fortunately, such cases are infrequent at the present time; unfortunately, they may become more frequent in the future."

Medical Economics, a national physicians' journal, carried a piece describing the participation of doctors in the funeral society movement. A Kentucky pediatrician is quoted as saying, "We should encourage people to use educational, health, or welfare funds as a memorial to the dead rather than throw a lot of money into a barbaric funeral ceremony complete with gussied-up bodies, expensive caskets, parades, and regalia." Mr. Raether, analyzing the article for readers of *Mortuary Management,* explains the reason for such an attitude: "Some doctors report they have an almost automatic feeling of failure when they lose a patient. The funeral director in all but a few cases takes care of the remains after death. Therefore, many doctors have some sort of a subconscious feeling against them because of this situation."

"Death's High Toll," by Abe Magrisso and Donald Rubin, appeared in the Fall, 1961, issue of *I.U.D. Digest,* published by the AFL-CIO. The writers propose "A concerted drive" by organized labor to reduce the cost of dying: "1) Reduced rates for funerals could be obtained from morticians, who, in turn, would be assured a greater volume of business . . . ; 2) Cemetery land can be bought by the acre at greatly reduced prices . . . ; 3) experienced staff members could provide much needed advice to the bereaved and even serve as intermediary to the mortician; 4) such things as flowers and even gravestones could be purchased in quantity and at wholesale prices, with the savings passed on to the bereaved." Mr. Raether, in a convention speech: "There are millions of individuals who belong to labor unions, associations for older persons and other groups. Representatives of these organizations are asking about pre-arranged funeral plans. They are probing to see if they might want something at a greatly reduced price for their members. If, my friends, pre-arrangement is the thing to do and we are to push it then let us get in with both feet but let us at the same time forget about the future of funeral service as we know it today."

The future of funeral service as we know it today? Its fate may indeed be in the balance.

18

NEW HOPE FOR THE DEAD

In the fateful-for-funerals sixties, all sorts of people are sticking their noses in where noses have hitherto not been stuck. Two state legislatures, those of Illinois and Michigan, are conducting investigations into all phases of the funeral and burial business; antitrust lawyers in another state are investigating combinations in restraint of trade in the undertaking business; the California ash-scattering bill, although moribund, is N.Y.D., as Mr. Ashton would say. Two major developments may have a considerable effect on the character of American funerals: defection in the ranks of undertakers from diehard National Funeral Directors Association positions, and the work of memorial soicieities and other consumer groups.

Many of the official pronouncements of funeral industry leaders are falling on deaf ears. Your friendly neighborhood mortician, as Herb Caen calls him, is looking at the bizarre battle rather more realistically than are the full-time organization men who preach at him in trade association meetings and speak for him in public. Those who have contracts with the memorial societies are pleased with the extra business that comes their way because they find that as a practical matter, and in spite of the N.F.D.A.'s strictures to the contrary, the $100 and $150 funerals (in which the wholesale cost of the coffin is about $30) add up to profit at the end of the year. Some of them resent the dictation of the N.F.D.A. and the crude pressures that are brought to bear to get them to sever their ties with the memorial societies.

The contract funeral director for the San Diego Memorial Society wrote to *Mortuary Management:*

Do we have the right to impose on the American people our ideology of funeral rights? The memorial societies of today are the direct result of the funeral industry's efforts to do so, and if the funeral industry does not see the light soon and give this small portion of the American public the right to dispose of their dead in a manner of their choice, then the industry is on its way to self destruction. . . . I was greatly surprised at the gracious way I was accepted by this group, and to see that these people were banded together to procure a right I believe they are entitled to under our free enterprise system. . . . The public that believes in direct disposal and a memorial service later have a religious right to do this and should not be penalized the price of a complete funeral service because of our self-inflicted high overhead. . . . Today, it would seem that funeral directors in general have decided to fight the memorial societies by printing the so-called "blacklists" of cooperating mortuaries, by calling the societies "Socialistic." Yes, in some cases even "Communistic."

When the memorial society people get the chance to explain their position to those in the funeral business, instead of having it explained for them by Mr. Raether and the trade press, there is frequently a most harmonious understanding. In April, 1962, I received an astonishing and rather unnerving telephone call. Would I speak at the

Western Regional Group meeting of National Selected Morticians on the subject of the funeral societies? If they would agree to park their trocars outside, I murmured. . . . Actually, the speech went off very well. The N.S.M. members are awfully polite; they applauded when I was introduced and at the end of my speech. Not a trocar was aimed. Furthermore, I think they really wanted to hear about the memorial societies at firsthand and form their own conclusions. After the meeting, Mr. Robert MacNeur, who had chaired the session, told me that he was initiating a new service at $185 for those who wanted the "simple disposal"; his previous low had been $485.

Two days later, Mr. Francis Wilson, a former president of the California State Board of Funeral Directors and Embalmers, and the owner of one of the largest local funeral establishments, telephoned. He was interested in securing a contract with the Bay Area Funeral Society; he agreed that people should have full freedom of choice in these matters; he would welcome the opportunity to serve the Society's ten thousand members. Would he be expelled from the N.S.M. if he signed a contract with the Society? I asked. No, he had spoken to Mr. Krieger about that. Mr. Krieger had told him that his membership in N.S.M. would not be in jeopardy if he were to sign a contract with the society. And what about N.F.D.A.? He didn't particularly care.

There is no doubt that, impelled by the growth of the funeral societies and by the recent newspaper articles, serious re-evaluation is taking place within the industry. An important indication of this is a current move on the part of the California Funeral Directors Association to get the whole question of prearrangement and pre-financing of funerals re-examined by the national organization.

The memorial society advocates, encouraged by the public response, picked up the odd ball they had chosen to run with and ran. "Power is lying in the streets!" might well have been their slogan.

In April, 1962, the first national gathering devoted to the subject of funeral reform was held in Chicago. More than two dozen societies were represented, out of eighty-five or more now operating in the United States and Canada. Delegates and observers came from California, Washington, Ohio, and a number of Eastern states. There were clergymen, sociologists, housewives, a few trade unionists. The tone of the meeting was far from crusading —it was moderate, reasoned, mild.

Mr. LeRoy Bowman, a sociologist and author of *The American Funeral: A Study in Guilt, Extravagance and Sublimity,* set forth the objectives of the funeral societies in these words.

This is the time to branch out or rather take in those people who always have been interested in this problem. We are concerned not only about the cost of dying, but about the subversion of values practiced by many funeral directors. Most societies believe in simple funerals and lend support for the spiritual rather than the physical. We should not however be a propaganda organization but a cooperative organization. It is valuable to have pamphlets to explain the nature of simple funerals but we should leave the final arrangements to each family or group. We cannot object should people wish more elaborate or expensive funerals.

Mr. Ernest Morgan, from the Society of Friends in Yellow Springs, Ohio, had some words of comfort for the funeral industry:

I will say that the funeral directors have a great deal to gain from the memorial society. They are in a very serious situation. There is a rising tide of bitterness and resentment against them. When people are "taken for a ride" in a financial or emotional situation they become hostile. The memorial society can save funeral directors from the rising tide of resentment against them and can provide the opportunity for people who want simplicity to get it.

The conference voted to establish the Continental Association of Funeral and Memorial Societies, based in Washington, D.C. The function of the association is to keep the member societies informed of new developments, to provide avenues for the establishment of reciprocal membership agreements between societies, to furnish help and advice to groups that are seeking to form new societies.

Are the funeral societies the solution to the problem? There will be those who say the funeral societies do not go nearly far enough. Some will favor the do-it-yourself approach of the burial committees, with perhaps a suitable adaptation for urban areas along the lines of cooperatively owned funeral establishments and crematoria. Others may think the French have provided an answer in offering several classes of state funerals in a wide range of prices that may be purchased directly from the government. Still others will enviously eye Switzerland, where there have been no private undertakers since 1890 and where a free state funeral, carried out by municipal attendants, with free grave, free coffin and free hearse, is the right of every citizen regardless of his financial status.

Whether the narrow passageway to the unknown, which everybody must cross, will continue to be as cluttered and as expensive to traverse as it is today, depends in the last analysis entirely on those travelers who have not yet reached it.*

*Since first publication of *The American Way of Death* in 1963, the state legislatures of Colorado and California have initiated investigations of the funeral business, and the Attorney General of New York State has announced that his office is investigating fraudulent selling techniques by undertakers.

19

POST MORTEM*

THERE HAVE been many changes in the funeral scene and more are on the way, but I must say at the outset that I should be very loath to take credit for these. At most, I may have opened up the subject—in those days, as taboo as sex had been a generation or two earlier—but it was the media, the churches, the growing consumer movement that took up the cry against what the funeral industry refers to as "the traditional American funeral." By this, the funeral men mean the full treatment: display of the embalmed and beautified corpse reposing on an inner-spring or foam-rubber mattress in an elegant "casket"; "visitation" of the deceased in the mortuary "slumber room"; an open-casket ceremony in which the mourners parade around for a last look; a burial vault

*Fourteen years after *The American Way of Death* was published, *McCall's* magazine asked me to take another hard look at funerary customs. The following is adapted from "The Funeral Salesmen," *McCall's*, November 1977.

that allegedly affords "eternal protection"; elaborate "floral tributes" from family and friends; a "final resting place" in a "memorial park" or mausoleum.

The cost of all this? It depends largely on what the traffic will bear. If a widow has, say, $4,000 from her husband's insurance policy, that will likely be the price charged for his funeral. The average cost, nationwide, of a funeral exclusive of burial plot is now conservatively estimated at $1,650, up from $750 at the time I was writing *The American Way of Death*.

For those who prefer a less cluttered and expensive send-off, two major developments offer some hope:

After an intensive two-year study of funeral costs and practices, the Federal Trade Commission's Consumer Protection Bureau has promulgated a "trade rule" which, if adopted, would go far to protect the unwary funeral purchaser in his dealings with undertakers, and would put a stop to widespread abuses and exploitative sales tactics that are today routine, rather than exceptional, in the nation's funeral parlors.

In many part of the country there has been a phenomenal growth of commercial enterprises offering "direct cremation," meaning transportation of the unembalmed body to a crematory where it is reduced to ashes that may be scattered at sea or in a garden. Under this arrangement, which typically costs about $250, the ministrations of an undertaker—and the expense of casket, vault and cemetery plot—are dispensed with altogether. Survivors are then at liberty to plan, according to their religion, philosophy and life-style, whatever kind of memorial they see fit—from formal church obsequies to a community meeting to a simple gathering of friends at home.

The $4-billion funeral industry is not taking all this lying down. The funeral men, faced with the dire prospect of losing their grip on the mortal remains of the Loved One, are fighting back with every means at their command: in the courts through their powerful lobbies in Congress and state legislatures, by developing within their trade associations innovative, evermore subtle selling techniques designed to manipulate the funeral purchaser into doing things their way.

FTC announced its proposed rule in 1975 and as required by law held public hearings in six cities around the country at which consumer groups, industry representatives, clergymen and other interested parties testified for or against the rule and were cross-examined by the other side.

The industry swung into action, responding with its usual belligerence as to a call to arms: "It Will Be a Costly War," declared *The American Funeral Director* in a headline. "The defense will cost a bundle, about $500,000 will be needed for a start . . ." Industry leaders exhorted the rank-and-file undertakers to bring pressure on their elected representatives, and were able to report occasional victories, as when Mr. Thomas H. Clark, counsel for the National Funeral Directors Association, congratulated the Conference of Funeral Service Examining Boards for their successful lobbying efforts: "Many of you were instrumental and helpful in trying to get to the various Congressmen of the United States. . . . You know, we got seventy-three Congressmen and thirteen Senators who signed resolutions condemning the FTC."

Why are the undertakers so deeply upset? The FTC rule would merely bring the funeral transaction into line with normal fair business practices. At the heart of it are these requirements:

Prices must be itemized. The present practice of many mortuaries is to quote a package price based on a multiple of the wholesale cost of the casket, stating that this "includes our full range of services." In states such as New York, New Jersey, Connecticut, California and Minnesota, where recently-enacted laws require a further breakdown, a price will be assigned to the casket (anywhere from a few hundred to several thousand dollars), to which is added "Cost of Professional Services" and a variety of related items: arrangements, counseling, use of slumber room for visitation, embalming, etc., which will typically run from $700 to $800. FTC proposes that the purchaser be given a price list showing the exact cost of each, thus enabling him to choose or refuse such "services" as "counseling," "embalming," "cosmetology," with a corresponding reduction in price of the funeral for any items not wanted.

Permission of next-of-kin must be obtained before embalming. At present, American undertakers embalm routinely without consulting corpse or kin—frequently in violation of the family's wishes or religious beliefs; the Orthodox Jewish faith, for example, expressly forbids embalming as repugnant to Jewish teachings.

Prices must be quoted over the telephone if requested. Attempts by the funeral purchaser to make price comparisons by telephone are generally frustrated by the undertaker, who will politely but firmly insist that "price is too sensitive a matter to be discussed over the telephone."

The most inexpensive casket must be displayed along with the others. Often the cheaper caskets are hidden away in some dim basement or garage, so the purchaser may not even be aware of their existence.

In addition, the rule would penalize undertakers for misrepresentations of fact, such as claiming that embalming and "sealer" caskets afford "eternal protection," or telling survivors that embalming is "required by law" (not true in any state); and it would prohibit efforts on the part of undertakers and their trade organizations to prevent or restrict the offering of low-cost funerals and direct cremation services.

Thus, the rule would guarantee a freedom of choice in funerary matters that does not effectively exist today. It would enable the funeral customer to know what he is paying for, to refuse certain items he may not want, to go to the inexpensive rather than the expensive way if he should so desire. In no way would it inhibit the person who, with eyes open, opts for the funeral of his or her dreams, costing perhaps many thousands of dollars. By requiring disclosure of prices it would stimulate competition based on informed consumer demand — surely, a cardinal principle of American free enterprise.

Yet the funeral industry's response has been to cry "Un-American!"—even to conjure up the specter of Communism; *The American Funeral Director* describes the FTC hearings as "the Soviet-style set-piece staged by FTC."

The rhetoric gets pretty wild. Howard C. Raether, still the industry's most influential spokesman, writing in *The Director,* house organ of the NFDA, lambasts the proposed rule as "a veiled attempt by the FTC staff to reverse the philosophy of American funeral customs, which have been historically developed within our society by the American public to effectively meet their needs when confronted by a death in the family . . . . There is an implication that these rules may bring about that which will be revolutionary."

Mr. John J. Curran, past president of the New York State Funeral Directors Association, goes him one better: testifying at the New York FTC hearing, he called the rule "a threat to the American way of life," and accused FTC of "tampering with the soul of America." The same thought is voiced in *Mortuary Management:* "FTC are trying to force their agnostic, atheistic ways on the God fearing, traditional family-oriented American. . . ."

Thus did the leading spokesman for the industry continue, as they did when I was researching *The American Way of Death*, to equate the fine and fancy open-casket funeral with patriotism, love of God and Country, while condemning as un-American the desire of some for a simple, inexpensive disposal of the dead.

For a breath of sanity, I sought the views of a number of clergymen of various faiths: Catholic, Jewish, Protestant, Unitarian. What did they think of the FTC proposals? Had they noticed any change in attitude on the part of parishioners in funerary matters? Without exception, they reported that the trend in their congregations is away from elaborate, expensive funerals and they applauded the FTC trade rule as long being overdue.

Father Brian Joyce, chancellor of the Catholic Diocese of Oakland, California, says that in the early sixties "it was rare or unheard of" for parishioners to request a plain, inexpensive funeral. Today, he could cite many instances of families who insist upon the simplest — he knows several who have gone so far as to construct their own coffins, simple wooden boxes that can be stored until the need arises. He estimates that since the Catholic Church lifted its ban on cremation, some five percent in his diocese are now cremated, "up from zero a few years ago." In his view, there is a major need for consumer education within the Church, to counteract "peer pressure for ornate funerals as a matter of family pride, which is all wrong."

According to Dr. George Marshall, Unitarian Minister of the Church of the Larger Fellowship in Boston, there has been "a definite change to a more simple approach." A few years ago, Mr. Marshall wrote a doctoral thesis on emotional responses to death: "When people learned I was working on this, I was swamped with horror-stories about gross injustices at the hands of undertakers." These were borne out by his own experiences when accompanying survivors to the mortuary to make funeral arrangements: "I was amazed at the crass way families were treated; the undertaker would switch price cards on the coffins, tailoring the bill to fit the family's pocketbook." He thinks the FTC rule is "a great thing — an opportunity that comes once in a generation, a chance for a real breakthrough."

The Reverend Frederick Fenton, Episcopalian minister of St. Augustine-by-the-Sea in Santa Monica, California, officiates at some thirty funerals a year; about half of these, he says, are cremations. While parishioners are growing more aware of the need to make some provisions ahead of time—and those who do almost invariably decide on cremation followed by a church service without the body present—there are still "terrible things happening in the funeral parlors, the old games are still being played," said Reverend Fenton. "The so-called standard funeral is a consumer rip-off."

He cited an experience of his own family just last year. His father-in-law died suddenly at home. Three women—the widow, and Reverend Fenton's wife and sister-in-law—went to a mortuary in San Bernardino to make arrangements. Bent on securing the simplest possible coffin, they chose the cheapest, a cloth-covered pine box. "The undertaker turned to the widow, and said, 'Your husband was a big man, wasn't he? This casket won't be large enough,' and he led them to a casket in the next-highest price bracket. Upon which my sister-in-law whipped out a tape measure, measured the inner dimensions of both coffins, and found them identical!" Curiously, Reverend Fenton had encountered the exact same sales ploy once before, when accompanying a bereaved parishioner to a funeral parlor. He believes that while the FTC rule would go far to correct many abuses, the Church should provide stronger leadership: "We need more priests and bishops showing the way by bequeathing their remains to medical schools, and counseling parishioners in the direction of moderation."

In Minneapolis, the Adath Jeshurun Congregation has established its own funeral society, devoted to restoring simplicity to the Jewish funeral in accord with Jewish tradition. Rabbi Arnold Goodman, who believes the FTC report "affirms a national scandal," told me that some 150 members of his Congregation provide "a battery of support services: washing and purification of the body, guarding the body during the days between death and funeral, making calls on the family before and after the funeral."

Through arrangement with a local undertaker, who supplies a plain wood box designed b the society, cost is kept under $400 and this is paid by the Congregation rather than by the survivors. But Rabbi Goodman empahasized that lower funeral costs are merely a by-product of the operation: "We're not in it for economic reasons, but for religious reasons," he said. "Simple Jewish funerals just happen to be less expensive." What about open-casket ceremonies? "We have very few of these. It's not a Jewish custom to come and gape at dead people."

There are disturbing indications for the industry that, aside from widespread clergy disapprobation, the "traditional American funeral" may be facing the gravest threat of all in its short history, in the shape of a growing rebellion by the American public-at-large.

Two years ago the Casket Manufacturers Association commissioned a survey on American attitudes to death. The findings are discussed in the January, 1975, issue of *Mortuary Management* under the heading "Preferences for Smaller Funerals Reason for Sober Concern." According to *Mortuary Management,* "If there is any important area of dissatisfaction and unrest, it has to do with funeral prices—what the public erroneously perceives as exorbitant funeral home profits and the high cost of caskets . . . . Among the negative and even ominous findings of the survey are that . . . most people believe the funeral should be smaller and more private . . . . Sixty-four percent agree with the statement that 'funerals should be small and private,' and only thirty percent disagree. (Moreover, twenty-five percent agree *strongly*.)" (Italics in the original.) Furthermore, to the question, "What form of disposition would you prefer for yourself?" fifteen percent answered that they preferred cremation, and fourteen percent opted for donations of their remains to medical schools for scientific research.

This is indeed bad news: almost thirty percent of the potential customers would prefer to bypass the undertaker altogether en route to the Unknown. How is the industry responding to these "negative and even ominous findings"? Mainly, by pulling every conceivable string to assure that the wishes of the thirty percent will not be carried out.

Mr. Raether, moving along with the times, no longer justifies the curious practice of embalming all comers on health grounds, necessary (as he told me when I was preparing *The American Way of Death*) to prevent spread of disease among the living. This theory has been totally discredited—no health purpose is served; the dead do not transmit disease—he has created a new hat for the undertaker to wear: that of "Grief Therapist" or "Counselor" to the grieving family. "Grief Therapy" consists of "viewing" the undertaker's handiwork displayed in a suitable costly container. In his recent pamphlet, "The Funeral Director and His Role as Counselor," published by NFDA, he gives some pointers on how to cajole and bully the survivors into an "open casket" service replete with embalming, "viewing" and "visitation," even though the family does not want this and the deceased had left specific directions to avoid it.

From the first phone call, the funeral director in his "role as counselor" should stick as close to the family as possible; failure to do this, says Mr. Raether, "creates the possibility of other 'counselors' or self-appointed 'advisors' stepping into the void created by the funeral director." Friends, clergy and other third parties present a particular threat: "It is not infrequent that representatives of the family, such as a friend, nurse, doctor, clergyperson or lawyer, may notify the funeral home of the death on behalf of the family . . . . You must remember that sometimes 'third party' callers may seek to act as intervenors for the family. Also, some of these people have set ideas as to what should or should not be done regarding funeralization . . . in this instance it is even more demanding that you evaluate how and when you should make your initial contact for counseling with the family." (How disheartening, then, to run into categorical directives from religious leaders such as this one, issued by Archbishop Joseph T. McGucken of the San Francisco Catholic Archdiocese: "All arrangements regarding funeral services are to be made directly with the parish clergy and not through a funeral director.")

The alert grief counselor may get many a clue from the first phone call as to family preferences that should be nipped in the bud: "Many times the tone of voice of the caller, discussion in the background or the nature of certain requests (no embalming, no funeral, a private funeral or body donation) are indications of need for immediate and individual counseling," writes Mr. Raether. "Most times this counseling is best done on a person-to-person basis, not by phone, and *immediately,* especially prior to the actual arrangement conference"—the latter being mortuary jargon for the clinching of the sale.

Above all, the counselor must find ways of overcoming objections to embalming: "Today, more than ever since its inception, people are questioning the need for embalming . . . We should consider the counseling technique to be used when the family says, 'We don't want any embalming' . . . or 'I don't believe in prettifying the dead.' " The counselor, suggests Mr. Raether, "could counter beautification of the dead with 'body image'. . . ." In any case, he should emphasize that "the therapeutic value of funeralization begins with a properly prepared and presentable body. . . . Oftentimes when a counselor has adequately supported the psychological values in viewing and visitation, all objections by the family are dismissed and the funeral proceeds according to usual procedures."

Lastly, there is the knotty problem created by families who have actually talked things over and arrived at some decisions *before* death occurred. "Another difficult situation," writes Mr. Raether, "is one in which an alternative to the funeral is chosen because of some pre-death directive or agreement. . . . 'He made me promise him there would be no looking at him after he was dead,' or, 'We agreed we'd both have memorial services without the body present.' " The canny counselor can circumvent this, too, according to Mr. Raether: "The counselor should point out that the previous decisions were made in the belief that they were the best for all concerned. Now when that is not the case, certainly changing the decisions so that they will meet the *needs* of all concerned would also be the desire of the deceased." (Mr. Raether fails to caution the hapless counselor that he might then find himself in the toils of the criminal justice system, for the law in California is that the wishes of the deceased regarding disposition of his body must prevail.)

Even if the deceased has made ironclad legal arrangements to bequeath his body to a medical school, all is not yet quite lost, because "after the anatomical study is completed, the entire residue of the body may be claimed in a sealed container for a service of commital and burial." In this case, the counselor "should opt for as much funeralization as possible either before the donation or after or both."

Having overcome all hurdles, the counselor is now ready to get down to the crux of the matter: sale of the casket, in which, Mr. Raether says, "two things should become apparent—the arranger's belief that the casket is the last material gift that can be given to the body, which was once a person, and the desire to have something aesthetically pleasing and/or protective."

But what *is* aesthetically pleasing? After my testimony in favor of the FTC rule at the Los Angeles hearing, it was my privilege to be cross-examined by Mr. Raether himself. Seeking to demonstrate that the undertaker does, indeed, have an obligation as "grief counselor" to guide the funeral purchaser in choice of an aesthetically pleasing casket, he asked some hypothetical questions and I found myself led on a merry chase into the fantasy world of the mortuary:

RAETHER: John Jones dies of a kidney disease. He is jaundiced. His wife is looking at a casket with an interior which will bring out the jaundiced condition. Should he [funeral director] suggest other caskets which would make a more aesthetic picture for the wife and the members of the family?

MITFORD: Well, I like the ideas of the matching casket, the jaundiced-colored one. I mean, if *I* died of jaundice I would rather have a jaundice-colored casket for myself. Just so with scarlet fever, I should have a red one.

RAETHER: Johanna Smith is a heavy person.

MITFORD: We are all getting a little stout.

RAETHER: Her husband is looking at a casket in which the funeral director knows she will not look proper because of the size and the nature of the casket. Should he so advise the husband?

MITFORD: Well, maybe the husband is trying to guy her up a bit. Perhaps he was always saying to her, "You should go on a diet," and now he is just getting even. Who knows?*

For the ingrate who would as soon forgo that last material gift, who does not find aesthetic pleasure in such offerings as the Medallion casket "accented with fine gold shading and impressive antique gold ornamental decor," or "the New American Colonial, authentic American styling" (currently featured in *Mortuary Management*), and who would like to spare his survivors the attentions of Mr. Raether's gang of grief counselors, simple cremation may well be the answer. A family can arrange this at most funeral establishments, but there is a catch: the bill will likely be very little less than that charged for the "traditional American funeral," as the undertaker will still try to sell a casket, embalming and a funeral service with the body present, before cremation.

In most parts of the country, the best hope for the Ultimate Consumer is to join a funeral or memorial society, pioneering nonprofit organizations that through collective bargaining secure contracts with undertakers for "direct disposal" at a small fraction of the going rate. There are now 170 societies in Canada and the United States, with headquarters at the Continental Association of Funeral and Memorial Societies, 1828 L Street, N.W., Washington, D.C. 20036. Although the growth of these societies has been spectacular—up from 17,000 families nationwide in 1963 to 600,000 today—their appeal is necessarily limited to the minority of well-organized souls who look ahead and prearrange their own funerals; and in most cases, one still has to go through the mortuary in transit to the crematorium.

The really new factor, which may herald a fundamental upheaval in American funeral customs, is the sudden success in the past few years of the "burn-and-scatter outfits,"

*FTC transcript, page 7252.

as the undertakers call the proliferating commercial ventures that will do it all—and for all comers—for a fixed fee of around $250, roughly based on the Social Security death benefit. So far, these firms do business principally on the West Coast where their presence has already had a noticeable effect on cremation statistics. Thus, while nationwide the percentage of cremations has almost doubled in thirteen years—up from 3.76 in 1964 to 7.32 in 1976—the rise on the West Coast has been far more dramatic: in 1976, more than forty percent of the West Coast dead were cremated. Judging from the growing popularity—and profitability—of their offerings, it seems safe to predict that the direct cremations chains will eventually spread across the country.

Telophase (the name means "final stage of cell division") was first in the field, organized in 1971 by Tom Sherrard, a lawyer who had been a prime mover in the San Diego Memorial Society, an affiliate of the Continental Association. "I found that even members of the Memorial Society, supposedly well-informed people who knew their own mind, were still being turned around by the Society's contract funeral director," Mr. Sherrard told me. "Through subtle persuasion, he'd maneuver them into taking all sorts of extras when they were at their most vulnerable. I started thinking, Who needs a funeral director? Lots of people would just as soon avoid that firm and friendly handshake, that sincere and sympathetic smile. We were the first to bypass the traditional undertaker-coffin-cemetery routine."

The bypassing was not without its perilous moments. In the early days, Telophase was beset with lawsuits, brought by the Funeral Directors and Embalmers Licensing Board, the Cemetery Board, and by individual cemeteries. Judge after judge ruled for Telophase; to date it has prevailed in 27 separate lawsuits. Furthermore, the funeral-industry lobby caused legislation to be introduced designed to put Telophase out of business by requiring it to have an embalming room and chapel. This seemed likely to pass until the press took up the cry against it: "Mortician-Sponsored

Bill Deserves to Die!" declared the Los Angeles *Times* in an editorial headline, and die it did.

Membership in Telophase, which operates only in Southern California, is currently 23,000, growing at the rate of twenty percent annually. "Our prices are uniform," said Mr. Sherrard. "We offer no frills whatsoever. It's a take-it-or-leave-it proposition; if the family want extras, we send them elsewhere, and if they want a memorial service, that's up to them. We pick up the body, take it to our refrigerated repository, thence to the cemetery after the necessary paperwork is completed. The ashes are usually handed over to the San Diego Ecumenical Council and scattered at sea by a Navy chaplain."

In contrast, the Neptune Society, second largest of the direct cremation chains, offers "a real first-class service at sea," according to its founder, Dr. Charles Denning. Neptune's base price is $255, but for an extra $250 as many as twenty relatives and friends can attend the ash-scattering ceremony on Denning's elegant bar-and-galley equipped yacht. Or, for a fee, survivors may hold a sea-going wake aboard the yacht, complete with champagne and canapés. Dr. Denning, who advertises extensively on radio and television, has been described as the Colonel Sanders of the body disposal business. The comparison is apt, for the meteoric commercial success of these enterprises seems to have established them as fixtures on the American scene. Leave it to American business ingenuity to cash in on the undoubtedly widespread yearning for simpler disposal of the dead! Yet—is there a hint of a warning in Dr. Denning's imaginative bon-voyage parties? Will the same ingenuity be invoked to devise evermore sumptuous yachts and stylish send-offs? In the last analysis this will be up to those of us who have not yet embarked for the Stygian shore.

CHAPTER NOTES

Chapter 3: *The Veterans Administration Contract Burial Program*

The exception noted in the case of the Veterans Administration is instructive because it shows how easy it is, by intelligent administration, to protect recipients of government funeral allowances from price gouging.

The V.A. authorizes the superintendents of regional veterans' hospitals to contract with local undertakers to furnish complete funerals for men who die in the veterans' hospitals, at a price not to exceed $250. The bidding for these contracts is sometimes spirited, and contracts awarded for as little as $190 may provide for a casket and services that would in the same establishment otherwise retail for $450 to $600. The contract funeral program in this way makes available to the families of some deceased ex-servicemen complete funeral services at a cost well within the statutory funeral allowances of $250. It is a very modest program, covering at best only one out of five veterans—those who die in veterans' hospitals. The families of those who die elsewhere receive the $250 allowance in cash and are left to do their own bargaining with the undertaker. Nonetheless, the contract funeral program is regarded with apprehension and loathing by most funeral industry leaders. Apprehension because it is viewed as a cloud, no bigger than a mummy's hand, that might presage similar action by other government agencies. Loathing because the success of the program affords striking proof of the ability of some funeral establishments to furnish "quality merchandise" and services—at a profit—for $250. The contract burial program has, up until now, survived, but just barely, the lobbying efforts of the funeral trade associations to eliminate it.* Some state associations have tried to curtail the bidding for such contracts by adopting "Ethical Codes" which prohibit members from offering, by contract with any organization, funeral goods and services at prices lower than those charged the public at large.

CHAPTER 9: *New York Cemetery Scandals*

The schemes for extracting private revenue from ostensibly nonprofit cemeteries are as varied as the promoter's ingenuity can devise and his conscience permit, for cemetery operations are in most states unburdened by legislative control. An extraordinary catalogue of actual case histories can be found in the report of New York Attorney General Nathaniel Goldstein on the results of his 1949 investigation of nonprofit cemeteries. While remedial legislation was enacted in New York as a result of the disclosures, the types of operation he described continue to flourish in other parts of the country.

Mr. Goldstein's fire was directed specifically at the "so-called nonprofit cemetery corporations or associations," which composed 70 per cent of all the cemeteries in New York State at that time. Expressly excluded from censure were cemeteries operated by churches and municipalities, "since it is patent that monies paid by the public to these are never diverted to private gain."

The report emphasized that the buccaneering practices disclosed by the investigation "are in no sense unique, rather they suggest the typical," in commercial cemetery practices.

In one frequently used variation of the nonprofit cemetery scheme, the promoters buy control of a sleepy old nonprofit cemetery that has never been properly exploited, and install new and friendly directors who then sell large chunks of the cemetery's undeveloped acreage to the pro-

*Since this writing the V.A. ordered the program terminated as of July 1, 1963.

moters at bargain prices. The promoters then retail the cemetery space to the public. In the case of 73-year-old Maple Grove Cemetery, in Queens, New York, the middleman was Maple Grove Memorial Park, Inc., a corporation set up in 1942 to deal in real estate, with capital of only $200. The friendly cemetery directors set aside fifty acres of land for a "memorial park" type of development, and turned it over to the real estate corporation for resale to the public. From 1943 to 1948 the real estate corporation realized a gross profit of $1,600,000, after paying the cemetery corporation 50 per cent of moneys realized from grave sales. They were able to do all this without adding to their initial investment of $200, because the friendly cemetery directors did not require cash payment but permitted payment to be made out of the proceeds of the retail sales. The retail sales campaign was the now standard high-pressure operation; a telephone crew used telephone directories to get "leads"; these were followed up by a team of twenty salesmen who made house calls, offering grave space on an "easy payment" installation plan at 6 per cent interest.

In another variation, an official of the Pine Lawn (New York) cemetery, with the assistance of her nephew, who was president of the corporation, acquired 5,000 burial plots from Pine Lawn for $11,000. Each plot consisted of four graves, each grave permitting of two interments, one above the other. "Simple arithmetic shows," says the Attorney General's report, that the lady was thereby "equipped to make space available for 40,000 bodies, the space for each body having cost her only 27½¢." The going price for such spaces was then (1949) $50 to $100 each, a price which would enable the lucky holder of this property to realize a gross profit of over $2 million on her $11,000 investment. Another official of the cemetery bought 3,000 plots at about the same bargain rate. Looking at it from the cemetery's point of view, it received less than $18,000 for 64,000 burial spaces. Out of this $18,000 it must pay for the original cost of the ground, and provide for current and future maintenance of all the graves in the area.

Another money-maker, the investigators found, is the burial of stillborn infants. The S——— Cemetery Association made a flat charge of $30 for such burials, but stipulated that the interments would be in "unmarked graves." In actual practice these interments were made in what cemetery officials described as "the space between" two standard occupied graves. Since the graves are laid out in adjoining rectangles, the truth of the matter is that the stillborn infants were really buried at a shallow level above the other bodies, unknown of course to the parents of the dead infants or to the owners of the plots in which the burials were made.

A further space-saving practice is described in the report: "At M——— C——— Cemetery, a son had his mother interred in 1931. In a complaint late in 1948, he stated that other graves had been laid out in such a fashion around that of his mother that he was unable to reach hers except by walking on the others. To utilize every dollar-valuable foot of space, paths are frequently converted to burial use, isolating all but the graves on the fringe of a given section."

Concepts of propriety change with the times, however, and it is interesting to note that this device, which shocked the New York Attorney General a little more than a decade ago, is today standard practice in most cemeteries. And inconveniences created by the elimination of paths, such as the messy problem of getting to graves in the middle of a section in the rainy season, are characteristically regarded by cemetery men as merchandising problems rather than questions of public convenience. Frederick Llewellyn, executive vice-president of Forest Lawn Memorial-Park, of Glendale, California, discussed his solution in a recent address to the annual convention of the National Association of Cemeteries. In areas where there is difficulty in getting to center graves in the rainy season, he commends the practice of offering a higher commission to salesmen for selling the hard-to-reach center lots in the summertime when (in California) there is no rain. Salesmen, he said, "must be motivated to sell those things which make the most profit." The problem that will confront the dry-season buyer when he attempts to slog his way to his "memorial estate" in the wet season was not discussed. He would, after all, be an ingrate to complain to the public-spirited citizens who have established the cemetery as a nonprofit corporation. As he dons his gum boots he may find comfort in the words of Maytor McKinley, cemetery tycoon, casket manufacturer and president-director of the Utter-McKinley chain of sixteen mortuaries: "Funeral directors and cemeteries give a moral and spiritual uplift to their communities. In my opinion this is the greatest contribution they make."

CHAPTER 17: *Emily Post on Funerals*

Mrs. Emily Post, that woman of extraordinary prudence, that famed pacesetter in matters of taste and custom, had some severe words for "an occasional funeral director" in the first edition of *Etiquette,* published in 1923: "Whether the temptation of 'good business' gradually undermines his character—knowing as he does that bereaved families ask no questions—or whether his profession is merely devoid of taste, he will, if not checked, bring the most ornate and expensive casket in his establishment; he will perform every rite that his professional ingenuity for expenditure can devise; he will employ every attendant he has; he will order vehicles numerous enough for the cortège of a President; he will even, if thrown in contact with a bewildered chief-mourner, secure a pledge for the erection of an elaborate mausoleum."

She suggests that someone who "has the family's interest at heart and knows their taste and purse should go personally to the establishment of the undertaker," there to make all arrangements on behalf of the family. "One would be a poor sort who for the sake of friends would not willingly endure a little troublesome inquiry, rather than witness a display of splurge and bad taste and realize at the same time that the friends who might have been protected will be deluged with bills which it cannot but embarrass them to pay."

Evidently Mrs. Post got a reaction from the undertaking trade, for in the 1942 edition of *Etiquette* she prefaces her remarks about funerals with this statement: "Because of the criticism of a certain not admirable type of funeral director in the earlier editions of this book, it must at once be said that this was not meant to apply to any of the directors of high reputation, who are conscientiously considerate not only of the feelings of the family but also of their pocketbooks." However, she not only repeats the offending paragraph, but strengthens it: "The wrong type of director will refuse to give an itemized list of costs, but will, instead, do his best to hypnotize the family into believing that the more expensive the casket and the more elaborate the preparations the greater the love and honor shown to the deceased." In the current edition, revised in 1955, the offending passage is, without explanation, deleted in its entirety.

For specific information on how to deal wisely and creatively with death, send for *A Manual of Death Education and Simple Burial,* by Ernest Morgan ($2 postpaid from Celo Press, Burnsville, North Carolina 28714). This comprehensive booklet, which is frequently revised, includes a directory of memorial societies with detailed information about them, and directories of medical schools, Eye-Banks and other tissue banks with instructions for making anatomical gifts. Equally valuable are sections in the booklet on how to meet the social and emotional needs of the survivors at time of death, and on Death Education.

If only a list of memorial societies is wanted, this can be obtained by sending a self-addressed stamped envelope to The Continental Association of Funeral and Memorial Societies, 1828 L Street, N.W., Washington, D.C. 20036. Persons interested in organizing a memorial society can get active assistance from this association.

BIBLIOGRAPHY

Both Mr. Benchley and I subscribed to two undertaking magazines: The Casket *and* Sunnyside. *Steel yourself:* Sunnyside *had a joke column called "From Grave to Gay." I cut a picture out of one of them, in color, of how and where to inject embalming fluid, and had it hung over my desk until Mr. Crowninshield asked me if I could possibly take it down. . . .*

—DOROTHY PARKER (describing the circumstances that led to termination of her employment at *Vogue*), quoted in *Writers at Work: The Paris Review Interviews.*

FOR REASONS quite different from those of Miss Parker I have lately been subscribing to several funeral trade magazines. They are without a doubt the liveliest source of information about developments within the trade. Yet they are virtually unobtainable save by subscription.

The area in which I live is unusually fortunate in its library facilities. The University of California library subscribes to more than 30,000 periodicals, of which many hundreds are specialized trade or business journals for every conceivable commercial enterprise and its subdivisions—*Electrical Merchandising, Chain Store Age, Skyscraper Management* and the like. In all this vast collection of titles there is not one funeral trade magazine. In fact, according to the *Union List of Serials* (a list of periodicals carried by major libraries throughout the country), funeral magazines are to be found nowhere west of the Rockies. For example, *Casket and Sunnyside* is carried in only six Eastern libraries; *Mortuary Management* in none.

Even the library at the San Francisco College of Mortuary Science, while it contains much useful material not stocked in university or public libraries, does not carry a complete file of the trade magazines; neither does the National Foundation of Funeral Service library in Evanston, Illinois. My request to the editors of *Casket and Sunnyside* and *The American Funeral Director* for permission to visit their New York offices and examine back issues of the magazines was indignantly and flatly refused.

Books on the subject are extremely scarce. There are but three full-length studies of the American funeral by people outside the trade, two of them long since out of print. Books written by and for members of the trade are generally not found in public or university libraries.

For these reasons it has been thought unnecessary to burden the reader with footnotes or numbered source references in the text; for if he should want to trace the sources, it is unlikely that he would be able to do so. Instead, for those who wish to pursue the subject further, I have appended a list of books, a list of articles in magazines of general circulation, and a list of funeral trade magazines with addresses.

—J. M.
April, 1963

BOOKS AND PAMPHLETS

Adair, Maude Adams. *The Techniques of Restorative Art.* Dubuque: W. C. Brown Company, 1948.

Asbell, Bernard. *When F.D.R. Died.* New York: Holt, Rinehart & Winston, Inc., 1961.

Bowman, LeRoy. The American Funeral: A Study in Guilt, Extravagance and Sublimity. Washington: Public Affairs Press, 1959.

Browne, Sir Thomas. *Hydriotaphia, Urne-Buriall,* 1958.

Budge, E. A. Wallace. *The Mummy.* London: Cambridge University Press, 1894.

Davey, Richard. *A History of Mourning.* London: Jays of Regent Street, 1889.

Dowd, Quincy L. *Funeral Management and Costs.* Chicago: University of Chicago Press, 1921.

Earle, Alice Morse. *Customs and Fashions in Old New England.* New York: Charles Scribner's Sons, 1893.

Eaton, Hubert. *The Comemoral.* Los Angeles: Academy Press, 1954.

Eckles, John H. *Modern Mortuary Science.* Philadelphia: Westbrook Publishing Company, 1948.

Feifel, Herman, editor. *The Meaning of Death.* New York: McGraw-Hill Book Company, Inc., 1959.

Fellows, Alfred. *The Law of Burial.* London: Hadden, Best & Company, Ltd., 1952.

Forest Lawn Memorial-Park Association. *Art Guide of Forest Lawn,* 1956.

Franz, Anne H. *Funeral Direction and Management.* Florida State Board of Funeral Directors and Embalmers, 1947.

Gebhart, John C. *Funeral Costs.* New York: G. P. Putnam's Sons, Inc., 1928.

Gordon, Leland J. *Economics for Consumers.* New York: American Book Company, 1953.

Habenstein, Robert W. *The American Funeral Director: A Study in the Sociology of Work.* Unpublished dissertation, Department of Sociology, University of Chicago, 1954.

Habenstein, Robert W., and Lamers, William M. *Funeral Customs the World Over.* Milwaukee: National Funeral Directors Association, 1960.

———— The History of American Funeral Directing. Milwaukee: National Funeral Directors Association, 1955.

Hohenschuh, W. P. The Modern Funeral. Chicago: Trade Periodical Company, 1900.

Irion, Ernest F. The Funeral and the Mourners. Nashville: Abingdon Press, 1954.

Krieger, Wilbur M. Successful Funeral Service Management. New York: Prentice-Hall, Inc., 1951.

Martin, Edward A. Psychology of Funeral Service. Grand Junction, Colorado: The Author, 1950.

Mayer, J. Sheridan. Restorative Art. Graphic Arts Press, 1961.

Myers, James, Jr. "Cooperative Funeral Associations." Cooperative League of the U.S.A., 1946.

Nora, Fred. 'Memorial Associations." Cooperative League of the U.S.A., 1962.

Paton, Lewis B. Spiritism and the Cult of the Dead in Antiquity. New York: The Macmillan Co., 1921.

Polson, Cyril John, Brittain, R. P., and Marshall, T. K. The Disposal of the Dead. New York: New York Philosophical Library, 1953.

Post, Emily. Etiquette. New York: Funk and Wagnalls Company, 1923, 1948.

Puckle, Bertram S. Funeral Customs. London: T. Wermer Laurie, Ltd., 1926.

Robinson, William. God's Acre Beautiful. London: John Murray Publishers, Ltd., 1883.

Roosevelt, James, and Shalett, Sidney. Affectionately, F.D.R. New York: Harcourt, Brace and Company, 1959.

St. Johns, Adela Rogers. First Step Up Toward Heaven. New York: Prentice-Hall, Inc., 1959.

Strub, Clarence G., and Frederick, L. G. The Principles and Practices of Embalming. Dallas: L. G. Frederick, 1959.

Volkart, Edmund H., and Michael, Stanley T. "Bereavement and Mental Health," Chapter IX in Explorations in Social Psychology, edited by Alexander H. Leighton. New York: Basic Books, Inc., 1957.

Warner, W. Lloyd. The Living and the Dead. New Haven: Yale University Press, 1959.

Waugh, Evelyn. The Loved One. Boston: Little, Brown & Company, 1948.

Williams, Marc. Flowers-by-Wire: The Story of the Florists' Telegraph Delivery Association. Detroit: Mercury House, 1960.

Wilson, Arnold, and Levy, H. Burial Reforms and Funeral Costs. New York: Oxford University Press, 1938.

MAGAZINE ARTICLES

Belfrage, Cedric. "Be Happy—Go Cemetery," American Mercury, July, 1951.

Brown, Charles M. "Reducing the High Cost of Dying," The Christian Century, October 21, 1936.

Davidson, Bill. "The High Cost of Dying," Collier's, May 19, 1951.

Davis, Elmer. "The Mortician," *American Mercury*, May, 1927.

Elliott, J. Richard, Jr. "The Funeral Business," *Barron's National Financial Weekly*, April 11, 1955.

Glass, Robert E. "A Team of Tactful Men," *The New Republic*, April 21, 1947.

Harmer, Ruth Mulvey. "The High Cost of Dying," *The Progressive*, March, 1961.

Hart, Scott. "Swing Low, Sweet Chariot," *Esquire*, May, 1947.

Havemann, Ernest. "Are Funerals Barbaric?" *McCall's*, May, 1956.

Jacobs, Paul. "The Most Cheerful Graveyard in the World," *The Reporter*, September 18, 1958.

Kaye, Nancy. "Fighting Fancy Funerals," *Medical Economics*, January 29, 1962.

Kephart, William M. "Status After Death," *American Sociological Review*, October, 1950.

Lagemann, John Kord. "The Hurt that Heals," *Good Housekeeping*, April, 1960.

Magrisso, Abe, and Rubin, Donald. "Death's High Toll," *AFL-CIO Industrial Union Digest*, Fall, 1961.

———. "The High Cost of Dying," *National Maritime Union Pilot*, March 23, 1961.

McCluskey, Thorp. "Death on Parade," *Christian Herald*, February, 1949.

Morgan, Al. "The Bier Barons," *Playboy*, June, 1960.

Murray, Don. "What Should a Funeral Cost?" *Coronet*, October, 1961.

Nichols, Charles H. "The Psychology of Selling Vaults," *The Vault Merchandiser*, April, 1956.

Nichols, Wade H. "It's Your Funeral," *Liberty*, July, 1948.

Radcliff, J. D. "Let the Dead Teach the Living," *Reader's Digest*, August, 1961.

Sheed, Wilfred, and Feltman, Shirley. "The Funeral Business," *Jubilee*, November, 1960.

("A special correspondent"). "The High Cost of Dying," *Economist*, September 16, 1962.

Treuhaft, Decca. "St. Peter; Don't You Call Me," *Frontier*, November, 1958.

Tunley, Roul. "Can You Afford to Die?" *The Saturday Evening Post*, June 17, 1961.

(unsigned). "The Costs You Must Face When Death Occurs," *Good Housekeeping*, June, 1959.

(unsigned). "Funerals," *Which?*, February, 1962.

(unsigned). "Memorial Societies: A Plan for Simple, Inexpensive Funerals," *Good Housekeeping*, August, 1962.

White, Trentwell M. and Sandrof, Ivan. "The First Embalmer," *The New Yorker*, November 7, 1942.

FUNERAL TRADE JOURNALS

American Funeral Director, 607 Fifth Avenue, New York 17, N.Y.

Canadian Funeral Director, 60 Fremont St. W., Toronto, Ontario

Casket and Sunnyside, 487 Broadway, New York 13, N.Y.

De-Ce-Co Magazine, 656 Beacon Street, Boston, Mass. (Published by the Dodge Chemical Company)

Funeral Directors Review, 343 So. Dearborn St., Chicago 4, Ill.

Jewish Funeral Director, 4720 No. Broad St., Philadelphia 41, Pa. (Quarterly. Official publication of the Jewish Funeral Directors of America, Inc.)

Mid-Continent Mortician, 905 Lumber Exchange Bldg., Minneapolis, Minn.

Morticians of the Southwest, P.O. Box 2683, Dallas, Texas.

Mortuary Management, 810 So. Robertson Blvd., Los Angeles 35, Calif.

National Funeral Director and Embalmer, 730 E. 63rd St., Chicago 37, Ill. (Official publication of the National [Negro] Funeral Directors and Morticians Association)

National Funeral Service Journal, 210 E. Ohio Street, Chicago, Ill.

Northeast Funeral Director, 118 Summer Street, Boston 10, Mass.

Professional Embalmer, 621 Plymouth Court, Chicago 5, Ill. (Published by the Undertakers Supply Company)

Southern Funeral Director, 1070 Spring Street, N.W., Atlanta, Ga.

The Director, 1030 No. Water St., Milwaukee 2, Wisc. (Official publication of the National Funeral Directors Association)

CEMETERY TRADE JOURNALS

American Cemetery, 607 Fifth Avenue, New York 17, N.Y.

Cemeterian, American Cemetery Association, 12 No. 3rd St., Columbus, Ohio.

Concept: The Journal of Creative Ideas for Cemeteries, Northwestern Bank Building, Milwaukee 2, Wisc. (Published by the Interment Association of America)

ENGLISH FUNERAL
TRADE JOURNALS

Funeral Director, 57 Doughty Street, London W.C. 1. (Official review of National Association of Funeral Directors)

Funeral Service Journal, Hillingdon Press, Uxbridge, Middlesex.

INDEX